# Eating Disorders: Effective Care and Treatment

Félix E. F. Larocca, M.D.
Medical Director
BASH[SM] Treatment and Research Center
for Eating and Mood Disorders
Deaconess Hospital
St. Louis, Missouri

VOLUME 1

Ishiyaku EuroAmerica, Inc.
St. Louis • Tokyo • 1986

Editor in Chief: Félix E.F. Larocca, M.D.
Medical Director
BASH℠ Treatment and Research Center
for Eating and Mood Disorders
Deaconess Hospital
St. Louis, Missouri

Copy Editor: Andrew Cox, B.A., M.F.A.

Index By: Andrew Cox, B.A., M.F.A.

©Copyright 1986 by Ishiyaku EuroAmerica, Inc. St. Louis, Missouri

Ishiyaku EuroAmerica, Inc.
11559 Rock Island Court, Maryland Heights (St. Louis), Missouri 63043

**Library of Congress Catalogue Card Number 85-082385**

Larocca, Félix E.F.
    Eating Disorders – Effective Care and Treatment

ISBN 0-912791-19-5

Ishiyaku EuroAmerica, Inc.
St. Louis • Tokyo

Composition and design: Pulsar Publishing, Maryland Heights, Missouri
Printed in the United States of America

# Contributors

S.A. BIRTCHNELL, M.B., B.S., M.R.C. Psych.
Academic Department of Psychiatry
St. George's Hospital Medical School
Tooting, London, Great Britain

GWEN WEBER BURCH, Ph.D., Administrative Director
UNMC Eating Disorders Program
Omaha, Nebraska, U.S.A.

JEFFREY B. DALIN, D.D.S., Dental Consultant
BASH<sup>SM</sup> Treatment and Research Center
for Eating and Mood Disorders
Deaconess Hospital, St. Louis, Missouri. U.S.A.

MEIR GROSS, M.D., Head, Section of Eating Disorders
The Cleveland Clinic Foundation, Cleveland, Ohio, U.S.A.

A. HARTE, Dip.C.O.T., Academic Department of Psychiatry
St. George's Hospital Medical School
Tooting, London, Great Britain

JAMES I. HUDSON, M.D., Psychiatric Research Laboratories
Mailman Research Center, McLean Hospital
Belmont, Massachusetts, U.S.A.
Harvard Medical School, Boston, Massachusetts, U.S.A.

JEFFREY M. JONAS, M.D., Psychiatric Research Laboratories
Mailman Research Center, McLean Hospital
Belmont, Massachusetts, U.S.A.
Harvard Medical School, Boston Massachusetts, U.S.A.

J. HUBERT LACEY, M.B., Ch.B, M.Phil., F.R.C. Psych.
Academic Department of Psychiatry
St. George's Hospital Medical School
Tooting, London, Great Britain

FÉLIX E.F. LAROCCA, M.D., Medical Director
BASH<sup>SM</sup> Treatment and Research Center
for Eating and Mood Disorders
Deaconess Hospital, St. Louis, Missouri, U.S.A.

JAMES E. MITCHELL, III, M.D., Associate Professor
Department of Psychiatry
University of Minnesota Medical School
Minneapolis, Minnesota, U.S.A.

RODRIGO A. MUÑOZ, M.D.
Associate Professor of Clinical Psychiatry
University of California – San Diego
San Diego, California, U.S.A.
President, American Academy of Clinical Psychiatrists
President, Western Mood and Sleep Disorders Institute
San Diego, California, U.S.A.

PAUL H. PEARSON, M.D.,
McGaw Professor of Adolescent Medicine, Medical Director
UNMC Eating Disorders Program, Omaha, Nebraska, U.S.A.

EUGENE U. PIAZZA, M.D., Associate in Psychiatry
The Children's Hospital Medical Center
Instructor, Harvard Medical School
Boston, Massachusetts, U.S.A.

HARRISON G. POPE, JR., M.D.
Psychiatric Research Laboratories, Mailman Research Center
McLean Hospital, Belmont, Massachusetts, U.S.A.
Harvard Medical School, Boston, Massachusetts, U.S.A.

PAULINE S. POWERS, M.D., Associate Professor of Psychiatry
Department of Psychiatry, University of South Florida
College of Medicine, Tampa, Florida, U.S.A.

W.J. KENNETH ROCKWELL, M.D.
Assistant Professor of Psychiatry, Department of Psychiatry
Director, Anorexia Nervosa/Bulimia Treatment Program
Duke University Medical Center, Durham, North Carolina, U.S.A

ALEXANDER ROSEMURGY, M.D., Assistant Professor of Surgery
Department of Surgery, University of South Florida
College of Medicine, Tampa, Florida, U.S.A.

J. BRADLEY RUBEL, Th.D.
President, ANRED, Inc.
Eugene, Oregon, U.S.A.

CATHERINE STEINER-ADAIR, Ed.D., Associate in Psychology
The Children's Hospital Medical Center
Boston, Massachusetts, U.S.A.

FERNANDO A. TAPIA, M.D., Professor of Psychiatry
and Behavioral Sciences
University of Oklahoma Health Sciences Center
College of Medicine, Oklahoma City, Oklahoma, U.S.A.

MOSHE S. TOREM, M.D., Chairman, Department of Psychiatry
Akron General Medical Center
Professor of Psychiatry, Northeastern Ohio Universities
College of Medicine, Akron, Ohio, U.S.A.

WALTER VANDEREYCKEN, M.D., Psychiatrist, Head of
the Anorexia Nervosa Unit
University Psychiatric Center St. Jozef, Kortenberg, Belgium

JOHAN VANDERLINDEN, M.A., Clinical Psychologist
University Psychiatric Center St. Jozef, Kortenberg, Belgium

CONSTANCE A. WALSH, R.N., Department of Psychiatry
St. John's Mercy Medical Center, St. Louis, Missouri, U.S.A.

DION VAN WERDE, M.A., Research Assistant
University Psychiatric Center St. Jozef, Kortenberg, Belgium

# Dedication

The contributors to this volume wish to dedicate it to the cause and spirit of international cooperation and to all their patients who made this book possible.

# Contents

Contents

# INTRODUCTION TO EATING DISORDERS: EFFECTIVE CARE AND TREATMENT

In trying to assemble a curriculum guide for understanding of the broad issues involved in preparing courses of study for medical students, resident physicians, nursing students, dieticians, and other professionals interested in a thorough and detailed access to knowledge on eating disorders, I found that the many already available books are either too specialized, simplified, or not to the point. I, therefore, set out to fulfill the task of providing our readers—the clinicians and the general public—with a guide that would encompass scientific, up-to-date knowledge on anorexia, bulimia, obesity, treatment, self-help, and other related and important issues.

What has resulted is this book.

In order to facilitate the search for knowledge and orientate the reader, I would like to highlight the essence of each chapter with the enjoyment that I derived from having a first-hand knowledge on the erudition of our contributors.

Chapter One, "Anorexia Nervosa Treatment Perspectives" by Meir Gross, provides us with a comprehensive critique of treatment modalities for Anorexia Nervosa emphasizing why, in the opinion of Dr. Gross, it is necessary to treat patients with Anorexia Nervosa in hospital facilities exclusively dedicated for this purpose.

Chapter Two, "A Critique of Treatment Methods for Anorexia Nervosa" by W.J. Kenneth Rockwell takes further the issue of treatment in an inpatient facility. It also discusses all other treatment modalities, including the relevance and importance of the "team", self-help, and the role of the so-called "specialist". Dr. Rockwell's chapter contains much practical knowledge, providing the reader with caveats and evaluations of treatments that are currently being proposed as valid for the remedy of the Anorexia Nervosa condition. In this chapter, the reader will find information on a wide range of issues concerning management of eating disorders.

Chapter Three, "Recent Trends in Group Therapy" by Piazza and Steiner-Adair, is a "how to" chapter. Here, the authors stress the benefits of group therapy for female patients and give us a clear and concise explanation as to why females in general tend to do better while being involved in group psychotherapy. Throughout the chapter, the authors provide theoretical underpinnings for a wide range of groups with a specific discussions on their applicability from the inpatient and outpatient aspects of care to the follow-up procedures. This chapter effectively paves the way for the next one.

Chapter Four, "Directive Group Therapy for Patients With Anorexia Nervosa or Bulimia" by Vandereycken, Vanderlinden, and Van Werde. As if poised to carry the torch in a relay run, these authors move on to discuss the "pros and cons" of group techniques. They deal with some of the concerns professionals have had as to the possibility of anorectic and bulimics reinforcing each other's pathology. Then they conclude by giving in detail their own European views of eclectic pragmaticism. This chapter brings to a nice closure the issues of group therapy in this volume.

Chapter Five, "Oral Manifestations of Eating Disorders" by Dalin is placed in the middle of the book's progression on diagnostic and treatment issues of eating disorders. This is an excellent review based on the author's extensive experience in working with eating disorder patients, and is a must for students of dentistry and practitioners alike.

Chapter Six is entitled, "Bulimia: An Evolving Concept". The author, Munoz, participated in the devising of Feigner's et al. research diagnostic criteria makes a lucid effort at providing our readers with a research diagnostic criteria for bulimia research. Brief, concise, but useful.

Chapter Seven, by Mitchell, takes the concept of bulimia further than it has been advanced thus far and goes on to explore all aspects of the bulimia syndrome, including medical and psychological. Mitchell ends with an excellent therapeutic critique. Up to this point, this chapter has facilitated the introduction of the next chapter.

Chapter Eight, "Bulimia - Towards a Rational Approach to Diagnosis and Treatment" is by Lacey, Harte, and Birtchnell. This is another chapter providing the reader with a deeper insight into the parallels and differences between European and American classifications. The authors recognize three types of bulimia and establish clear treatment guidelines and prognostic implications for each. They discuss the effectiveness of various treatment methods and provide the reader with a clear understanding of strategies that work.

Chapter Nine, "An Intermediate Care Model for the Treatment of Eating Disorders" was based on the editor's own approach to the programming and planning for inpatient, outpatient, and intermediate care and treatment for individuals with eating disorders. This approach relys extensively on self-help and self-help groups. The wide variety of available resources is stressed, and difficulties encountered in providing this care are discussed.

Chapter Ten, "Eating Disorders and Dissociative States" by Torem, does not necessarily represent the editor's desire to provide an esoteric chapter to the reader, but much rather a review of the parallel lines that exist in clinically dissociated states with Anorexia Nervosa and bulimia. The author has done his research on individuals under hypnosis shedding some light as to the possibility that Anorexia Nervosa and bulimia may indeed have more in common with dissociative states than with so-called borderline states.

Chapter Eleven, "Treatment of Bulimia With Thymoleptic Medications" by Pope, Hudson, and Jonas, provide us with an opportunity to have the three names that are most associated with treating bulimia through anti-depressants. They come together and give a critique of the most recent medications for the treatment of eating disorders—particularly bulimia—with the latest addition to the therapeutic armamentarium. For those seeking this kind of information, this chapter alone is a must.

Chapter Twelve, "Anorexia Nervosa and Bulimia: The Role of the Nurse" by Constance A. Walsh, a registered nurse who has participated in the formation of one of the largest self-help organizations and one of the largest treatment centers for eating disorders, gives us a first-hand review of the issues involved in providing nursing care for individuals suffering from anorexia and bulimia. For anyone in nursing or psychiatry desiring to find information on training nurses in the care of eating disorders, this chapter constitutes an excellent if not the best, source.

Chapter Thirteen, "Anorexia, Bulimia, and Obesity in Adolescence: The Sociocultural Perspective" by Burch and Pearson, provides the reader with a detailed analysis of demographic and sociocultural influences on today's adolescents and is an excellent analysis of what could influence adolescents today to become afflicted by anorexia nervosa, bulimia, or obesity. By bringing in again the issue of obesity, the authors pave the way for Chapter Fourteen.

"Current Treatment of Obesity" by Powers and Rosemurgy. In the field of Obesity, Powers and Rosemurgy give us a systematic and scholarly review of obesity; from endocrinology to the gastric restriction and procedures, to self-help, we find that this is a comprehensive chapter that indeed may be said to contain all that is to be known for anyone interested in obesity from diagnosis to treatment.

Chapter Fifteen, "Burn-Out and Eating Disorders Therapists" by J. Bradley Rubel is a must. While most books discuss the pragmatic and theoretical speculations and formulations that lead to the creation of a therapeutic atmosphere or a therapeutic relationship for managing eating disorders, nowhere have I found a critique of what could happen to individuals practicing therapy with the eating disorders patient. Dr. Rubel gives us all her caveats in an impressive way.

Chapter Sixteen, "Self-Help on an Individual Basis" by Fernando Tapia, concludes the book. This is self-healing based on Dr. Tapia's own self-discovery, which lead to the publication of his celebrated "Magic Rooster". Down to earth and simplified, this chapter provides patients with a source for reading about hope themselves, a chapter that covers in detail the issues involved.

25 authors converge to provide us with a comprehensive, highly readable collection of chapters that flow in a way that few edited books I have read before have flowed.

The time spent in assembling these articles and the time spent in reviewing the papers was a most worthwhile experience.

To all the contributors of this book, I owe a personal debt as I feel that we have not just added another book to the growing literature on eating disorders, but that we have augmented and complemented the field. Let's let the judge be the readers.

Félix E. F. Larocca, M.D.

Medical Director,

BASH Treatment and Research Center for Eating and Mood Disorders

Deaconess Hospital

St. Louis, Missouri

Spring 1985

# CHAPTER 1

# Anorexia Nervosa - Treatment Perspectives

**Meir Gross, M.D.**

Since the increase in reported cases of anorexia nervosa during the last decade, more and more professionals became interested in the treatment of this disorder. Many treatment methods were promoted by various specialists. Pediatricians paid more attention to medical treatment, leaving psychotherapy to a psychiatrist or a psychologist as a liaison service. As the number of eating disorders patients increased in pediatric floors, more organized programs evolved, behavior modification therapy being the primary method. As it became clear that more organized programs were needed within the realm of psychiatry, child psychiatrists emphasized individual and family therapy, as well. Social workers also promoted the latter—usually in special settings such as child guidance clinics. As cases of anorexia grew to epidemic proportions, special inpatient programs—usually in a psychiatric hospital setting or in psychiatric units of general hospitals—started to organize.

These programs are now becoming more sophisticated, including a variety of treatment options such as assertiveness training, group therapy, biofeedback and therapeutic community, along with nutritional assessment and dietary counseling. It has also become clear that having only one treatment modality is not in the best interest of most patients. Better results are gained by a combination of treatment modalities. Such comprehensive programs are offered in numerous medical centers around the country.

This chapter outlines the treatment of anorexia nervosa including medical as well as psychological aspects of treatment. The discussion will focus first on the medical concerns and then move on to therapeutic aspects (Table 1).

1

## The Medical Treatment

If a patient is emaciated, the first concern should be to stabilize her condition. Depending on the patient's individual circumstances, supplementing food intake is essential. There are different methods of achieving this goal. The most direct and complex method is total parenteral nutrition or hyperalimentation (5). This method provides complete nutrition by the intravenous route. It involves the infusion of a protein solution made up of hydrolysate, glucose, electrolytes, minerals and vitamins at a constant rate through an indwelling catheter surgically placed in a major vessel such as the subclavian vein. Another method of supplementing nutrition is by inserting a naso-gastric tube and administering tube feedings. Tube feeding and regular intravenous therapy are proven methods for replacing body fluids.

The least invasive way of supplementing the patient's food intake is with oral nutritional supplements such as Ensure, Sustacal, etc. If any of these methods are chosen to re-hydrate the anorectic patient, it must be monitored and the patient weaned slowly since dependence on these artificial food concentrates for weight gain is common. Any nutritional supplement is considered a medication. Therefore, it is charted as such in the patient's files and patients are required to drink it in the presence of the medication nurse. By not considering it as food helps to avoid conflicts with the patient in regard to eating or not eating.

Special attention should be given to the level of the potassium since it could be below normal due to induced vomiting or abuse of laxatives by the patient. If potassium deficiency is found, immediate correction is needed to prevent cardiac arrhythmia or imminent lethal cardiac arrest.

Dietetic counseling is also important for nutritional assessment and planned feeding (13). Supportive advice by the dietitian is essential. Patients with mild conditions may respond to supportive counseling that deals with the serious consequences of starvation. Refractory patients should be made aware of the possibility of gastric tube feeding or intravenous feeding in order to prepare them ahead of time. (17).

The dietitian helps the patient plan a specific diet. The amount of calories are then increased gradually. The participation of the patient is important, since in the beginning of therapy many patients are fearful of weight gain. As a general rule, no specific diet is recommended for anorectic patients. Patients are allowed to eat whatever they like. The dietary consult serves to help patients maintain their weight after achieving the goal weight—which is usually in the low-normal range for height and body build. Anorectic patients are phobic about getting obese, and, therefore, a goal weight might be a reassurance to them.

Special attention should be paid to other possible medical problems such as anemia, leukopenia (7), abnormal liver functions, cardiac arrhythmias (22), peripheral edema, etc. It is important that all physicians working with the patient—the hematologist, cardiologist, gynecologist, gastroenterologist, general pediatrician and the psychiatrist—be part of a team that meets on a regular basis to coordinate treatment (8).

If the patient is anxious about weight gain, the use of minor or major tranquilizers might be needed. If the patient is depressed or has primary affective disorder along with anorexia nervosa, then use of anti-depressant medication is indicated—preferably one of the tricyclic anti-depressants (10). Lately it has been found that patients with chronic anorexia nervosa develop a condition similar to osteoporosis in post-menopausal women. This is due to the low level of estrogen in anorectic patients as in post-menopausal women. In these cases, it is recommended estrogen and calcium be administered in order to prevent osteopenia (2).

**The Psychological Treatment**

Psychotherapy for anorexia nervosa is complicated due to the resistance most patients have to any therapeutic approach. Patients may also be resistant to any change in their obsessive-compulsive habits. It is important, therefore, that the therapist be aware of the typical manipulative behavior of anorectic patients.

It is unlikely that any one mode of treatment will be successful in the treatment of this disorder. It is important to tailor treatment to the specific problem of each patient using a variety of modalities. The best results are being achieved in a milieu setting of a large medical center in which a special treatment program for eating disorders is established (23). The therapist in charge of the treatment should collaborate with all team members to prevent the patient from manipulating one therapist against the other. Frequent meetings between the team members are also important to assess progress in therapy.

The individual therapy of patients should focus on the patient as a person and not on eating habits or weight unless indicated by critical physiological factors. If the therapist gets stuck on issues of weight or food, it will only reinforce the patient's game and allow the patient to avoid dealing with the underlying causes of the disorder. Patients have a need for discussing weight and eating behaviors, but this should be provided for in specific terms. The patient should only be allowed to discuss these matters with the dietitian or a designated nurse or therapist. In this way food and weight issues are not allowed to pervade therapeutic relationships.

The anorectic patient deals with unconscious conflicts in areas crucial to all adolescents—conflicts that adult anorectics have yet to resolve. There is a great deal of regression involved in the disorder. Patients with anorexia nervosa are still struggling with impulses that surround their basic drives. These issues are: independence, self-esteem, and the resolution of strong and ambivalent feelings towards significant others (16).

The therapist can expect each of these conflicts to be acted out in the therapeutic setting. Such acting out behavior can serve as a guide for understanding the underlying conflict behind the overt behavior.

The conflict of independence versus dependence is a major developmental issue for any adolescent. Testing limits and having the opportunity to make both right and wrong choices are components of a healthy adaptation. This conflict is perhaps the one most consistently acted out by anorectic patients. It is the key factor to their persistent manipulating attitude.

Self-esteem and confidence are also vital to a healthy psychological adjustment. They are outgrowths of the adolescent's attempt at self-independence and identity. Adolescents learn much about who they are from the responses of others—whether it is from the individual therapist or the members of the therapeutic team.

As a result of these underlying conflicts, negative impulses may arise. The patient feels a need to control. Therefore, anorectic patients tend to exhibit very high levels of anxiety which often become unbearable. Their behaviors are a response to these stresses and are primarily a means of anxiety reduction. This is particularly true of the ritualistic denial of symptoms or feelings these patients have. Ritualistic behavior, denial of reality, and resistance to treatment are pervasive—especially in the early stages of treatment—and should be dealt with before progressing further in therapy (23).

Behavioral therapy is used after the patient has accepted the responsibilities of a behavior contract. The patient is thus able to control her own eating habits and face the contingency of the contract whenever unsuccessful in fulfilling its requirements. The contract enables the patient—with the help of a dietitian—to learn how much food is required to attain and maintain a certain weight. The contract spells out what is the expected weight goal as assessed by nutritional assessment. It specifies the expectation of a certain weight gain per day—usually one-quarter of a pound. For being above the average weight gain privileges and rewards are given based on the patient's preferences. The contract also specifies the loss of privileges for a failure to gain the expected daily weight. If the patient is below the graph line for the average expected weight gain, the patient is restricted to bed.

This contractual idea is based on the principle of operant conditioning with clearly spelled out positive contingencies. The patient is weighed every morning in a hospital gown. As long as the patient is "above the line" she can apply for privileges specified in the regulations of the milieu.

The behavior contract is drawn by the team after an observation period of at least ten days. This allows team members to know the patient well enough so the most effective rewards will be used. This way the patient will be better motivated to gain the expected weight. Moreover, before the contract is constructed, it is necessary to estimate the weight goal the patient is expected to reach. This weight goal should be based on a nutritional evaluation.

Behavior therapy as a treatment for anorexia was used successfully by Halmi et al. (12), Leitenberg et al. (19), Bhanji and Thompson (3), Agras et al. (1) and others. It is a promising method. If behavior therapy is used in such a way that the responsibility of weight gain is given to the patient, a conflict about eating between the staff and the patients is eliminated. Consequently, patients do not transfer any negative aspects of family dynamics to the staff. Therefore, resistance is minimized.

It is important behavior therapy not be used without the patient signing an agreement before it is started. Otherwise, it might become a source of conflict and lose effectiveness. Forcing a behavior contract on the patient has negative results. These perils have been discussed by Bruch (4).

There is another danger to watch for, however, while treating a

5

patient with a strict behavior contract. There are patients who will try to gain their expected daily weight by all means, including excessive water drinking. This can cause severe seizures (Jos, 14). These seizures may be caused by the changes in electrolytes in the brain's nerve cells and evidenced by hyponatremia in the blood. Severe seizures could also lead into status epilepticus and death. Abnormalities in vasopressin metabolism are suggested by Gold (9). Jos sees self-induced water intoxication as the reason for generalized seizures (15). Silber describes a 15-year old anorectic girl that developed grand mal seizures to the degree of status epilepticus (25). For this reason occasional screening of serum electrolytes and urinary specific gravity are necessary while patients are on a strict behavior therapy contract.

The above danger emphasizes the importance of concomitant need to pay attention to the emotional needs of the patient while on behavior therapy. Behavior therapy should not be the only treatment given to the patient. Psychological problems and the emotional state of the patient should be attended to at the same time.

In summary, it would be easy to ignore the psychological factors and force patients to gain weight against all protestations via forced feeding or rigid controls of behavior therapy. But this has been shown to produce an increased rate of recidivism. Neither forced feeding or behavior therapy should be used as the only treatment method.

Milieu therapy is an integral part of an inpatient program for treating anorexia nervosa. Opportunities for therapeutic interventions exist when the patients unconsciously act out their developmental conflicts daily within the therapeutic milieu. This milieu includes all personnel and physical facilities which are part of the patients daily living on the unit—from the various technicians, maintenance personnel, peers, etc., to the nursing staff and doctors. The milieu is similar to a real life situation where patients identify roles significant others play in their lives. The milieu helps provide a structure in order to compensate for anorectics' executive ego deficits.

The milieu also promotes a sense of community and personal responsibility. In such a milieu there should be a constitution which incorporates the team's philosophy and provides concrete guidelines for dealing with everyday ward issues. Such a constitution could establish provision for the concept of a ward government. Meetings for patients should be held every weekday. Attendance should be required by all patients and as many nursing and other staff as possible. These daily therapeutic community meetings provide a foundation for information sharing. The meetings also serve as a clearing house for various ward issues or patient conflicts as they might arise.

In a milieu setting there is a place for a judicial committee comprised of a certain number of patients and a staff advisor. Such a judicial committee can act as the governing body. It can impose restrictions, suspend privileges and otherwise help make patients accountable for their own behaviors on the ward. The committee's decisions, however, should get approval from the staff. Weekly meetings should be held to review attendance and to see that the various patient committees are functioning (24).

The purpose for such a system is twofold. It fosters interdependence among members of the ward community and helps patients to learn to deal with decisions made by peers—something they failed to do in life. Feedback from peers is also more effective than feedback from authority figures such as nurses or doctors.

Family therapy is a treatment modality used to treat the patient in the context of her family. In this regard, the therapeutic perspective should deal with the family as the unit for therapy. Family therapy in a comprehensive treatment plan should take into consideration the patient's capacity to respond to the family's interaction. The family's ability to engage in conjoint meetings should be considered as well. It is important to recognize that family dynamics—control, guilt, symptom maintenance and the ability of members within the family to change or keep rigid—are part of any family functioning. Therefore, any expectation for change in the patient will affect issues in the family as well. Any successful and lasting change in symptoms should include involvement of the family as a whole.

Family therapy, therefore, should be directed towards achieving flexibility of expression within the family. At the same time, ongoing family therapy should be directed towards eliminating faulty relations that could have caused the symptoms in the first place. The therapist should address any dysfunctional patterns found in the family. These patterns may be found in the immediate (nuclear) family or in the extended family that may include multigenerational problems. Pathological family patterns found in "psychosomatic families" are: enmeshment, overprotectiveness, rigidity and lack of any ability for conflict resolution. In families of anorectic patients, patterns of pseudomutuality and pseudohostility are often seen (21).

Biofeedback is a form of treatment that is not yet widely used for anorexia nervosa patients. The basic benefit from biofeedback therapy is the teaching of relaxation techniques to counteract the typical high activity level of these patients. The anorectic patient tends to deny fatigue and typically displays an inability to relax. These patients pursue their activities with high levels of compulsiveness. This compulsiveness can produce excessive levels of autonomic arousal which could lead to psychophysiologic stress reactions.

By being connected to the biofeedback machines through sensors (muscle or temperature sensors), the patient learns to become an active participant in the process of relaxation training. Cold fingers are seen typically in patients who have suffered substantial weight loss. Patients find it difficult not to accept their pathology, especially when the evidence can be seen on a sound or light monitor. Biofeedback may make it easier for the therapist to break through the denial process of anorectic patients (20).

Hypnosis can also be used effectively as part of a therapeutic strategy for anorexia nervosa. Hypnotherapeutic intervention is most effective in symptoms such as hyperactivity, distorted body image, feelings of inadequacy, perfectionistic tendencies, and failure of interoceptive awareness. It may also help patients to overcome their resistance to therapy (11).

Crasilneck and Hall (6) have described the use of hypnosis for anorectic patients. They have used hypnotic suggestions to increase a patient's awareness of hunger by equating it with the pleasure of eating. They have also used hypoanalysis for uncovering psychodynamic conflicts behind the anorectic symptoms. They treated 70 cases of anorexia and achieved marked improvement in more than half. Kroger and Fezler (18) have also combined behavior therapy with hypnosis. They gave post-hypnotic suggestions to their patients, associating food and good appetite with pleasant memories while helping the patients to ventilate feelings of aggression and hostility.

Regardless of what method is used to treat anorectic patients, coordination and collaboration between the various team members is essential. Anorectic patients are known to be resistant and manipulative. They will try to split the staff in the inpatient unit or the therapist, dietitian and parents when seen on an outpatient basis. Open communication between professionals at all stages of evaluation and treatment are of paramount importance in any successful therapy.

**TABLE 1.** Treatment of Anorexia Nervosa

1. Medical
   a. Correcting dehydration and electrolyte imbalance
   b. Supply of necessary nutrients by eating, nasogastric tubing or intravenous route including total parenteral nutrition (TPN)

2. Psychotherapy
   a. Individual insight oriented (psychoanalytic)
   b. Individual supportive
   c. Group (general including patients with other problems)
   d. Special group for anorexia nervosa patients
   e. Assertiveness training group
   f. Family therapy
   g. Biofeedback
   h. Hypnosis
   i. Creative or art therapy
   j. Recreational therapy
   k. Behavior therapy (behavioral weight contract)
   l. Vocational rehabilitation
   m. Psychopharmacotherapy (medication)
   n. Milieu therapy, including therapeutic community

# REFERENCES

1. Agras, W.S., Barlow, D.H., Chapin, H.N., Abel, G.G., Leitenberg, H.: Behavior modification of anorexia nervosa. Arch. Gen. Psychiatry, 30:279–286, 1974.
2. Ayers, J.W.T., Gidwani, G.P., Schmidt, I.M.V., Gross, M.: Osteopenia in hypoestrogenic young women with anorexia nervosa. Fertil Steril, 41:224–228, 1984.
3. Bhanji, S., Thompson, J.: Operant conditioning in the treatment of anorexia nervosa: A review and retrospective study of eleven cases. Br. J. Psychiatry, 124:166–172, 1972.
4. Bruch, H.: Perils of behavior modification in treatment of anorexia nervosa. JAMA, 230:-1419–1422, 1974.
5. Chiulli, R., Groves, M., Steiger, E.: Total parenteral nutrition in anorexia nervosa. Gross, M., Ed. Anorexia Nervosa - A Comprehensive Approach. Lexington, MA, The Collamore Press, 1982, pp. 141–152.
6. Crasilneck, H.B., Hall, J.A.: Clinical hypnosis: Principles and applications. New York: Grune and Stratton, 1975.
7. Dyment, P.G.: Hematological changes induced by anorexia nervosa. Gross, M., Ed. Anorexia Nervosa - A Comprehensive Approach. Lexington, MA, The Collamore Press, 1982, pp. 27–30.
8. Doering, E.J.: The role of the primary care physician in the diagnosis and management of anorexia nervosa. Gross, M., Ed. Anorexia Nervosa - A Comprehensive Approach. Lexington, MA: The Collamore Press, 1982, pp. 15–25.
9. Gold, P., Kaye, W., Robertson, G.L., et al.: Abnormalities in plasma and cerebral spinal fluid orginine vasopressin in patients with anorexia nervosa. N. Engl. J. Med., 308:1117–1123, 1983.
10. Gross, M.: An in-hospital therapy program. Gross, M., Ed. Anorexia Nervosa - A Comprehensive Approach. Lexington, MA: The Collamore Press, 1982, pp. 91–102.
11. Gross, M.: Hypnosis in the therapy of anorexia nervosa. Am. J. Clin. Hypnosis, 26:175–181, 1984.

12. Halmi, K.A., Powers, P., Cunningham, S.: Treatment of anorexia nervosa with behavior modification. Arch. Gen. Psychiatry, 32:93–96, 1975.

13. Huse, D.M., Lucas, A.R.: Dietary treatment of anorexia nervosa. J. Am. Dietetic Assoc., 83:687–690, 1983.

14. Jos, C.J., Perez-Cruet, J.: Incidence and morbidity of self-induced water intoxication in state mental hospital patients. Am. J. Psychiatry, 136:221–222, 1979.

15. Jos, C.J.: Generalized seizures from self-induced water intoxication. Psychosomatics, 25:153–157, 1984.

16. Kernberg, O.F.: Borderline conditions and pathological narcissism. New York: Jason Aronson, 1975.

17. Kovach, K.M.: The assessment of nutritional status in anorexia nervosa. Gross, M., Ed. Anorexia Nervosa - A Comprehensive Approach, Lexington, MA: The Collamore Press, 1982, pp. 69–79.

18. Kroger, W.S., Fezler, W.D.: Hypnosis and behavior modification: Imagery conditioning. Philadelphia: Lippincott, 1976.

19. Leitenberg, H., Agras, W.S., Thomson, L.E.: A sequential analysis of the effect of selective positive reinforcement in modifying anorexia nervosa. Behav. Res. Ther., 6:211–218, 1968.

20. McKee, M.G., Kiffer, J.F.: Clinical biofeedback therapy in the treatment of anorexia nervosa. Gross, M., Ed., Anorexia Nervosa - A Comprehensive Approach. Lexington, MA: The Collamore Press, 1982, pp. 129–139.

21. Minuchin, S.: Psychosomatic Families. Camridge, MA: Harvard University Press, 1978.

22. Moodie, D.S.: Cardiac function in anorexia nervosa. Gross, M., Ed. Anorexia Nervosa - A Comprehensive Approach. Lexington, MA: The Collamore Press, 1982, pp. 45–58.

23. Reece, B.A., Gross, M.: A comprehensive milieu program for treatment of anorexia nervosa. Gross, M., Ed., Anorexia Nervosa - A Comprehensive Approach. Lexington, MA. The Collamore Press, 1982, pp. 103–109.

24. Rubin, S.R.: The community meeting. A comparative study. Am. J. Psychiatry, 136:708–711, 1979.

25. Silber, T.J.: Seizures, water intoxication in anorexia nervosa. Psychosomatics, 25:705–706, 1984.

## CHAPTER 2

# A Critique of Treatment Methods for Anorexia Nervosa

W. J. Kenneth Rockwell

## INTRODUCTION

The crescendo of interest in anorexia nervosa during the past ten years has led to a proliferation of articles and books on the subject, both lay and scientific. But Drossman (18) has pointed out there have been no major breakthroughs in knowledge about the illness or how to treat it. The effort to advance knowledge is intense and hopefully we are on the threshold. The mortality rate of six to eighteen percent (27, 47) makes anorexia the most lethal psychiatric illness. Even if this were not so the morbidity rate (27, 31, 46, 48), chronicity, and debilitating effects on families would make the effort worthwhile.

Lucas (35) has traced the history of anorexia nervosa as an illness and has defined five eras: descriptive, pituitary, rediscovery of the illness, psychoanalytic, and modern, the last commencing in 1961 and being characterized as the biopsychosocial era. In the United States during the past twenty years Bruch (4–12) has been the single most influential person in shaping our conception of eating disorders as psychiatric illnesses and our ideas as to how to approach them with psychotherapy. Hsu (28) has briefly reviewed the six current etiological theories of anorexia. In a review of research findings on follow-up studies, Steinhausen and Glanville (45) conclude that research on this illness does not constitute a unified whole—we still have an incomplete picture of the illness, treated or untreated. In fact, the issues are not settled as to the classification of eating disorders or their diagnostic criteria (2, 24, 26).

As is usually the case in illnesses with multi-determined (21) or unclear etiologies and pathogeneses there are a variety of treatments, the greatest rationale for each of which is the personal style and theoretical orientation of the therapist administering it. Excellent reviews of treatment are available, among them Bliss and Branch (3), Sours (44), and Garfinkel and Garner (20). If any generalizations have emerged recently they would seem to be: 1) that the immediate focus of attention should be on the eating disorder and the behaviors involved, and that physiological control, stabilization, and restitution need to be achieved first. Afterwards the major focus should shift to changing the attitudes that underly such behaviors 2) treatment should be multi-modal—a variety of interventions should be applied simultaneously and/or sequentially 3) the necessary characteristics of a therapist treating an anorectic patient must include persistance, patience, and a refusal to be intimidated.

## Inpatient and Outpatient Treatment

The current approach in treatment of anorectic patients is similar to that with illnesses in general: hospitalize only when necessary. The indications for hospitalization always depend on clinical judgment. The following criteria are usually among the guidelines: 1) weight loss to 20-25% below Ideal Body Weight (IBW) 2) failure of outpatient treatment: no substantial weight increase after six to twelve months of continuous treatment 3) severe metabolic abnormality with particular reference to potassium depletion: repeated serum potassium levels below 2.5 mEq/L; one episode of serum potassium below 2.0 mEq/L. Metabolic abnormalities are usually associated with vomiting and/or laxative or diuretic abuse (or severe emaciation from food restriction). The patient may need to be hospitalized to bring under control the pattern of vomiting or medication abuse. 4) Psychic status: severe psychic stress with special reference to: a) suicidal ideation 2) family turmoil and conflict with patient.

The most frequent reason for hospitalizing an anorectic patient is disordered eating behavior that has resulted in unremitting emaciation. The great majority of in-hospital treatment programs now focus on restoration of physiology - proper nutrition and weight gain - as the first priority after the correction of any immediately threatening medical complications. The second phase of treatment—interdigitating with the first from the outset—is psychosocial habilitation. In inpa-

12

tient care programs, there is usually a shift in focus toward the second phase as hospitalization progresses.

The goals of these two phases are as follows: Physiological: 1) "nutritional rehabilitation," "refeeding," "weight restoration" 2) weight stabilization 3) cessation of use of laxatives, diuretics, diet pills, or emetics, if any. Psychosocial: 1) assumption by patient of responsibility for eating and related behaviors and weight control 2) reducing intensity of obsessive focus on eating, weight, and body image 3) broadening range of activities and interests; 4) examining family relationships, achieving disentanglements, and establishing self-boundary within family 5) examining peer relationships and effecting age-appropriate socialization processes 6) assuming responsibility for own feelings and behaviors and establishing self-boundary in relation to all others.

Also, large numbers of anorectics have been and continue to be treated in hospital medical units by pediatricians, family practitioners, and internists. The numbers of such patients are not known. But it would be worth knowing, particularly those who are treated successfully, and presumably there are some. For this subgroup, perhaps Hurstian psychotherapy suffices: a ". . . few straightforward conversations are sufficient to reveal and straighten out most mental tangles" (29). In collusion with their families, some more severe patients continue to deny any but the most dire physiological consequences and pursue medical treatment only. The remainder become involved with formally trained mental health professionals.

There has been some controversy between behaviorally oriented therapists and others about the use of behavioral techniques to help promote weight restoration. (Hopefully, no professional seriously believes that weight restoration via behavior therapy is all there is to the treatment of anorexia nervosa.) Ironically, Bruch, who for a time inveighed against the dangers of behavior modification (7), indirectly lent support to its use. Her claim, supported by the work of Keys et al. (30), was that the effects of malnutrition—e.g., poor concentration, obsessionality and perhaps even the tendency toward concrete thinking—severely diminished patients' capacity for psychotherapy. Her findings and claims have been disputed by Wilson et al. (51), however. Due to her undisputed stature in the field, though, her assertions about the effects of malnutrition on mental/emotional processes have become virtually reified in current clinical lore. But these effects are

13

worthy of further study, such as in the work of Rippere (39, 40) and Maxwell et al. (36). The issue is simply how much and what kind of talk may be useful to a malnourished patient.

The difficulty in "reaching" many anorectic patients with psychotherapy alone has produced a need for alternate means of treatment modalities. Applied with various degrees of complexity along with a positive reward system, behavior modification is useful in the nutritional rehabilitation phase of treatment. Patients often spontaneously acknowledge that they "feel better physically" even if they "don't like the weight." This better feeling plus the reduction of tension levels in their interactions with others—particularly their families—are the trade-offs for the feeling of having been controlled that patients complain of who have been treated with behavior modification.

The period of hospitalization should be sustained long enough for the accomplishment of the physiological phase of treatment. In terms of weight this might be ninty-five percent of Ideal Body Weight (IBW) —for women, a few pounds above the weight at which they could be expected to resume menses (19). Both figures allow for some weight loss after discharge—an expectable event—without physiological compromise. The patient should also demonstrate for more than just a few days proper nutritional practice, which includes sufficient and balanced dietary intake and excludes vomiting and use of laxatives, diuretics, and diet pills.

With respect to the goals listed in the psychosocial phase, it can be seen that with the exception of the first two, only a beginning will be made in accomplishing these during hospitalization. It follows that the thinking of patients and their families must be shaped, as well as can be in advance, to the idea that hospitalization is but a first (or intermediary) phase in treatment. They will have a much longer term of outpatient work—many people seeking hospitalization or referral speak as if with the magical belief that they will be "cured" in the hospital.

The criteria for psychic improvement sufficient to instigate discharge are less easily quantifiable than weight or eating behaviors. But factors do exist. They include the degree of emotional stability, engagement with the psychosocial habilitation process through treatment, and sufficient change in the milieu to which the patient will return, or in the patient's ability to cope with it.

It can be seen also that behavior modification has no relevance to the last four of the six goals in the psychosocial phase of treatment. In a general sense these goals cover development from that of the small child to the mature adult. Anorectic patients vary widely in the extent of their regression and developmental arrest. But if psychosocial treatment is to be a part of the program as a whole most of it will have to be done on an outpatient basis.

For some patients relatively brief family therapy appears to suffice. Others may succeed with psychoanalysis, although the selection criteria for this procedure are unclear. The majority of patients are seen in individual psychotherapy with or without other concurrent therapies. Up to the present no specific "type" of individual psychotherapy has been demonstrated to be superior with anorectic patients, either to another "type" of individual therapy or to other treatment forms. Bruch abandoned interpretive psychoanalytic psychotherapy for a "fact finding" variety and was quite successful with the latter (5, 6, 9–12). But her method minus her person has not arisen as a distinct treatment approach. Garner et al. (20, 22, 23) have described a cognitive behavioral method—similar in many respects to Bruch's approach —that holds promise, particularly for the many anorectic patients who cannot talk about their feelings or have difficulty in doing so. Garner specifies a number of misconceptions, false assumptions, and cognitive distortions commonly found in anorectic patients and sets forth in some detail many issues to be addressed and maneuvers that can be undertaken by therapists. Since this approach has proved successful, it is to be developed further and subjected to a more rigorously controlled application (22).

## Drug Treatment

The following medications in the treatment of anorexia nervosa have been reviewed elswhere (41): neuroleptics, tricyclic anti-depressants, lithium carbonate, cyproheptadine, and $^9$-tetrahydrocannibinol. Since then, Vandereycken (49) has reported a double-blind, placebo-controlled crossover (three-week "active" treatment) trial of the selective dopamine antagonist sulpiride with eighteen female patients. With respect to daily weight gain sulpiride was superior to placebo but not significantly so. Comparison of drug and placebo effects on behavioral and attitudinal measures demonstrated indifference. In his discussion, Vandereycken concludes—as did we in our review—that weight resto-

15

ration can be achieved without medication. As he points out: "It is far more important to change the patients' weight phobia and their distorted attitudes toward their own body (sic)" (49, p 290). If a medication could be found that would do such things, then the search for such a compound is worthwhile. In the meantime, drugs remain a minor adjunct in treatment. Crisp's recommendation still stands: ". . . judicious use of small doses of phenothiazines or benzodiazpines during the process of gaining weight is the best guideline currently offered for treatment" (15, p 857). As much could be said for weight restored patients.

## Psychoanalysis

Psychoanalysis has had the longest time to establish its position in the treatment of anorexia nervosa. So far it has failed to do so. One might assume after so long a time that some quantitative data would have accumulated on the treatment efficacy of psychoanalysis. One would think characteristics of a subgroup of patients who had been treated with some success would have been delineated, too. At the present time there are no criteria for determining a subgroup of anorectic patients who might have a reasonable chance of benefiting from psychoanalysis. Nevertheless, it has its advocates, for example Sours (44) and Wilson et al. (51). While setting forth an analytic approach with which he has had success, however, Sours is restrained: "But just as there is no unitary concept of anorexia nervosa, there is no unitary treatment for anorexia nervosa" (44, p 370). The final paragraph of his book defines the key factor to the treatment of almost any anorectic: "All this takes time." (44, p 377).

More sanguine, Wilson et al. start with the ". . . hope that we will be able to make it clear that psychoanalysis is the treatment of choice for abstaining bulimics and anorectics" (51, p XI), but then mount no serious effort to do so. We can accept to a certain extent global clinical assessments in such well known and observed patients—i.e., conversion during treatment from individuals with disordered eating behavior, physiology, and relationships, to people reasonably free of such deficits. For comparative treatments purposes some quantification and specification are necessary but are missing from their accounts. There is no characterization of the pool from which patients were drawn. How was selection for psychoanalysis really done? Were there any failures? Treatment intensity and total times are not clear nor is method (psychoanalysis vs. analytic psychotherapy). Impressions and conclusions based on cases treated by the authors and cases known through supervision are commingled. Follow-up data are ragged.

Wilson et al. succeed in establishing that psychoanalysis can be applied with success to some patients with anorexia nervosa. These include patients with long histories and difficult presentations that many therapists would not consider candidates for analysis. They elaborate many important psychodynamic issues, including in particular countertransference issues. Repeated references to the talent of many their patients suggest, but do not characterize, ego assets in their population that may have been treatment enabling. Most anorectics seen in psychiatric treatment have beneath their symptoms moderate to severe degrees of psychopathology without any special countervailing endowment. While undertaking to treat an emaciated anorectic with office psychoanalysis is heroic and occasionally successful, the implication that it might be proper routine for fifty percent underweight patients is mischievous.

## Family Therapy

It is the opinion of many therapists and investigators that family therapy is important in the treatment of anorexia nervosa. There are, however, no reported controlled studies to document this. Family therapy became more prominent as a treatment form through the defection of Selvini-Palazzoli from an individual psychoanalytic to a family systems approach (38). Hsu (28) has briefly reviewed studies of family pathology in relation to etiology and Yager (53) has dealt in more detail with family issues in pathogenesis.

The current clinical stance is that in anorexia it is always beneficial to involve families in treatment—at least initially, where they are available geographically and psychologically. Nevertheless, in reality the first order of business for the therapist is to determine the likelihood that family therapy will be of benefit to the patient. This may involve a prolonged assessment and preparation phase involving one or both parents. Such assessment may result in the recommendation that one or both parents engage in individual therapy prior to or concomitant with the onset of family therapy. Or, there may be a recommendation for prior or concomitant marital therapy. (Occasionally, it will be determined in advance that family therapy will in all probability be a negative force.)

The situation becomes more complicated with patients who are married. But the same considerations as in family therapy apply to marital therapy and spouses. Nor can family of origin members be ignored or discounted in the case of married patients. It does little for treatment when the patient is brought to the hospital one day by her husband only to be whisked out the next by her mother and sister.

Once family therapy sessions proper begin, the first issues to be dealt with are the beliefs and attitudes of the designated patient, family members, and therapist in regard to the family's role in the cause and perpetuation of the illness. In practical terms the parents' posture is most usually either to assume total responsibility for causing the illness or to deny the illness exists. Neither posture leads to constructive change. Regardless of the therapist's basic beliefs about etiology and pathogenesis it is better to evaluate each family member individually as well as the total family ethos.

Minuchin et al. (37) have offered a challenge to all other modalities in the treatment of anorexia nervosa by claiming recovery from both anorexia and its psychosocial components in eighty-six percent (43/50) of patients treated by their method of family systems therapy. Follow-up was from one and one-half to seven years with eighty percent followed for two or more years. Median age of the patients was fourteen and one-half years, median interval of illness onset to start of treatment was six months, and median course of treatment was six months (range 2-16 months). Follow-up ratings were global-clinical. One of the interesting features of this study was that sixteen different therapists were employed. These therapists came from different disciplines and levels of experience, thus suggesting an effect of the method rather than the practitioner. Another feature was the flexibility in formal characteristics and specific goals of treatment. These goals depended on the developmental status of each patient, most of whom were adolescents. Again this suggests an effect due to the family systems treatment framework.

Factors other than treatment may have contributed to the positive outcome of this study. In addition to a relatively young population with short duration of illness, case selection may have been biased in favor of good outcome. The families in treatment were difficult enough, to be sure, but the struggles to get the families into treatment and maintain them there on any consistent basis appeared to have been resolved outside the treatment study. Perhaps the employment of the "family meal"—a weekly occasion during which family interactions and attitudes toward eating could be observed and during which therapeutic points could be made—was one of the tools in the program that helped to select families more committed to treatment. Nevertheless, Minuchin et al. make a very strong case for the use of family systems treatment, at least with younger anorectic patients.

Family systems treatment needs further study—from patient/family selection to follow-up—before it can lay true claim to being the best treatment even for a defined sub-group of anorectic patients.

## Self-Help and Support Groups

Eating disorders self-help organizations and support groups are a new and useful addition to the treatment of anorexia nervosa (25, 32-34). In an admirable review Rubel (42) points out that these resources have existed for less than ten years. With more than one hundred groups developing independently in different parts of the country, their structures, formats, and goals are quite variable. The "ideal" self-help group should not involve professionals. In practice, however, the most stable eating disorders groups to date do involve them. Professional therapists seem to assist these groups best by acting as organizers, teachers of social and counseling skills, and technical consultants. When they act as therapists they begin to undermine the self-help concept and impair the group's purposes.

Accessibility to a group is desirable for families as well as patients since many of both's needs can be served in the support group setting —it reduces social isolation and provides a noncritical environment for issue exploration. Through shared experiences parents can learn strategies in how to cope with their children's problems and their own feelings. In groups that mix parents and children of different families, the greater emotional distance can sometimes enable the older generation to hear and appreciate better what the younger generation has to say about the illness.

For refractory patients in particular, the contact with someone who has "been there" but has found herself capable of changing destructive attitudes and behaviors is beneficial. Such contact may also reinforce the sicker patient's negative feelings, however, so groups must be prepared with outreach plans that will help sustain membership contact, particularly with newer and sicker members. A group also must be prepared to acknowledge a member's bid for self-reliance by supporting nonattendance at some point.

In the largest such self-help group, BASH (Bulimia/Anorexia Self-Help, St. Louis), several hundred people are on the rolls and once a month up to four hundred of them—including patients and their families—gather for the better part of a day. During these meetings there is an educational presentation followed by small group sessions. These sessions are led by facilitators, some of whom are improved and/or recovered patients. The groups contain both parents and children but families are separated intergenerationally. One of the outstanding features of this model is the use of facilitators: lay people who have completed a comprehensive training program in eating disorders and self-help.

Self-help groups are not a substitute for other forms of treatment. In fact, a valuable function these groups can serve is to refer individuals to qualified treatment resources (some support groups are integral parts of multi-modal treatment programs). This does not necessarily mean referral away from the group, however, as patients and families can participate in support group activities during different phases of treatment. By the same token, self-help groups may be the only resource available to a substantial number of anorectic patients and their families. This is due to 1) financial reasons and/or 2) personal choice. The latter may be based on unrealistic fears about treatment by professionals or on previous unsuccessful encounters with them.

Factors intrinsic to self-help groups make study difficult, but evaluation studies are needed on the effects of the self-help group experience. Positive effects attributable to that experience would in all likelihood be seen as having been achieved by cost-effective means. Likewise, at this stage of our knowledge, it is quite possible that a sub-group of anorexia nervosa patients may be identifiable for whom a self-help group experience is the best treatment.

## Programs, Teams, and Iatrogenesis

Nowadays it is fashionable to be slim. If one carries this to excess it is fashionable to be treated in an eating disorders program by a team of specialists. Perhaps the sequence of events leading to this was inevitable, but social cyberneticists should be at work attempting to determine if reinforcing feedback circuitry is beginning to develop in this system. From the standpoint of patients, their families, and their therapists, the connotations of the words "program", "team", and "specialist" are unfortunate for a few reasons. Taken together the three terms imply a potential for treatment power that doesn't exist today. It is one thing to offer hope and quite another to ignite unrealistic expectations.

Take the words individually. The word "program" is most commonly associated with TV and/or some other entertainment at which one is a passive observer. "Team" in a treatment connotation is likely to conjure up fantasies of the surgical team—the patient lies unconscious while a swarming group of specialists perform a miracle. And finally, consider the word "specialist". Is it someone who spends most of his or her time treating the illness in question? Is it someone with special training, experience, and expertise? With respect to anorexia nervosa there are very few of the latter around at present. The connotations of these terms reinforce notions that the patient is a passive participant in the proceedings.

Since the terminology is already in place, some steps need to be taken to mitigate the myths it has [since this refers to "terminology"] created. At the individual level the practitioner can attempt to educate patients and their families about how difficult an eating disorder is to treat. The therapist can point out the extended time usually required, the variability of course during treatment, and the unpredictability of outcome. Although this approach seems to make little impression at first, when it is applied repeatedly it begins to make sense to patients and their families as they experience the vicissitudes of treatment over time. If applied consistently by the treatment community at large, it may serve to reduce the frenzied level of expectation currently present in the treatment seeking atmosphere.

Practitioners can assist at the public education level as well by making a greater effort to influence the tone of news media accounts, particularly in local papers. Feature articles continue to appear and their form has become almost as stereotyped as the classical symptoms of the illness (43). Art work consists of the "Anorexia Logo": cartoon of elephantine girl, full face, peering from the mirror at concentration camp victim, seen rear view. Lately there has been a second wave of eating disorders articles. These new articles deal with bulimia (1, 13, 14, 16). Accompanying these is usually the photo of a healthy looking, attractive, young woman reported in the article as cured or recovering. In these articles the symptom descriptions are usually good. Then comes epidemiology, with incidence/prevalence figures cited based on the highest guesses. In short, the impression is conveyed that there is an epidemic of crisis proportions. The story continues with pods of information gathered from distant expert sources followed by the young woman's case history. She has been successfully treated by a local expert, who also comments knowledgeably on the diseases in general. The major flaw in the treatment story is that it does not convey—no newspaper feature story could—the degree of turmoil and distress the illness occasions in patients and those around her.

The format of these feature stories is simple: human interest story of attractive young girl in crisis with a happy ending. They tend to glamorize the illness. But an illness with a six to eighteen percent mortality rate (27, 47) and such a high morbidity rate (27, 31, 46, 48) is not glamorous.

Perhaps public attention could be gained only by such glamorization, but the recognition phase should be over. Now is the time for all responsible editors to find a way of enticing their readerships into a realistic comprehension of anorexia nervosa and the difficulty in treating it. And it is up to the directors of the suddenly ubiquitous eating disorders programs to help them accomplish this.

The stuff of anorexia (and bulimia) is material incompatible with popular weekly magazines. Diet books are already under bombardment from serious eating disorders professionals (17, 52). As for TV presentations, to subdue the carnival atmosphere and project a message in sober perspective requires the combination in one person of experienced television showman and eating disorders expert. Only one or two such persons may exist.

Perhaps, counter to what the media project, no eating disorders "epidemic" exists. But if there is a real increase in incidence, if suggestibility plays any part in inducing the syndromes, current media practices and coverage may be contributing to the problem. Likewise, the efflorescence of programs and teams designed especially to deal with eating disorders may be contributing also. They may be fueling the unhealthy narcissistic tendency of these patients to believe that their disorder makes them worthy of special notice. Possible counters to this trap are for professionals to emphasize the serious nature of the business at hand. Once a given program has become established, it should merge with a broader division of disorders—e.g., "Psychosomatic," "Dietary Dyscontrol." Otherwise, we may be contributing to the illnesses we treat (50).

# ACKNOWLEDGEMENT

This work was supported by the Tom and Sarah Kern Anorexia Nervosa Fund.

## REFERENCES

1. AP: Fitness Guru's Second Child Changed Her Eating Habits. *Durham Morning Herald,* Dec. 26, 1984.
2. Askevold, F.: The diagnosis of anorexia nervosa. *Int. J. Eating Disorders,* 2(4):39–43, 1983.
3. Bliss, E. L., and Branch, C. H. H.: *Anorexia Nervosa: Its History, Psychology and Biology.* New York, Hoeber, 1960.
4. Bruch, H.: The psychiatric differential diagnosis of anorexia nervosa. In J. Meyer and H. Feldmann (eds.): *Anorexia Nervosa.* Stuttgart:Georg Thieme Verlag, 1965.
5. Bruch, H.: Family transactions in eating disorders. *Comprehensive Psychiatry,* 12:238–248, 1971.
6. Bruch, H.: *Eating Disorders: Obesity, Anorexia Nervosa, and the Person Within.* New York, Basic Books, 1973.
7. Bruch, H.: Perils of behavior modification in treatment of anorexia nervosa. *JAMA,* 230(10):1419–1422, 1974.
8. Bruch, H.: Psychological antecedents of anorexia nervosa. In R. Vigersky (ed.): *Anorexia Nervosa.* New York, Raven Press, 1977.
9. Bruch, H.: *The Golden Cage: The Enigma of Anorexia Nervosa.* Cambridge, Harvard University Press, 1978.
10. Bruch, H.: Island in the river: The anorexic adolescent in treatment. In S. C. Feinstein and P. L. Giovacchini (eds.): *Adolescent Psychiatry.* Chicago, Chicago University Press, 1979.
11. Bruch, H.: Anorexia nervosa: Therapy and theory. *Am. J. Psychiatry,* 139(12):1531–1538, 1982.
12. Bruch, H.: Psychotherapy in anorexia nervosa. *Int. J. Eating Disorders,* 1:4:3–14, 1982.
13. Caudill, P.: Bulimia: The Road to Thinness is Paved with Food. *The Fayetteville Times,* Section G (Lifestyle), Jan. 30, 1983, pp 1–2.
14. Caudill, P.: One Victim's Tug of War with Food. *The Fayetteville Times,* Section G (Lifestyle), pp 1–2, Jan. 30, 1983.
15. Crisp. A. H.: Anorexia nervosa. *Br. Med. J.,* 287:855–858, 1983.
16. Davis, B.: The End of Binge and Purge: Eating Disorders Can Be Relieved Through Program. *The Altanta Constitution,* Oct. 25, 1984.
17. Dazzi, A., and Dwyer, J.: Nutritional analyses of popular weight-reduction diets in books and magazines. *Int. J. Eating Disorders,* 3(2):61–79, 1984.
18. Drossman, D. A.: Anorexia nervosa: A comprehensive approach. *Adv. Intern. Med.,* 28:339–361, 1983.
19. Frisch, R. E. and McAruthur, J. W.: Menstrual cycles: Fatness as a determinant of minimum weight for height necessary for their maintenance or onset. *Science,* 185:949–951, 1974.
20. Garfinkel, P. E. and Garner, D. M.: *Anorexia Nervosa: A Multidimensional Perspective.* New York, Brunner/Mazel, 1982.
21. Garfinkel, P. E., and Garner, D. M.: Multidetermined nature of anorexia nervosa. In Darby, Garfinkel, Garner, and Coscina, (eds.): *Anorexia Nervosa: Recent Developments in Research.* New York, Alan R. Liss, Inc., 1983, pages 3–14.
22. Garner, D. M. and Bemis, K. M.: A cognitive-behavioral approach to anorexia nervosa. *Cog. Ther. and Res.,* 6(2):123–150, 1982.
23. Garner, D. M., Garfinkel, P. E., and Bemis, K. M.: A multidimensional psychotherapy for anorexia nervosa. *Int. J. Eating Disorders,* 1(2):3–46, 1982.
24. Garner, D. M., Olmsted, M. P., and Garfinkel, P. E.: Does anorexia nervosa occur on a continuum? *Int. J. Eating Disorders,* 2(4):11–20, 1983.
25. Gartner, A., and Riessman, F.: *Help: A Working Guide to Self-Help Groups.* New York, New Viewpoints/Vision Books, 1980.
26. Halmi, K. A.: Classification of eating disorders. *Int. J. Eating Disorders,* 2(4):21–26, 1983.

27. Hsu, L. K. G.: Outcome of anorexia nervosa: A review of the literature (1954 to 1978). *Arch. Gen. Psychiatry,* 9(37):1041–1046, 1980.
28. Hsu, L. K. G.: The aetiology of anorexia nervosa. *Psychol. Med.,* 113:231–238, 1983.
29. Hurst, A.: Discussion on anorexia nervosa. *Proc. Roy. Soc. Med.,* 32:744–745, 1939.
30. Keys, A., Brozek, J., Henschel, A., Mickelsen, O., and Taylor, H. L.: *The Biology of Human Starvation.* Minneapolis, University of Minnesota Press, 1950.
31. Kohle, K., and Mall, H.: Follow-up study of 36 anorexia patients treated on an integrated internistic-psychosomatic ward. *Int. J. Eating Disorders, 2(4):215–219, 1983.*
32. Larocca, F. E. F.: The relevance of self-help in the management of anorexia and bulimia. *Res Medica* magazine, 1(2):16–19, St. Louis, St. John's Mercy Medical Center, 1983.
33. Larocca, F. E. F.: *A Public Primer On Eating Disorders: The BASH Approach.* St. Louis, Mo. BASH, Inc. 1984.
34. Larocca, F. E. F., and Kolodny, N. J.: *Anorexia & Bulimia: Facilitator's Training Manual. A Primer: The BASH Approach. St. Louis, Midwest Medical Publications, 1983.*
35. Lucas, A. R.: Subject Review: Toward the understanding of anorexia nervosa as a disease entity. *Mayo Clin. Proc.* 56:254–264, 1981.
36. Maxwell, J. K., Tucker, D. M., and Towner, B. D.: Asymmetric cognitive function in anorexia nervosa. *Intern. J. Neuroscience,* 24:37–44, 1984.
37. Minuchin, S., Rosman, B. L., and Baker L.: *Psychosomatic Families: Anorexia Nervosa in Context.* Cambridge, Harvard Univ. Press, 1978.
38. Palazzoli, M. S.: *Self Starvation: From Individual to Family Therapy in the Treatment of Anorexia Nervosa.* Arnold Pomerans, tr. New York and London: Jason Aronson, 1978; London: Human Context Books, Chaucer, 1974.
39. Rippere, V.: Dietary treatment of chronic obsessional ruminations. *Br. J. Clin. Psychology,* 22:314–316, 1983.
40. Rippere, V.: Can hypoglycemia cause obsessions and ruminations? *Medical Hypotheses,* 15:3–13, 1984.
41. Rockwell, W. J. K., Nishita, J. K., and Ellinwood, E. H.: Anorexia nervosa: Current perspectives in research. *Psychiatric Clin. N. Am.,* 7(2):223–233, 1984.
42. Rubel, J. A.: The function of self-help groups in recovery from anorexia nervosa and bulimia. *Psychiatric Clin. of N. Am.,* 7(2):381–394, 1984.
43. Sill, M.: A Fat Image May Hide Behind a Thin Body. *The News and Observer,* Raleigh, N.C., Oct. 22, 1983.
44. Sours, J. A.: *Starving to Death in a Sea of Objects: The Anorexia Nervosa Syndrome.* New York & London, Jason Aronson, 1980.
45. Steinhausen, H-C., and Glanville, K.: Follow-up studies of anorexia nervosa: A review of research findings. *Psychological Medicine,* 13:239–249, 1983.
46. Steinhausen, H-C., and Glanville, K.: Retrospective and prospective follow-up studies in anorexia nervosa. *Int. J. Eating Disorders,* 2(4):221–235, 1983.
47. Theander, S.: Research on outcome and prognosis of anorexia nervosa and some results from a Swedish long-term study. *Int. J. Eating Disorders,* 2(4):167–174, 1983.
48. Vandereycken, W., and Pierloot, R.: Long-term outcome research in anorexia nervosa: The problem of patient selection and follow-up duration. *Int. J. Eating Disorders,* 2(4):237–242, 1983.
49. Vandereycken, W.: Neuroleptics in the short-term treatment of anorexia nervosa: A double-blind placebo-controlled study with sulpiride. *Br. J. Psychiatry,* 144:288–292, 1984.
50. Wallach, M. A., and Wallach L.: *Psychology's Sanction for Selfishness: The Era of Egoism in Theory and Therapy.* San Francisco, W. H. Freeman & Co., 1983.
51. Wilson, C. P., ed.: *The Fear Of Being Fat: The Treatment of Anorexia and Bulimia.* New York, Jason Aronson, 1983.
52. Wooley, O. W., and Wooley, S.: The beverly hills eating disorder: The mass marketing of anorexia nervosa. *Int. J. Eating Disorders,* 1(3):57–69, 1982.
53. Yager, J.: Family issues in the pathogenesis of anorexia nervosa. *Psychosomatic Med.,* 44:43–60, 1982.

## CHAPTER 3

# Recent Trends In Group Therapy For Anorexia Nervosa and Bulimia

Eugene A. Piazza, MD and Catherine Steiner-Adair, EdD

(This chapter was supported in part by the *Nancy Rollins Anorexia Nervosa Research Fund* and the *Gilbert H. Hood Family Fund.* Nina Piazza, M.S.W provided editorial and technical assistance.)

Group therapy has become a common form of treatment for anorexia and bulimia. In addition to its usefulness as a treatment modality, group therapy has become more frequently used because of the proliferation of eating disorder programs over the past ten years. There remains controversy in various aspects of group therapy, however, and a continuing need exists for adequate evaluation and assessment of outcome. Reports of group therapy for these disorders have been increasing in literature since 1980. Few indications of the use of group therapy appear before then.

Numerous articles are now available on group therapy for eating disordered patients, each presenting its own theoretical and clinical evolution. In this chapter we will attempt to provide a selective overview of what theoretical approaches are being considered, how groups are being designed and structured, and what seems to be working. In order to do this, we have chosen a small number of representative group programs, realizing that the limited scope of this chapter could not include all group programs. We have purposely excluded group programs that have already been widely represented in literature.

The purpose of this chapter is to inform readers of the variety of issues and options in designing a group therapy program for patients with eating disorders. Our assumption is that the interested reader will use this chapter as a springboard to the primary sources for further information.

At present there are group therapies for patients, their parents and families, and support and self-help groups. These will be discussed separately. These three kinds of groups, both inpatient and outpatient, fall into four different theoretical approaches: cognitive-behavioral, psycho-educational, insight, and self-help.

## NORMAL FEMALE ADOLESCENT DEVELOPMENT AND THE USEFULNESS OF GROUP THERAPY

The recent proliferation of group therapy has sprung from a general feeling of significant potential for this treatment modality. Several authors (Vandereycken, Polivy, Fernandez, and Mitchell among others) have discussed the application of group therapy theories for eating disordered patients.

Perhaps some additional insight into the success of group therapy for females with eating disorders can be found in the literature on normal female adolescent development. Although the usefulness of group therapy for both sexes cannot be disputed, this section will deal with developmental differences between males and females that may shed light on why groups are particularly helpful for teenage and young adult females with eating disorders.

Females may be especially good candidates to benefit from group therapy because they are socialized to be dependent on an external audience for their self-definition (Douvan and Adelson 1976) and are perhaps best able to integrate change when receiving peer support. Although separation, individuation and autonomy are upheld as the goals of development in current psychological theories—as well as in the culture at large (Rothchild 1979)—recent research on female adolescence points to a different conceptualization of female identity formation. This concept emphasizes the relational and social context for female identity formation.

More recently, developmental psychologists have shifted the paradigm of female adolescent development from the male based traditional model—which emphasizes detachment in movement towards autonomy—towards a model which presents the identity process for adolescent females as one of self-differentiation within the context of relationships. In other words, females develop their identity as they experience themselves through attachment in relationships. (Chodorow, 1974, Gilligan, 1979, 1982, Marcia, 1980). As a result, females tend to be more aware of the impact of individual decisions on others, and they are more likely to make changes in themselves when they feel others support them.

The tendency for females with eating disorders to "rely solely on acceptance from others as the criterion for positive self-evaluation" (Garner, 1982, p. 24) is described in clinical literature as a disturbance. However, females are naturally more dependent on and vulnerable to external references impacting on their sense of identity since they develop their identity in the context of relationships. Because girls are socialized to rely heavily on external acceptance and feedback to inform their identity, they are more vulnerable to peer pressure and cultural values. In contrast to boys—who are encouraged to make independent decisions—girls are oriented towards an external audience for making judgments, and are encouraged to remain fluid and ambiguous between their self-definition and external confirmation in that self-definition (Douvan and Adelson, 1976).

Another example of how female socialization differs from that of males relevant to eating disorders can be found in comparing the family systems' understanding of the role of the eating disordered child and the literature on self-initiated conflict by teenagers within the family. Minuchin (1978) along with others has described the anorectic's peace-keeping familial role and describes the potential eating disordered patient as the loyal family member who avoids and smooths out conflict within an enmeshed family system. However, there is a significant sex role difference found in self-initiated conflict within the family by male and female teenagers. For the adolescent boy who is socialized to make independent life decisions which can lead to conflict or crisis with authority figures, creating conflict within the family can be an identity confirming event. This is different for the female, who from toddlerhood on has been socialized to be proficient in interpersonal relationships. For a teenage female, initiating a decision or disagreement within her family can be experienced as a disconfirmation of her identity and can have a different meaning for her rather than a boy (Marcia, 1980, p. 179). Clearly, females with eating disorders have a difficult time developing the capacity to take a stand apart from their family or culture and still feel connected to them. One can see how helpful group support and the opportunity to practice these social skills would be.

27

Today's female adolescents have been socialized to be concerned with and to value relationships. However, suddenly at adolescence they are taught to devalue the importance of relationships towards which they have been socialized and to value independence and autonomy (Steiner-Adair, 1984). This developmental double bind confronts the teenage adolescent girl with the challenge of valuing parts of herself that society suddenly teaches her to devalue, and requires that the female adolescent take a stand apart from the culture—a task for which she is often poorly prepared (Steiner-Adair, 1984). As the cultural values and expectations of women have shifted over the last twenty years, women's consciousness-raising groups have sprung up all over the country to help women integrate new values and opportunities, and to resist adopting unhealthy values which err in denying the fundamental importance of interdependence. There is a striking parallel between the nature of women's groups and the psycho-educational and supportive nature of group therapy for women with eating disorders. The group enables the eating disordered female to take a stand apart from cultural values which are developmentally detrimental, without feeling isolated.

Perhaps the most obvious way in which group therapy helps girls with eating disorders take a stand apart from the culture is in the area of resisting the cultural messages about dieting and thinness. Clearly girls with anorexia have an exaggerated and distorted preoccupation with thinness (Garner et al., 1982, p. 13-14). However, the literature on normal female adolescent development affirms that the symptomatic self-destructive dieting behavior is culturally supported. There is a striking sex role difference concerning the impact of socio-cultural influences on teenage boys and girls—girls being far more directly affected by and therefore dependent on a narrowly defined cultural beauty ideal. While numerous psychodynamic interpretations have been generated concerning the anorectic's inability to accept her body as it is (Galdston 1974, Masterson, 1977, Bruch, 1978), the recent literature on normal female adolescent development indicates that today's girls are being socialized to be unable to accept their bodies. This presents female teenagers with yet another developmental double bind: one of adolescence's challenges is coming to terms with one's body and developing a positive body image. Yet at the same time, today's society tells its female teenagers that they should struggle to change their body to fit a narrowly defined beauty ideal and that they will be judged according to the extent to which they are able to change their bodies. They are not supported for their ability to accept their bodies (Wooley and Wooley, 1980, Steiner-Adair, 1984).

Numerous studies have been done which indicate that it is not socially adaptive or rewarding for a girl to accept her body as she metamorphoses into a full-rounded female during adolescence and young adulthood. By age three, girls have been socialized to accept a standard of thinness that is dangerously close to the minimal required weight for reproduction, and to hate obesity (Wooley and Wooley, 1980). Paradoxically, as females reach puberty and their bodies begin to mature and fill out, they are simultaneously more vulnerable to socio-cultural standards of beauty impacting their self-esteem. Adolescent girls are more harshly judged and punished on the basis of their bodies (Elder, 1969). In evaluating females, our culture places a high value on physical beauty. Not surprisingly, self-esteem, self-confidence and anxiety levels fluctuate more in women because of their body-image than in men (Fisher, 1974). Girls are more comparative, critical and self-conscious about their bodies and therefore worry more about them than do boys (Rosenbaum, 1979). Unfortunately, rather than help the female teenager relate to her body and live in it in a creative way, today's culture tells her that to compromise on her looks is "crazy" (Steiner-Adair, 1984).

All therapists who work with eating disordered patients are acutely aware of the struggle confronting patients on the road to recovery when they must reject the cultural imperative to define themselves in terms of their body size, and to maintain a low body weight by staying on a diet. Similarly, most therapists are familiar with the patient's complaint that the therapist's support of a healthier body weight and dietary style exists in a vacuum ("you're just saying I look good because you're my therapist"). Group therapy offers an unparalleled milieu in which eating disordered patients can begin to question cultural imperatives that contribute to their disordered behavior, and to take a stand against rigidly defined beauty without feeling terrified and isolated. Patients can identify with one another's gains, and develop an internalized voice that is self-supporting through the support of others. Group therapy provides eating disordered patients with a social context in which they can develop a more healthy identity within the context of the network of group relationships, an arena to practice and develop interpersonal skills, and a shared experience in which the importance of relationships and communication is supported and rein-forced. Furthermore, the group provides a safe and supportive envi-ronment in which the patients can begin to question cultural values concerning beauty ideals, eating behaviors and the overemphasis on independence which have all been distorted in the eating disordered syndrome, as well as the culture at large.

# INSIGHT GROUP THERAPY: INPATIENT

Insight-focused group therapy is based on the psychoanalytic concept of insight into one's own feelings, thoughts, and dreams, and into one's manner of relating. Additionally, the mechanisms of transference and feedback play a central role in the workings of insight-oriented group therapy.

## Goals

While there is much theoretical overlap among the various practition-ers, Lieb et al., Piazza et al., Polivy and Maher have reported on insight-oriented inpatient groups. Piazza, et al. (1983), on the Psy-chosomatic Unit at Boston's Children's Hospital, observed a natural clustering together of anorectic patients (with good and ill effects) and decided to restructure the informal group interactions into a formal therapy group for purposes of maximizing the positive influences of socialization, role modeling, and mutual support in a non-threatening, non-punitive atmosphere. Lieb also noted the importance of those treatment goals as well as the goals of gaining insight into feelings and behavior and improving staff's effectiveness through better under-standing of their anorectic patient's concerns. Maher corroborated other's awareness of the socializing aspect of the group, and noted also that the group setting provided better opportunities for improved reality testing, especially with regard to body image distortions. He also discusses the importance of family dynamics in anorectic symp-tom formation and therapy, and sees possibilities within the group for "family reenactment." Polivy finds in this modality a means for achieving goals that include "consensual validation," peer feedback, coping models, and increased self-esteem. Hall, on a more cautious note, feels that goals relating to expressions of assertiveness, recogniz-ing and dealing with anger, dealing with fears of displeasing others, hopelessness and isolation should be handled gradually and at later stages of the group's experience. Vandereycken and Meermann observe that, by virtue of a common symptomatology, the anorectic in a well-structured group can have a corrective influence on the individual's distortions and manipulations. For example, deceptions and "tricks of the trade" (hiding pennies in pockets, "water loading") are quickly revealed by other anorectics who may also have used those same tricks. These clinicians also find the group model useful for reasons previously mentioned: goals of mutual support and reality testing.

## Leadership

To counteract the common complaint that "other people" cannot understand, Piazza et al. turned to a recovered anorectic with group experience to co-lead an inpatient anorectic group. The leader also served as a role model for group members. Milieu staff on the Psychosomatic Unit of Children's Hospital were sought out as the other half of the leadership team and as observers—their knowledge of patient issues and personalities was seen as helpful in running the group. Hall found her role as individual therapist useful and advantageous in her simultaneous position as group therapist. Whereas group leadership at Children's was always female—in consideration of the sexual and feminist issues often raised—Huerta reports success with himsef as group leader. Hall sees the need for a more active and encouraging stance on the part of the leader in contrast to the interpretive, silent traditional role. Certainly staff on the Psychosomatic Unit found a more active style of leadership effective in providing a positive atmosphere for the patients' interactions and mutual support and disagreements, and helpful in reducing tension that can occur from the anorectic's experience of herself as "empty" in group settings. These patients require a more interactive and relational form of individual insight oriented therapy (Surrey). The same is also true for insight-oriented group therapy.

## Patient Selection

Patients who present severe cachexia and emaciation, and whose body vital signs—blood pressure, pulse and temperature—are markedly below normal, have been found to have cognitive deficits and disordered thinking which adversely affect their ability to benefit from group therapy. Also, their psychic impairment can have deleterious effects on the fragile and tenuous efforts towards health of other group

31

members. Other clinicians report similar findings regarding the physical condition of group members. Inpatient group members are, on the whole, needy. As Polivy points out, smaller group size is important "so patients do not feel compelled to vie for group time." On the Unit of Children's Hospital we found the most workable size ranged from six to eight members. Hall, on the other hand, prefers limiting membership to a somewhat smaller group (4-6). Because these are inpatient groups, however, one is limited by the availability of patients, and therapy groups are formed with the population at hand. Inpatient groups are usually open-ended—as newly admitted patients become physically ready, they join the group. Likewise, as patients are discharged, they leave the group.

For the first four years of the anorectic groups on the Psychosomatic Unit, discharged patients were encouraged to continue attending their group during the vulnerable six-week period after hospitalization. The healthier, discharged patients were sometimes noted as having a positive influence on their inpatient fellow members. On the other hand, the fragility of the post-discharge period was sometimes endangered by the regressive pull of those less healthy, newly admitted members.

Regarding group mix, some authors (Hall, 1985, Maher, 1984) feel that anorectics should be in a homogenous group. We have on many occasions included bulimics and anorectics with histories of binging and vomiting in our anorectic group therapy. When a male anorectic has been admitted on the Unit, he, too, has been included in the group. We do not find the occasional male or bulimic patient to be overly influenced or affected adversely by the group.

However, a more important distinction, we feel, is that of age. We assume patients within the 13-19 year range are dealing with a common set of adolescent issues. The 20+ group is dealing with marital, job adjustment, life satisfaction, and chronic illness issues, and is better served within one group. Frequency of meetings varies, as does the length of individual sessions. Most therapists find weekly sessions adequate, and limit sessions to one hour or so. Longer sessions seem too exhausting for leaders and members, even though the "tempo" of the group often picks up just before the time is up.

## Benefits and Disadvantages to Group Therapy with Inpatients

One of the initial findings on follow-up at Children's Hospital was the relationship between subjectively experiencing friendships on the Unit as helpful and having a favorable medical outcome (Piazza & Rollins, 1981). It is within the safety of the group that these friendships and general socialization are nurtured and encouraged to extend outside the group.

As mentioned in an earlier section, the anorectic group benefits the individual by offering—perhaps for the first time—an atmosphere where everyone there knows how it feels to be anorectic and that "just eating" isn't as easy as it sounds. Concerns about weight, body size, sexual matters, and family issues are tested out within the group setting, with other members helping to validate or correct the individual's statements and beliefs. The advantage of this built-in feedback is that it can be an invaluable tool for growth and intergrating change.

Many anorectics find beginning individual therapy difficult. They identify the therapist with parental authority figures, thus interfering with the formation of a trusting therapeutic alliance. The patient-therapist relationship in the group setting is less intense and threatening, and may yield a more comfortable setting in which to share real concerns and to allow the development of trusting relationships. Although it is unusual to observe an anorectic patient challenge a peer's symptomatic behavior outside the group milieu, group therapy seems to support and elicit members confronting their peers denial and manipulations in a healthy and productive way.

What are the disadvantages of group therapy for these patients? Hall and Maher find the anorectic's denial of feelings and problems prevents them from forming the kinds of meaningful social relationships needed to even begin to make use of group treatment. We feel that some of these issues, though difficult, can often be dealt with in the group. Identification of themselves as "anorectics" to the exclusion of other healthier qualities can be a potential hazard, as can be the negative influence members sometimes exert on each other: for instance, an anorectic, stuck in her sick role, may occasionally attempt to tear down any thrust towards health by other members. This is certainly a serious problem and must be addressed by group leaders through consolidating the forces for health and optimism of the better functioning group members. Through their modeling and influence, these healthier patients may well dislodge the sicker member from her sick role.

Extreme dependency of patients on each other was found by Polivy within anorectic groups. At Children's Hospital, however, we were not concerned about over-dependence and encouraged the extension of these friendships beyond the group—which usually took the form of a network of telephone contacts and visits. In interviewing patients as they approach discharge, they often say that the friendships formed in the group were the most beneficial aspect of their recovery. Although Polivy found that over-involvement in the group can sometimes serve to split the anorectic patient from involvement in her individual therapy, the staff at Children's found that this usually can be dealt with by maintaining good communications between co-leaders, individual therapist, and milieu team.

## TRANSITION GROUP

In meeting the needs of discharged anorectics and bulimics, the Childrens' Hospital team found they could no longer include these former patients effectively in the ongoing inpatient group. Newly arrived inpatients were dealing with entirely different issues from those of patients in the vulnerable post-discharge period. Consequently, a new "Transition Group" was begun in 1984. It is a time-limited (ten-week) series of sessions, spanning the two weeks prior to and eight weeks after discharge. The primary goal is to prevent recidivism and provide early intervention to prevent rehospitalization. Group issues dealt with concerned separation from the safety and structure of the hospital milieu and adjustments back into home, school, and social environment. Eighteen of the nineteen patients in the group over a six-month period did not require rehospitalization.

The group varies in size, from four to ten, each member contracting for a ten-week period. Since individuals are beginning their ten-week periods at different times, the group is open-ended because of the rolling admissions to the group—the "older" members often serve as role models for those who are just about to leave the hospital. The group is co-led by one of the authors (Steiner-Adair) and the staff nutritionist (Flynn). A nutritionist was chosen to co-lead the group in response to the high amounts of anxiety and interest expressed concerning the complexities of maintaining newly acquired eating skills as patients return to their pre-hospital environment or new residential programs. The therapy model is multidimensional, drawn from the following approaches: cognitive-behavioral, psycho-educational, psychodynamic, family systems, psychodrama, and nutritional management.

# INSIGHT GROUP THERAPY: OUTPATIENT

The general theoretical framework for outpatients is similar to that of the inpatient groups discussed earlier, except that outpatients may be less impaired physically and functioning slightly better psychologically. Because they lack the support of inpatient milieu staff, they may turn to the group for their sole support and comfort. Outpatient group members may never have been hospitalized or may have come from earlier experiences with inpatient groups. While Huerta used the open-ended format with his outpatient groups, our personal experience included a closed outpatient group of adolescent anorectics who were also in individual therapy with the same leader (Piazza). Following the expressed interest of the individual patients in meeting with others with like problems, the leader formed the group of outpatients which met during the spring term of 1980. In contrast to Polivy—who reported that 7 of her 14 patients dropped out (most of the dropouts were the younger patients)—our experience was that the teens in our group, perhaps because more homogeneous in age, remained and finished the period of group therapy. At recent follow-up three of the four were doing well, while one later had a recurrence of her symptoms.

Maher, in reporting on group therapy for 12 anorectic outpatients over a nine-month period, at first was favorably impressed with the group becoming cohesive, being able to identify similar problems, and finding a general feeling of comfort. Using a traditional psychodynamic approach with little structuring by the group leader, there were later major problems of the group members relying increasingly on the therapist, a loss of optimism, and decreasing attendance. This progressed to "a sense of depression, despair, and extreme isolation" (p. 270). Communication among members diminished markedly and half the members dropped out. Maher's general assessment of the group was that it provided limited, if any, benefit in doing psychodynamic insight-oriented group therapy with these patients. This was not found to be true in the cognitive-behavioral, psycho-educational, or multidimensional groups. In part, the experience at Children's Hospital was similar, but over four years of continuous group therapy, there were recurrent cycles of depression, despair and fragmentation of the group process followed by cohesiveness, mutual support and optimism. The leaders also experienced these cycles, and required continuous support from each other and from supervision following each group therapy session. The leaders reacted to the "down" cycle with a sense of frustration and emotional depletion. Hall has emphasized the "loneliness and hunger that can be provoked in the group leader" (p.223).

# COGNITIVE-BEHAVIORAL AND PSYCHO-EDUCATIONAL GROUPS

## General Theory

Outpatient cognitive-behavioral groups and psycho-educational groups are based on combining therapeutic modalities which specifically address symptomatic behavior at a behavioral level which is aimed at symptom reduction, and through education, which is aimed at cognitive restructuring. Mitchell et al. also drew from the chemical dependency model in establishing their approach. Based on the Alcoholics Anonymous model, Mitchell et al. require abstinence of binging and vomiting upon entry (although one is not expelled from the group for a failure to maintain abstinence immediately) and use group pressure and confrontation to reinforce abstinence.

In essence, both cognitive-behavioral therapy and psycho-educational therapy are best described as multidimensional, since there is a great deal of overlap in the different treatment techniques utilized. These include: behavioral contracts, keeping charts which monitor binge-purging behavior and mood changes, identifying trigger thoughts and attitudes, supplying new educational information to change thinking, and teaching stress reduction and relaxation techniques. The shift away from a more traditional insight-oriented therapy to a cognitive-behavioral and psycho-educational approach stems from the observation that although psychodynamic treatment can lead to improvement in well being, it has comparatively little effect on symptomatic behavior and thought disorder, and can in fact increase tension when the patient feels that insight cannot help her with her behavioral problems. Also, the research on psychodynamic insight-oriented groups supports a need for a more structured group experience for patients with eating disorders, and a concomitant need for group leaders to take an active role in all areas of group process. Furthermore, it appears that bulimic behavior is best treated in a group context where patients have the opportunity to learn from their identification with other patients' increased understanding of what triggers destructive cycles. Another benefit is that as an increasing number of requests for help occur, group therapy is far more effective in reaching a broader number of patients when resources are limited.

The shift from more traditional cognitive-behavioral and psycho-educational groups to a multidimensional approach evolved from the observations that behavioral therapy alone, although effective in reducing or temporarily abating symptoms, lead to an increase in tension and denial of intrapsychic problems (Mitchell). Hence, most groups which call themselves either cognitive-behavioral or psycho-educational use a multidimensional approach which utilizes behavioral therapy, cognitive therapy, psychoeducation and insight-oriented therapy. These are groups which have a high degree of built-in structure (around attendance, absences, payment, diaries, dietary prescriptions, and expectations about contributing to group process) which are combined with insight-oriented group discussion.

All of the multidimensional groups stress the connection between bulimia and interpersonal problems, although groups differ in when and how they choose to introduce the connection. Roy-Byrne (1984) retrospectively reported that after an initial period of experimentation, his team found that the connection should be highlighted from the very beginning of any program.

Outpatient group therapy for bulimia is recommended for treatment at various stages or junctures of an individual's road to recovery. Groups have been used as an initial and sole form of therapy, as a beginning introduction to be followed by intensive, individual therapy, or to occur concurrently with individual therapy. Groups may be used as a "transitional object" in the passage out of a hospitalization or after terminating individual therapy. Some groups require that the individual also be in individual therapy. Some groups provide individual therapy as part of their group program (Lacey). And some programs feel that the group is all encompassing, while others suggest but do not require it.

It was hard to distinguish between the goals of treatment programs labelled psycho-educational and those labelled cognitive-behavioral. The most noticeable difference occurred between the one group that was strictly for anorectics: Vandereycken and Meermann's goal was short-term weight restoration for their inpatient cognitive-behavioral group. Weight restoration goals were established in a variety of areas and then were scaled according to predictions of outcome if goals were attained or unattained. Clearly, weight restoration would not have the same salience in groups for bulimics. In fact, changes in weight were forbidden in some groups.

In general terms, goals for cognitive-behavioral groups were aimed at eliminating bulimic behavior, restructuring attitudes towards the self, and improving stress management (Dixon and Kiecolt-Glaser, 1981). Different approaches placed different values on the importance of intra- and interpersonal difficulties. Using the behavioral model of learned helplessness, Connors et al., in their psycho-educational groups discussed the goals in terms of interrupting the symptomatic behavior and the accompanying feelings of helplessness and hopelessness. Fernandez shifted the goals' emphasis towards a more generalized understanding of one's self and emotional problems. Lacey stressed the connection between behavior and interpersonal difficulties. In a program designed to quickly eliminate bulimic behavior and connect behavior to relational problems, his first goal was the removal of dietary manipulation without the development of another weight disorder. The second goal was the recognition and management of the link between emotional and social factors and symptomatic behavior. The final goal was the acquisition of new ways of dealing with emotional and social factors and the interpersonal difficulties associated with them.

Connor's psycho-ed group had an active structured three-stage goal approach aimed at interrupting the symptomatology. In phase one, education and self-monitoring was used to foster cognitive change. Patients are provided with much information concerning socio-cultural, emotional and physical factors, and taught setpoint theory. Phase two consisted of short-term goal contracts which stressed small success and the importance of expressing feelings rather than turning to food. Phase three concluded the program with goals directed toward assertiveness, relaxation, and new coping skills.

## Leadership

All of the cognitive-behavioral and the psycho-educational groups were co-led. The levels of training in both group dynamics and eating disorders varied, although most groups were led by professionals who had some familiarity with eating disorders. The male/female team in Lacey's groups had some knowledge of psychiatry, but no specialized training in group therapy. Medical supervision was provided. Many groups were co-led by staff members who were highly trained in the area of eating disorders (Roy-Byrne, Connors, Fernandez, Boskind-White, Mitchell). Mitchell's program was outstanding in its utilization of leaders representing seven disciplines, each specializing in a different aspect of the treatment of eating disorders (3 psychiatrists, 1 psychologist, 1 social worker, 1 chemical dependency worker, 2 practical nurses, and 1 dietician). Although it was not always possible to determine the sex of group leaders from the articles, three programs specify the advantages of male/female teams.

As a pioneer in the field of group therapy for women with bulimia, Boskind-White initially co-led her groups with another female. However, she quickly discovered the usefulness of co-leadership with a male, but she specified that both leaders should have a strong feminist orientation. Along with Boskind-White's stated advantage of having a man in the group, Lacey described the added advantage of having the parental dyad represented, and the importance of discussing parent-related transference issues. Roy-Byrne et al. also had a male/female team.

Concerning extra-group patient contact, in some programs the group leaders met with some of the patients individually before the group for behavioral contracting (Lacey, Roy-Byrne, Mitchell). In one group (Roy-Byrne et al.), three members were in individual psychotherapy with one of the group leaders. No program reported difficulties resulting from the extra group contact. Concerning the overall perception of the relationship between group leaders and group members, Lacey's description of the alliance as one in which "The therapist and rational self of the patient ally against the dietary and emotional chaos" (Lacey, p. 213) best describes the dynamic impact of the co-leaders.

### Patient Selection

Several authors found mixing anorectic patients in heterogenous groups (i.e. groups with non-eating disordered patients) difficult for numerous reasons. Vandereycken found that mixing anorectics with other patients not only embedded anorectics in accepting their illness but had the adverse effect of promoting specific behaviors and entrenching the identification with the "anorectic" role and identity. In keeping with the psuedo-sociability so often seen in anorectics, Vandereycken observed anorectics playing a superficially and minimally supportive role with others, while internally withdrawing and remaining isolated from the group interaction. This is counterproductive to the opportunities group therapy can offer for developing and practicing new social skills, real interaction, sharing vulnerability, and initiating connection to others.

Until recently, there have been few attempts to run all-anorectic groups due to the concern that anorectics would emulate, imitate, reinforce each other, and even defend each other (Vandereycken p. 126). Furthermore, one can speculate that the anorectics' difficulty with initiating any kind of reflective, vulnerable statements about the self would lead to a painful group of silent, highly anxious females, who would sit comparing their weight in self-rejecting ways—a potentially overwhelming picture for any experienced therapist. However, initial forays into all anorectic groups are demonstrating that multidimensional group therapy with anorectics can in fact be highly beneficial. In contrast to anticipated concerns that anorectics in an all-anorectic group would be as withdrawn as observed in a heterogeneous group, Vandereycken, Polivy, and Yager all found that anorectics are most likely to confront one another in all-anorectic groups. Although some competition for "whose symptoms are most serious" was observed, the common thread of a shared debilitating illness and an accepting group therapy milieu seems to enable anorectics to perceive the psychological meaning of their illness in a collaborative way. While Polivy stresses the importance of the group leaders guarding against the elusive bonding around the anorectic identity that can occur, the benefits gained from the group experience that cannot be attained in individual therapy appear to outweigh the risks.

Roy-Byrne et al. found that in previously heterogeneous groups attended by bulimic patients, the bulimics found the shift to an all-bulimic group preferable. Reasons centered around a sense of shame and embarrassment among people whose problems were not food centered and who weren't purging. Furthermore, the bulimic patients seemed to benefit greatly from the opportunity to identify with other bulimics and learn from them. In an all-bulimic group, patients were more able to comprehend that binging and purging were caused by underlying psychological problems, and to shift their attention from the behavior to the issues.

As the differences between normal-weight bulimics and bulimics with a history of anorexia became increasingly clear, the utility of attending to the differences in patient selection becomes possible. Lacey distinguishes between normal-weight bulimia—as an extension of normal adolescent periodic binging and an intensification of neuroticism—and a more serious history of anorexia that has developed into bulimia. After an initial period of mixing bulimic patients with restricting primary anorectics in a group, Yager established separate groups for bulimics and anorectics. Fernandez found it important to keep the number of bulimics with a history of anorexia small in a group for patients with bulimia. Yager found it valuable to limit the number of borderlines or severely disturbed patients as well.

Several variables have been identified and associated with a poor prognosis in group therapy. Lacey and Fernandez found that a history of alcohol and drug abuse were indicative of poor prognosis. Fernandez found that married patients experienced more difficulty. Patients with personality disorders and sexual disinhibition also did not do as well. Polivy found that anorectics living with their family of origin did less well. Yager did not find this to be significant. Yager found it important to limit the number of patients with intense dependency needs, although a few could benefit from the group without draining it.

All of the psycho-educational and cognitive-behavioral groups were closed groups. The one long-term group (Roy-Byrne et al.) began with far more members (19) than it ended up with (9), and following the high attrition rate, implemented a ten-member policy with strict rules about membership. The veracity of Roy-Byrne's rules about attendance and closing group membership comes out of his experiences which led him to conclude that open groups can be support groups, but cannot provide the same quality of cohesion which builds trust. If new members are to be introduced to an already existing group, they suggested the leaders wait until it is possible to introduce two members simultaneously, in order to diffuse the group reaction to new members.

## Length and Frequency of Therapy Sessions

Most psycho-educational groups are short-term groups. Dixon's groups met for 10 weeks and Connors et al. met for a total of 12 weeks, each session for 2 hours, with 2 meetings a week for the first three weeks, and once a week for the remaining sessions. There were a variety of configurations in the cognitive-behavioral groups concerning length and frequency. Fernandez' groups met for 12 sessions (and paid a fixed fee for the total program in advance). Boskind-Lodahl and White groups met for eleven two-hour sessions with a six-hour marathon session midway.

Boskind-Lodahl and White also do marathon weekend sessions that begin Friday night and continue through most of Sunday. Lacey's program took place over ten weeks, and met for a half-day each time. Each week every individual had a half-hour individual session in which behavioral contracts were established for the week ahead, and then members went into a one and one-half hour therapy group. Mitchell's groups met for 8 weeks at varied frequency. In the first week the patients were seen every night, and then three times a week for the next three weeks, each evening consisting of a 45-minute lecture and group discussion, dinner with the group and group leaders, and then one and one-half hour group therapy which focused on the lectures and homework. In weeks 5-8, patients attended two sessions per week, combining group therapy meetings and support. At the end of the first and second month, patients were seen for individual sessions to evaluate how the treatment was progressing and further needs at termination. In addition to the meetings that were exclusively for patients, during the first month, two sessions for family members or friends were held. In the first meeting, family members and friends were provided with information about bulimia and the treatment program. At the second meeting, they and the patient met to discuss family dynamics, how they related to bulimia, and other interpersonal problems that were linked to the illness.

The longest multidimensional therapy group in the literature was that of Roy-Byrne et al., which met for 12 months, for 90 minutes each session. Initially undertaken as an experiment in long-term group therapy for bulimics, Roy-Byrne et al. shifted their concern to the aspects of attendance, absences, and duration. Because the early stage of the group had problems with attendance, they evolved a policy in which the door to the room was locked after five minutes. Equally strict rules were soon established concerning attendance. After a short period of requesting but not requiring attendance or notification of absences, they established a policy of expelling from the group those with more than two unexplained absences. Three absences within a period of several months had to be discussed privately with the group leaders and in the group sessions. In contrast to short term groups, they did not find it optimal to have a rigidly scheduled duration time for long-term group therapy. A more flexible open-ended long-term commitment that could acknowledge the natural process of long-term group therapy was recommended.

### Techniques and Formats for Outpatient Bulimic Groups

A consistent dimension of all the cognitive-behavioral and psycho-ed groups was the use of contracts. Contracts were generally introduced early in the program or at the very beginning. For example, Lacey had patients contract from the initial interview to attend all the meetings and related sessions. Contracts were both long- and short-term— agreeing to maintain a certain weight for the twelve-week period (Lacey), or asserting oneself in a difficult social situation within the next week (Boskind Lodahl-White). Sometimes contracts were used at the end of each group session to summarize what had been learned and to extend individual goals a step further (Connors, Lacey). Whether the contract be about attendance or weight or practicing a new social skill, the use of contracts and contract negotiations were a major component of this multidimensional therapeutic approach, which places a strong emphasis on the need to analyze behavioral antecedents to binging and purging (Mitchell).

Another consistent dimension of the cognitive-behavioral and psycho-ed groups is the use of diaries in which behaviors and feelings, thoughts and observations are recorded and reviewed. The diaries are used to teach self-monitoring techniques which identify patterns of eating, feelings, and triggers associated with binging and purging. In the area of dieting and eating behavior, there are a wide variety of the combined usage of contracts and diaries to interrupt the symptomatic dieting behavior. In some groups, diaries are used to contract and outline sensible meals, and observe behavior and one's ability to follow a healthy meal plan.

Fernandez tried to implement a reward plan for those group members who successfully attended all meetings and maintained their present weight (which was contracted early in the group). The reward system consisted of two $25 gift certificates purchased at a local department store which would be returned at the successful completion of the group. However, although many patients completed the contracts and the group, they all had a difficult time rewarding themselves and cashing in on their accomplishments. This is not too surprising for those who work with eating disordered patients and are familiar with the difficulty these patients have with any kind of positive self-reinforcement and self-appreciation. Mitchell et al. taught patients to positively reinforce and restructure themselves for unproblematic cognitions and behaviors, making positive reinforcement a self-regulated aspect of cognitive restructuring.

Lacey also had each individual member contract to maintain weight within a prescribed range, and patients in Lacey's program are weighed on the same scales consistently throughout the twelve weeks. It is noteworthy that Lacey found the diaries the single most important element of his multidimensional program, and attributed the highly successful outcome to the strict reinforcement of utilizing diaries. In contrast to this, Roy-Byrne et al. suggested the use of diaries but did not require it because of some patient's experience of keeping a diary as demeaning. In their long-term program, Roy-Byrne et al. also worked with dieting and eating behavior by having the group go out to dinner with the leaders every two months. Lacey also had patients contract from the very beginning to eat a prescribed diet of three meals and to eat only at these times. A diet sheet was contracted which could not be altered without the therapist. If binging occurred, the patient had to continue to eat the three meals, and a new behavior was added and monitored in the diary to reduce the binging.

In most approaches the emphasis eventually shifted to connecting problems in relationships and interpersonal difficulties. In contrast to psychodynamic groups, which tend to employ a more historic approach, these groups focused on the here and now. Connors' program has promoted the message that the decision to binge is a personal choice, and along with Boskind-Lodahl White, highlights the notion of personal accountability. In addition to the keeping of diaries, she uses sensory awareness and guided fantasy exercises to increase awareness of the patterns that lead to binging and purging, and to offer alternative behaviors.

A variety of techniques is suggested to deal with the thought disorder—which is so much a part of bulimia. Cognitive restructuring and psycho-educational materials are applied in several groups. Connors' program has provided much psycho-ed material with particular emphasis on the sociocultural pressure to be thin. This information, combined with information on dieting and setpoint theory offers a reframing of bulimia as an illness involving cultural and biological forces rather than an illness which is exclusively tied to individual failures in personality and willpower. The value of health and the normalcy of eating is repeatedly stressed. This is helpful in changing disordered thinking that leads to symptomatic behavior. Roy-Byrne et al. have dealt more with self-acceptance and focus on individual irrational beliefs.

Several group programs hand out written material, including nutritional information, homework work sheets used for group discussion, and handouts emphasizing both general and specific aspects of bulimia. For example, Fernandez et al. have a handout on the problem of relapse, which they pass out fairly early into the 12-week program, since termination is immediately a factor. In Mitchell's program, group members hear a lecture, receive handouts, and discuss the evening's topic in group. This provides three structures to reinforce new behavior based on new information. Yager also has a printed informational booklet which is distributed at the beginning of the program. Relaxation techniques (Boskind-Lodahl, White) and biofeedback (Connors) are also taught to deal with difficult transitions.

In the area of interpersonal difficulties that are related to bulimia, a combination of exercises and insight-oriented group discussion was described in the cognitive-behavioral and psycho-ed literature. Role playing of feared situations and to introduce new social skills to actual situations was used by Boskind-Lodahl and White and Roy-Byrne. Connors, Dixon, Mitchell and Boskind-Lodahl and White found assertiveness training to be a valuable method of enhancing interpersonal skills and increasing self-expression. Themes related to eating such as revenge, fear of success, need for approval, difficulty in relationships, having a "fat" identity, feeling out of control, and perfectionist expectations (Dixon) are among many described in the literature. Connors found that feelings of sadness and learned helplessness decreased with successes in behavioral changes (which were part of goal setting) and in turn, individuals learned how to assert themselves and had new experiences of personal efficacy. A common arena utilized by many groups for practicing social skills—especially reaching out to others and maintaining connection to others over time—was the suggestion or requirement (Mitchell) of contacting other group members in between sessions.

In conclusion, Mitchell et al. conducted what appeared to be the most extensive and multi-faceted research on outpatient therapies with bulimics and came to several conclusions, many of which are confirmed in the literature. For one and one-half years, nine therapists of different clinical backgrounds led different kinds of therapy groups with strategies as broadranging as behavioral contracting to nondirective, psychodynamically-oriented groups. After weekly meetings to discuss the results of a total of seven groups (with all members meeting

DSM-III Criteria, with 6 to 12 patients per group), Mitchell et al. came up with the following conclusions about outpatient therapy with bulimic patients:

1. Eating behavior and associated problems with food should be discussed in the group. The absence of addressing eating behaviors was associated with an inability to deal effectively with other problems, as well as with little or minimal change in eating behavior.

2. An approach requiring a confession of the bulimic behavior from the onset of the group seemed to be most effective.

3. Although self-esteem and mood improved with abstinence, additional help from cognitive restructuring, assertiveness skills, and relaxation techniques were needed to improve self-concept.

4. Many patients found it helpful to be in additional support groups like Overeaters Anonymous, and referrals were offered.

5. Group members benefited from contact with each other outside the group, including phone calls and increased contact for support to avoid a binge.

6. Although most members could refrain from a binge immediately following the group, some could not sustain this effort toward the end of the group, so a more intensive design was implemented utilizing behavioral constructs and techniques (Mitchell, p. 241-242).

## GROUPS FOR PARENTS OF ANORECTIC INPATIENTS

The use of group therapy for parents as an adjunct to treatment of the anorectic patient points to the already established importance of family dynamics in the overall treatment of anorexia. There have been few reports, however, of the use of parental group therapy for either inpatients or outpatients. Rose and Garfinkel have reported on their use of the group mode at Clarke Institute for parents who either refused or were inappropriate for family treatment. Their goals were to provide these parents with information about the illness, support during the period of their child's hospitalization, and insight into family dynamics. Piazza, Piazza and Rollins (1980), had also reported on a parent group on the Psychosomatic Unit at Children's Hospital. Their goals in setting up the group were to provide a medium in which insight could be made into aspects of parental involvement which related to their child's symptoms, and then to deal therapeutically with these findings. The mutuality of their problems, feelings of sadness and guilt, soon became obvious, and the resultant support was a welcome benefit to all. Guilt-ridden parents discussed in the group their feelings and fears about having a child with such a devastating illness, described the pain of separation, and drew upon the strength of the group to help them not bow to the pressures of their child or to their own internal pressures to remove the child from the hospital prematurely.

Leadership of these parent groups has taken different forms. Rose and Garfinkel have utilized a volunteer adult recovered anorectic to co-lead the group with the social worker. This volunteer leader was well received by the parents who looked to her for better understanding of what their child was experiencing. They could also test out ideas with this recovered anorectic and she in turn could understand their problems and frustrations. Piazza and Rollins were the primary co-therapists for their group of parents, but in addition had an observer-recorder from the milieu staff and periodic attendance by one or two other milieu staff. Group size was usually between 10 and 20 parents, and as children were discharged and admitted, the composition of the parent group changed.

In spite of the turnover, however, there was a sequence of issues and progression in the group process—not a continuous flow, but a spiralling with "forward movement," regression to earlier issues, then on again. While parents wondered what they had done to contribute to the child's problem, they also sought to be absolved from blame. When this wish was not gratified they openly expressed guilt at having caused harm, often with potent emotional release. At this point, the atmosphere would improve and a degree of comfort and trust prevailed. However, their frustrations and anxieties would later reappear to be followed by negative reactions to the group experience with expressions of criticisms that the doctors were withholding and complaints that their expectations were unmet. Many issues regarding changes in themselves and in their understanding of their childrens' illnesses were dealt with in the group process. A variety of sub-groups were formed in which common experiences were explored, disbelief and sympathy shared, and support received from the larger group.

## GROUPS FOR PARENTS OF OUTPATIENT ANORECTICS AND BULIMICS

Recently, Eliot (1982) began a "family crisis" group available to parents of outpatients being evaluated and treated at the Anorexia Nervosa and Associated Disorders Clinic at Children's Hospital. As co-therapists, Eliot has enlisted the aid of two parents of a recovered anorectic patient. The group meets bi-monthly and is open-ended, including parents of children currently being evaluated and/or treated at the Clinic. The purpose of the group is to provide education, support, and help to parents dealing with an anorectic child. The co-therapist parents invited by the leader to join her provide the other parents with support, understanding, and practical suggestions for dealing with the often frustrating and exhausting interactions between them and their anorectic child. These parent co-therapists help others to recognize the need for their own involvement in their child's treatment. As parents who have been through a similar ordeal, they also offer a model of hope and encouragement.

# SELF HELP, INPATIENT AND OUTPATIENT GROUPS

Self-help groups, also sometimes called support groups, are defined by Miller and Powers (p.292) as "the gathering of individuals who, sharing a common problem, work together towards increased understanding of the problem and its consequences, while offering each other empathy and help."

The numerous self-help groups existing now for eating disorders also provide public information and awareness, promote research and development of treatment programs, as well as offer patients and families important support and understanding of their situations.

The concept of self-help has been developed by Larocca for bulimic and anorectic patients as an important adjunct to an all-inclusive program of inpatient and outpatient treatment. The program includes diagnostic assessment of patient and family, hospitalization, use of medication when necessary, family therapy, and self-help. Larocca also uses "facilitators"—recovered anorectics trained in group leadership (see Larocca chapter).

Another use of self-help groups is as independent gatherings of individuals around a common problem. While therapy may be encouraged and supported, it is not an integral part of the organization's program. An example of this latter self-help organization is the Anorexia Nervosa Aid Society of Massachusetts, where leadership of the groups is conducted by both a recovered anorectic and a professional group leader, both of whom are trained and supervised in group process. In the Anorexia Nervosa Aid Society of Massachusetts, parent support group leadership is by trained parents who provide support and education in the form of speakers with special knowledge about the illness (Warner 1984). Many self-help organizations (ANAS, ANAD, BASH, BRIDGE, . . .) produce a newsletter which can be an important source of information and networking for people who feel isolated with their eating disorder. In addition, the newsletter creates an extended feeling of commonality, a feeling that seems to reinforce the positive effects of the self-help support groups.

## Benefits and Disadvantages

For frightened, highly defensive anorectics, the self-help group can be a less threatening, more acceptable means of dealing with their problems. If successful, the self-help group can act as a conduit to further therapy. For parents, family, and friends, the support group can offer information, support and guidance in getting further care for their anorectic or bulimic friend or family member.

The potential disadvantage of self-help is that group members may so overvalue participation in the group, that they come to devalue or withdraw from their individual treatment. There is concern that quality of leadership among some of the many self-help groups may be inadequate. In response, several self-help organizations are implementing program evaluations. However, most participants report that belonging to a self-help group—whether prior to individual therapy, as an adjunct to therapy, or as a transition out of therapy—is a highly valued aspect of their road to recovery.

## REFERENCES

Boskind-Lodahl, M., & White, W. C. (1978). The definition and treatment of bulimarexia in college women: A pilot study. *Journal of the American College Health Association*, 27, 84–97.

Bruch, H., (1978). Anorexia nervosa. In S. Feinstein & P. Giovacchini (Eds.) *Adolescent Psychiatry, Vol. 5*, New York: Jason Aronson.

Bruch, H., (1978). *The Golden Cage*. Cambridge: Harvard University Press.

Chodrow, N., (1974). Family structure and feminine personality. In M. Rosaldo & L. Lamphere (Eds.) *Women: Culture and Society*. Stanford: Stanford University Press.

Connors, M.E., Johnson G.L., & Stuckey, M.K. (1984). Treatment of bulimia with brief psychoeducational group therapy. *American Journal of Psychiatry*, 141, 1512–1516.

Dixon, K., & Kiecolt-Glaser, J. (1981). Group therapy for bulimia. Paper presented at the meeting of the *American Psychiatric Association*, New Orleans.

Douvan, E., & Adelson, J. (1976). *The Adolescent Experience*. New York: John Wiley.

Elder, C.H., (1969). Appearance and education in marriage mobility. *American Sociological Review*. 34:519–533.

Eliot, Alexandra (1985). Personal communication. Boston.

Fairburn, C.G. (1981). A cognitive behavioral

approach to the treatment of bulimia. *Psychological Medicine,* 11, 707–711.

Fairburn, C.G. (1985). Cognitive-behavioral treatment for bulimia. In D.M. Garner & P.E. Garfinkel (Eds.), *Handbook of Psychotherapy for Anorexia Nervosa and Bulimia.* New York-London: The Guilford Press.

Fernandez, R.C., (1984). Group therapy of bulimia. In P.S. Powers & R.C. Fernandez (Eds.), *Current treatments of anorexia nervosa and bulimia.* New York: Karger.

Fisher S., (1975). *Body Consciousness.* New York: Jason Aronson.

Galdston, R., (1974). Mind over matter: Observations on 50 patients hospitalized with anorexia nervosa. *Journal of the American Academy of Child Psychiatry.* 13:246–263.

Garner, D.M., Garfinkel, P.E., & Bemis, K.M., (1982). A Multidimensional psychotherapy for anorexia nervosa. *International Journal for Eating Disorders,* 1:3–46.

Garfinkel, P.E., & Garner, D.M., (1982). *Anorexia Nervosa: A Multidimensional Perspective.* New York: Brunner/Mazel.

Gillian, C., (1979). Woman's place in man's life cycle. *Harvard Educational Review.* 29:4.

Gillian, C., (1982). *In A Different Voice.* Cambridge: Harvard University Press.

Hall, A., (1985). Group psychotherapy for anorexia nervosa. In D.M. Garner & P.E. Garfinkel (Eds.) *Handbook of Psychotherapy for Anorexia Nervosa and Bulimia.* New York-London: The Guilford Press.

Huerta, E., (1982). Group therapy for anorexia nervosa patients. In M. Gross (Ed.), *Anorexia Nervosa.* Toronto: The Collamore Press.

Kagan, J., (1964). Acquisition and significance of sex typing and sex role identity. In M.L. Hoffman and L.W. Hoffman (Eds.) *Review of Child Development Research (Vol. 1)* New York: Russell Sage Foundation.

Lacey, J.H., (1983). Bulimia nervosa, binge eating, and psychogenic vomiting: A controlled treatment study and long-term outcome. *British Medical Journal.* 286:1609–1613.

Lacey, J.H. & Phil, M. (1983). An outpatient treatment program for bulimia nervosa. *International Journal of Eating Disorders,* 2,209–214.

Larocca, F.E.F., (1984). An inpatient model for the treatment of eating disorders. *Psychiatric Clinics of North America.* 7:287–297.

Lieb, R.C., DeGroot, V. & Thompson, T.L. (1980). Group psychotherapy in the treatment of anorexia nervosa. Presented at annual meeting of *American Academy of Child Psychiatry.* Chicago.

Maher, M.S., (1984). Group therapy for anorexia nervosa and bulimia. In P.S. Powers & R.C. Fernandez (Eds.) *Current treatment of anorexia nervosa and bulimia.* New York: Karger.

Marcia, J., (1980). Identity in adolescence. In J Adelson (Ed.) *Handbook of Adolescent Psychology.* New York: Wiley & Sons.

Masterson, J.F., (1977). Primary anorexia nervosa in the borderline adolescent: an object-relations view. In P. Martocollis (Ed.) *Borderline Personality Disorders: The Concept, The Syndrome, The Patient.* New York: International Universities Press.

Miller, S.G. & Powers, H.P., (1984). Support groups for eating disordered patients. In P.S. Powers & R.C. Fernandez (Eds.) *Current treatment of anorexia nervosa and bulimia.* New York: Karger.

Minuchin. S., Rosman, B., & Baker, L., (1978). *Psychosomatic Families: Anorexia Nervosa in Context.* Cambridge: Harvard University Press.

Mitchell, J.E., Hatsukami, D., Goff, G., Pyle, R.L., Eckert, E.D. & Davis, L.E. (1985). Intensive outpatient group treatment for bulimia. In D.M. Garner & P.E. Garfinkel (Eds.), *Handbook of Psychotherapy for Anorexia Nervosa and Bulimia.* New York-London: The Guilford Press.

Orbach, S. (1984). Fat is a Feminist Issue. New York: Berkeley.

Piazza, E.A., Carni, J.D., Kelly, J. & Plante, S.K. (1983). Group psychotherapy for anorexia nervosa. *Journal of the American Academy of Child Psychiatry,* 22,3:276–278.

Piazza, E.A., Piazza, N., & Rollins, N. (1980). Anorexia nervosa: Controversial aspects of therapy. *Comprehensive Psychiatry,* 21:177–189.

Polivy, J. (1981). Group therapy for anorexia nervosa. *Journal of Psychiatric Research and Treatment Evaluation.* 3:279–283.

Rollins, N., Piazza, E.A. (1978). Diagnosis of anorexia nervosa: A critical reappraisal. *Journal of American Academy of Child Psychiatry,* 17:126–137.

Rose, J. & Garfinkel, P.E., A parents' group in the management of anorexia nervosa. *Canadian Journal of Psychiatry,* 25:228–233.

Rosenbaum, M.B., (1979). The changing body image of the adolescent girl. In M. Sugar (Ed.) *Female Adolescent Development.* New York: Brunner/Mazel.

Rothchild, E., (1979). Female power: Lines to development of autonomy. In M. Sugar (Ed.) *Female Adolescent Development.* New York: Brunner/Mazel.

Roy-Byrne, P., Lee-Benner, K., & Yager, J., (1984). Group therapy for bulimia. *International Journal of Eating Disorders.* 1:97–116.

Steiner-Adair, C., (1984). The body politic: Normal female development and the development of eating disorders. Doctoral thesis. Harvard Graduate School of Education. Forthcoming in Amer. Acad. of Psychoanalysis, Vol. 14:1, 1986.

Surrey, J., (1985). The "Self-In-Relation": A Theory of Women's Development. *Working Paper #13* Wellesley College.

Surrey, J., (1984). Eating patterns as a reflection of women's development. *Working Paper #9.* Wellesley College.

Vandereycken, W. & Meermann, R. (1984). *Anorexia nervosa.* Berlin-New York: Walter de Gruyter.

Warner, Patricia (1984). Personal communication. Lincoln, MA.

Wooley, S.C., & Wooley, O.W., (1980). Eating disorders, obesity and anorexia. In A. Brodsky & R. Hare-Mustin (Eds.) *Women and Psychotherapy.* New York: The Guilford Press.

# CHAPTER 4

# Directive Group Therapy For Patients With Anorexia Nervosa Or Bulimia

*Walter Vandereycken* [1], M.D.
*Johan Vanderlinden* [2], M.A.
*Dion Van Werde* [3], M.A.

## Synopsis

In the last few years there has been a trend to treat anorexia and bulimia patients in homogeneous groups. The first part of this chapter summarizes the literature on group therapy for these patients—in particular the pros and cons—and its different forms. The second part focuses on our own experience with directive group therapy for hospitalized anorexia and bulimia patients. The following issues will be addressed: some formal characteristics, the treatment philosophy, the eclectic-pragmatic procedure, major therapeutic factors, and the process of group therapy. Although this approach seems promising, further investigation on its cost-benefit ratio is required.

## Introduction

In view of the ever increasing amount of publications about psychotherapy with anorexia nervosa (AN) and bulimia (or bulimia nervosa, BN) patients, reports on group therapy are rather scarce. The main part of this paper's contribution is the sediment of two years clinical experience with more than 100 patients who have been hospitalized for serious dysorexia (AN or BN) in a specialized unit at the University Psychiatric Center St. Jozef in Kortenberg. Directive group therapy is an important part of our specific residential program. There are two groups of 8 to 10 patients each. Within a well-structured setting or sociotherapeutic milieu, maximum use is made of group dynamics in its different forms.

As to specific dysorectic symptomatology (weight and eating behavior), a standardized behavioral contract system is applied. On the sociotherapeutic level, each group is "coached" by two nurses who twice a week lead a one-hour, task-oriented discussion centered around concrete topics such as contacts with family, organizing a weekend at home, planning activities in or outside the hospital. Group dynamics also play an important role in the body-oriented therapy, and are aimed at affecting body awareness by means of various techniques such as relaxation, dance-movement therapy and video-confrontation. Through family sessions and parent counseling groups, family members are also involved as much as possible in the treatment program.

Hence, the directive group therapy we will discuss in this chapter must be viewed against the background of a multidimensional treatment approach, the details of which we have reported elsewhere (1). Although a great deal of what will be described hereafter can also be applied to outpatient group therapy, one must take into account that our experience is coloured by the specific residential setting we are working in.

## A SHORT LITERATURE SURVEY

Reports on the group treatment of AN/BN patients are recent. The Dutch psychiatrist Christien Lafeber (2) is an exception to this rule. She was probably the first to experiment with group therapy for AN patients. However, she gave up quickly and her report about the experiment remained practically unknown. Only fifteen years later did other clinicians start to report on their experience. Possible explanations for the recent interest in the group approach to eating disorders are the growing popularity of self-help groups and the increasing number of patients referred for treatment. Recently, several articles about this subject have been published and presumably many more are to be expected.

Up until now most descriptions are rather impressionistic and fragmentary. In the first place, group psychotherapy with AN/BN

1 Psychiatrist, Head of the Anorexia Nervosa Unit
2 Clinical Psychologist
3 Research Assistant

patients is not only possible but has specific benefits as well. However, as to the theoretical framework of group therapy and the way in which concepts are "translated" into concrete procedures within the group sessions, the articles become more vague. No wonder that, up to the present, systematic (process-effect) investigations have not been reported yet. The following discussion of the literature is restricted to the pros and cons and the concrete course of group therapy in AN/BN patients.

## Pros and cons of group therapy

One of the recurring themes in literature on AN is the denial of illness by patients and their lack of insight together with a resistance to treatment. AN patients are called a "nightmare" for the therapist who tries to reach them in an individual psychotherapeutic contact because they are capable of rigid defensive maneuvers (3). But Lafeber (2) came to the conclusion that it is in mixed groups defense mechanisms may exist: AN patients play a pseudonormal role (the model patient) or remain the silent background figures who give the initiative to others, while echoing impersonal opinions and acting like co-therapists.

In AN-only groups, however, patients seem to neutralize each others' sham fights. Moreover, a homogeneous group contains a strong factor of universality: everyone has a similar problem, one recognizes oneself in others, so one feels at ease and understood. Patients are much more willing to accept a confrontation with their own weaknesses from "companions" than from "outsiders". Another advantage is that some patients will only succeed in building up a trustworthy relationship within the protecting climate of a group of fellow patients.

Some authors (4,5) have shown that on a mixed ward with several AN patients, a subgroup spontaneously formed. Furthermore, patients who made friends in the informal group, showed better treatment results. Schmitt and others (6–8) notice that AN patients have a shortage of socialization and that their relations with peers usually are poor on the emotional level. AN patients learn to isolate themselves (with particular attention to individual, mostly intellectual performances). This is both cause and consequence of a growing gap with their surrounding (family, peers). A therapeutic peer group experience could mean a help for breaking this circle. Group therapy is also economical, especially since the number of patients is constantly increasing.

As opposed to these advantages, many authors have uncovered possible risks. In homogeneous groups, typical resistance could be installed. First, a collective resistance to insight and the enhancement of a pseudo-identity ("us, AN patients") could develop. The patients might protect one another and reinforce their symptomatology (e.g. by learning each other's tricks of controlling body weight). Patients could start rivalling and lapse into negative competition ("the slimmer, the better"). Also strong dependence can be created by patients. Group contacts may become a substitute for social relations that are being avoided (especially heterosexual ones).

Most authors, however, admit that these dangers can be avoided by experienced therapists. As a matter of fact, a positive group setting appears to counteract negative tendencies—the escape from symptoms (9) and preventing negative competiton (5). As such, patients in a group often confront and correct each other with respect to their distorted body perception (6). The homogeneity of the group facilitates the acceptance of direct and often hard feedback and self-confrontation (10). In other words, if the forementioned risks do occur—which we assume to happen often in self-help groups (1)—it is first of all owing to the therapist's inability to direct the group process in a proper way.

## Forms of group therapy

In view of the limited experience with the homogeneous group approach, we can only mention some general impressions. Most of the time it consists of open groups that meet once a week. In some places only outpatients participate (4), in other, only inpatients (10). In still other settings the two are combined (5). "Pure" AN groups are concerned with mostly adolescents (2,6,9), while BN groups are concerned mostly grown-up women (11,12). Others are mixing both types (13). Up to the present, we cannot judge upon the pros and cons of these formal aspects.

There are many theoretical schools involved: client-centered (3,6), psychoanalytic (9), eclectic-directive (11). Some are based on feminism (14). Others are theoretically action-oriented usually emphasizing non-verbal elements (2,15). Still others describe specific procedures showing little difference with assertiveness training groups

(16), or even with the average social support self-help groups (17).

In most publications, group therapy seems to be combined with other forms of treatment. Although often nothing is said about how this was integrated. Apart from the forementioned warnings against negative group effects, little or nothing in literature is discussed about the role and place of the therapist. In fact, because most experiments with group therapy are quite new, many authors can only describe their personal trial-and-error process as therapist. In the following, we in our way will try to describe our experience, attempting to be more explicit than most of the authors discussed so far.

# OWN CLINICAL EXPERIENCE
## Formal characteristics

The AN unit at U.P.C. Kortenberg consists of 16 to 20 patients, divided in two groups. Each group has three group therapy sessions of one hour per week (Monday, Wednesday and Friday) led by one or two therapists. Sessions may be viewed by other team members from behind a one-way mirror, thus creating the possibility for intervision.

As to group composition, no specific criteria are used: AN and BN patients are not separated, and the age of the group members can vary from 15 to 45 years, the majority of the patients being between the age of 18 and 25. This means that adolescents and adults (possibly married) are mixed. Groups have a total turnover of 55 patients per year. Apart from a few individual sessions (intake and general clinical assessment) during the first week after admission, no other individual contacts are provided, except in special cases.

In advance, arrangements are made with each patient about the concrete course of the sessions:
- Beginnings and endings are strict; absences are not tolerated.
- Questions and/or discussions about practical topics are referred to the group meeting with the nursing staff.
- Each session starts with the patients making a general schedule themselves about the topics and/or members they would like to focus on.
- A great part of one session each week is devoted to the evaluation of two members' progress (this means that each group member will be evaluated at least once a month).
- The patients know that sessions can be recorded on videotape

or followed from behind the one-way mirror for intervision purposes.

These rules give the patients a clear-cut structure and provide an active working atmosphere.

Besides enforcing the rules, the group therapist has an important coordinating role to fulfill also. Apart from the task within the group therapy, he or she is also the major contact figure for the patient's family. This central position of the group therapist contrasts considerably with the strong division of therapeutic functions which is usual in psychotherapeutic communities.

Although centralization of different functions within one therapist definitely demands a great amount of knowledge and therapeutic skills, it has some important and specific benefits:

- It avoids the patient's almost notorious game of playing therapists against off each other (splitting the team).
- It enhances consistent action and avoids endless discussions among therapists.
- Information from different angles (individual, group, family or partner) is gathered in a more efficient and integrated way, which helps the planning and realization of treatment strategy.
- Centralization often brings about some extra motivation on behalf of the therapist.
- It is reassuring for the patient's relatives to know that there is one person they can call on.

## Treatment philosophy

The notion 'directive therapy' means here that it is time-limited and action oriented and works toward concrete, well-defined goals by means of an eclectic-pragmatic approach (18).

Directive group therapy does not aim at personality changes as an end in itself. Its intent is to stimulate the patient into learning how to formulate and how to reach well-circumscribed goals for themselves. Consequently, the treatment is in the first place directed to change in the 'here-and-now' situation. We are more interested in the future than in the past, so to speak. This, of course, does not mean that we don't work with 'the past' in our group sessions. On the other hand, we are well aware of the risk of a merely rational analysis and interpretation of the past. As a matter of fact, this is one of employed defensive devices of A/N patients.

Treatment is limited to an average stay of 3 months in the hospital. This means for some patients that we actually counter regression inside the hospital by presetting a certain date for discharge. Our approach is eclectic. It combines behavioral, experiential and interactional concepts and methods from different therapeutic orientation. We deliberately exploit the so-called non-specific factors in therapy (19). As a result, a lot of attention is paid to the establishment of a profound therapeutic relationship that creates trust, hope and positive anticipation.

Though specific symptoms get much attention, they are not allowed to become of primal interest in group sessions. Group members are encouraged to look at the interactional function of their symptoms (weight and eating problems) in their personal life, especially within the context of their family or marital relations. We work on constructive problem solving in order to make the pseudo-solution of the eating disorder superfluous. The therapist serves as a model and a facilitator who does not hide him/herself behind a curtain of mysterious omnipotence. During sessions, clear communication and active participation are required on the part of the therapist.

**The eclectic-pragmatic procedure**

Our eclectic-pragmatic approach combines concepts and methods from behavior therapy, cognitive therapy, communication and systems theory. The behavioral approach has led us to the design of a treatment-oriented problem analysis and evaluation procedure. Each patient has to formulate her own treatment plan whose merits and shortcomings are discussed in the group. Considerable time is spent on how to analyze problems (functional analysis), how to formulate aims (pin-pointing) and how to proceed with small steps (successive approximation and shaping). The therapist uses his/her modeling function when proposing concrete tasks, reinforcing assertive behavior, etc. Special attention is paid to the analysis of 'typical' cognitions. Some focus is put on irrational beliefs and perceptions (about one's body, about nutrition and weight, about performances and achievements, etc.) and on their influence in the development and maintenance of the eating disorder (20). The questioning and changing of these irrational belief systems is an important task of the group therapist.

Whereas the cognitive-behavioral approach provides a lot of person-centered strategies, we also try to work with interactions between group members. AN/BN patients are known for having poor communicative skills. Therefore, therapists should take care to give feedback on ways of communicating (verbal and non-verbal) within the group. The group setting is a situation in which different kinds of communication can be experimented with: talking in the I-form, speaking loud enough, asking for attention, the importance of eye contact, the way somebody sits and so on.

Systems theory—especially the structural family therapy approach (21)—made us consider the group as a whole, as a system consisting of different parts or subsystems which may interact and communicate according to specific patterns that resemble family structures. The functioning of a system depends on clear boundaries between subsystems, not too rigid, not too permeable. The therapist should base interventions on important information about the group structure: are there special coalitions and conflicts, and do they ressemble the respective home situations of the patients involved? The group therapist must try, as soon as possible, to avoid attempts on the part of patients to act as a co-therapist, since such a position endangers the necessary boundary between the group members and the therapist(s).

At the beginning of the treatment, many patients exhibit a rigid boundary between themselves and the others. They occupy a position in the group reminiscent of their social isolation before being admitted to the hospital. Techniques from structural and strategic therapy (21,-22) are useful in aiming interventions at the stimulation of group interactions: the creation of a warm contact with every patient (joining), the redefining of the complaints (relabeling), the translation of the problems in the here-and-now situation (enactment), the direct provocation of crisis through confrontation within a climate of support and security, etc. Finally, we use different rituals in our group sessions—for instance, welcome and farewell rituals when a patient enters the group or leaves the hospital (23) to promote communication.

In conclusion, it seems to us that this eclectic orientation—an integrated blend of various therapeutic skills and techniques from different theoretical models—fulfills the need for a multidimensional approach to eating disorders (24).

**Therapeutic factors**

Regardless of any particular theoretical frame and concrete treatment strategy, the group therapist has to be attentive to "therapeutic factors"—i.e. those factors that are supposed to influence the final result as a function of the therapist's actions, the other group members, and the patient herself (25). The following "therapeutic factors" are of great importance in group therapy with AN/BN patients:

(1) *Self-disclosure* or the expression of relevant personal experiences that might have a cathartic effect when combined with the release of intense emotions. AN patients are reluctant to self-disclosure because they often fear a loss of control over their emotions. They rationalize their feelings or use an impersonal "book language"— expressions they have heard from (former or actual) therapists or learned from literature on eating disorders. Stereotyped verbalizations and intellectualizing language have to be countered by therapists through non-verbal or action-directed techniques.

(2) *Insight,* a therapy process whereby two interrelated forms are differentiated. First, is psychogenetic insight—i.e. the understanding of own psychological processes (feelings, thoughts, fantasies, ideas). This refers to the patient's understanding of her motives (why she behaves this way). Next comes insight in interactions—i.e. the understanding of the nature of the relations with others. This form of insight is connected with interpersonal learning processes (feedback from the therapist and other group members).

The therapist is faced here, once again, with the risk of intellectualized insight—especially for those patients who have had psychotherapy before or have 'psychoanalyzed' themselves by means of lay literature. The therapist should be attentive to this kind of impersonal intellectualism as well as to the patient's irrational ideas and interpretations. Typical features of intellectualized insight are: overgeneralization, all-or-none reasoning, negative self-talk and superstitious thinking (20). The therapist must tackle the patients' idea of insight in order to discover true recognitions that are an important part of patients' recovery.

(3) *Acceptance and cohesion:* This refers to the degree of positive meaning and attraction the group has for its members—a patient's feeling of acceptance and value inside the group. In a homogeneous group this acceptance can be established through the process of mutual recognition (the mirror effect). Major problems have to be recog-

nized, however: negative competition ("which one of us has the most serious condition"), power struggles comparable with the tensions at home (e.g. sibling rivalry), and excessive altruism. The latter factor refers to patients' tendency to take care of others in order to obliterate themselves. Patients also like to play the role of co-therapist or 'model' patient in order to please the group therapist.

In our opinion, these are the most relevant therapeutic factors and pitfalls in group therapy with AN/BN patients. We like to point out here that working with mixed groups of adolescents and adults has extra benefits. Against the background of individuation-separation, issues which are often lying at the heart of the disorder can be brought out in such mixed groups. Confronted by a group member that could be her mother evokes powerful interpersonal dynamics that might lead to an intense learning process for a youngster. This is because attachment-autonomy conflicts are thereby actualized (re-enacted) within the group.

## Therapeutic process

It is remarkable how different groups tend to go through a similar evolution during the course of therapy (26). The main factor in the first phase is the *breakthrough of both the denial of illness and the resistance* towards change. Most AN/BN patients declare at the beginning of treatment that they have no problems—certainly no psychological ones. Moreover, they often deny both their eating and weight problems.

We developed a specific therapy-oriented assessment procedure, the 'Goal Attainment Evaluation' (G.A.E.), to break down and work with the patients' powerful resistances so that engagement in therapy will be more effective. When entering our program, every patient receives a list of problems commonly associated with AN/BN (see Appendix 1). The patient has to choose at least two items from each of the three problem areas that are mentioned (eating or weight problems, self-experience, interactions). Each problem or long-term goal has to be translated, then, into concrete steps or short-term goals.

This results in a treatment plan that, both for the patient and the staff, functions as a guide and as a point of reference for the evaluation of the patient's progress during treatment (1, 27). Within a fortnight (after entering the program), every patient has to present her own G.A.E. form (see Appendix 2) in a group therapy session. At least once a month, every patient's evolution is evaluated by herself, the entire group and the treatment staff. Each of these three parties specifies their own judgment on a special evaluation form (see Appendix 3). These judgments are compared and discussed in a special group session devoted to the evaluation of two members' evolution during the last month. This procedure is an effective contribution to the breakthrough of resistance.

Once denial and resistance are bypassed, patients should start searching for the psychological meaning of their symptoms, using the support and confrontation of patients who have already gone through this treatment phase. This means the patient is now a step further in the treatment process and enters *the exploration phase.*

Patients are encouraged to talk about their opinions and feelings in the group. In the beginning this all happens slowly since most of the patients are too afraid to utter a personal opinion and prefer to hide themselves behind a pseudo-identity—an "eating disorder patient." In this phase, patients still show a low level of self-differentiation with respect to their fellow group members. The quest for personal meaning and interactional function of their symptoms implies that the symptom-mask must be thrown off. For most patients this phase leads to emotional confusion.

Old ways of communicating and behaving ought to be substituted gradually by new and more adequate ones. The basic treatment factors facilitating this important step to radical change are a good therapeutic relationship and a solid group cohesion. The therapist has to be both emphatic and confronting at the same time. Gradually, patients in the last phase manage to become more independent and reach a higher level of *self-differentiation.* The acquisition of more independence, however, often clashes with opposition from fellow group members, relatives, partners etc. Change always means a step in the dark. This can mobilize resistance in the patient's social surrounding. In this last phase, it is quite possible that patients take up 'old habits' but usually this drawback is quickly detected by the group and the staff so that a complete regression can be prevented.

Patients in the last phase of treatment can also be elected by the other group members as the official group representative. As such, they learn how to work with the staff and their co-patients in a proper way. The group representative holds a key function as mediator between staff and patients. She has to take care of the newcomers (for instance introducing them to the treatment program) and make sure that all patients attend all facets of the program.

When a patient is about to be discharged, all members are asked to say goodbye. During these often emotional moments, every group member is confronted with the finiteness of the treatment as well as the challenge and threat of an uncertain future.

## Conclusion

The group approach is a promising innovation in the treatment of AN/BN problems, both from an economic and a therapeutic point of view. But we do not claim to have presented here a totally new 'product'. The methods and experiences we describe are inspired and shared by other clinicians. Experience with other new "waves" in therapy, however, has taught us that enthusiasm for a new approach is not a guarantee for success. Enthusiasm or personal satisfaction cannot be a sufficient basis for a new approach. Evaluation and the appropriate research are still needed. So like many of the authors we mention, we have plans for evaluative research. This kind of evaluation is complex because there are no prerequisites—research on the outcome of any kind of treatment for AN/BN patients is scarce or unreliable (28). Nevertheless, in the future we hope to present some well documented self-criticism on the group approach we have presented here.

## References

1. Vandereycken, W., and Meermann, R.: Anorexia Nervosa: A Clinician's Guide to Treatment. Berlin-New York, Walter de Gruyter, 1984.
2. Lafeber, C., Lansen, J., and Jongerius, P.J.: A group therapy with anorexia nervosa patients. Paper presented at the 7th International Congress of Psychotherapy, Wiesbaden, April 21–26, 1967.
3. Franke, A.: Ueberlegungen zur Anwendungen klienten-zentrierter Psychotherapie bei Anorexia nervosa. In Meermann, R. (ed.): Anorexia Nervosa. Ursachen und Behandlung. Stuttgart, Ferdinand Enke Verlag, 1981.
4. Huerta, E.: Group therapy for anorexia nervosa patients. In Gross, M. (ed.), Anorexia Nervosa: A Comprehensive Approach. Lexington, Collamore Press, 1982.
5. Piazza, E., Carin, J.D., Kelly, J., and Plante, S.F.: Group psychotherapy for anorexia nervosa. J. Am. Acad. Child Psychiatry, 22: 276 –278, 1983.
6. Schmitt, G.M.: Klientenzentrierte Gruppenpsychotherapie in der Behandlung der Pubertätsmagersucht. Prax. Kinderpsychol. Kinderpsychiatrie, 29: 247–251, 1980.
7. Schmitt, G.M., and Wendt, R.: Die stationäre Behandlung magersüchtiger Jugendlicher unter dem Gesichtspunkt der sozialen Reintegration. Z. Kind. Jugendpsychiatrie, 10: 67–73, 1972.
8. Schmitt, G.M., Wendt, R., and Jochmus, I.: Stationäre Behandlung magersüchtiger Jugendlicher mit vorwiegend klientenzentrierter Einzel- und Gruppentherapie. In Meermann, R. (ed): Anorexia Nervosa. Ursachen und Behandlung. Stuttgart: Ferdinand Enke Verlag, 1981.

9. Frisch, F.: Psychothérapie d'un groupe d'anorectiques mentales. Rev. Méd. Psychosom., *18:* 292–294, 1976.

10. Polivy, J.: Group therapy as an adjunctive treatment for anorexia nervosa. J. Psychiat. Treat. Eval., *3:* 279–283, 1981.

11. Roy-Byrne, P., Lee-Benner, K., and Yager, J.: Group therapy for bulimia: A year's experience. Int.J.Eat.Dis., *3* (2): 97–116, 1984.

12. Stevens, E.V., and Salisbury, J.D.: Group therapy for bulimic adults. Am.J. Orthopsychiatry, *54:* 156–161, 1984.

13. Neuman, P.A., and Halvorson, P.A.: Anorexia Nervosa and Bulimia. A Handbook for Counselors and Therapists. New York, Van Nostrand Reinhold, 1983.

14. White, W.C., and Boskind-White, M.: An experiential-behavioral approach to the treatment of bulimarexia. Psychother. Theory. Res. Pract., *18:* 501–507, 1981.

15. Schütze, G.: Anorexia Nervosa. Bern-Stuttgart-Wien: Verlag Hans Hubert, 1980.

16. Lawrence, M., and Lowenstein, C.: Self-starvation. Spare Rib, 42–43, 1979.

17. Vaughan, E.: Counselling anorexia. Marriage Guid.J., *18:* 230–236, 1979.

18. Lange, A., and van der Hart, O.: Directive Family Therapy. New York, Brunner/Mazel, 1983.

19. Rabkin, R.: Strategic Psychotherapy. Brief and Symptomatic Treatment. New York, Basic Books, 1977.

20. Garner, D.M., and Bemis, K.M.: A cognitive behavioral approach to anorexia nervosa. Cognit.Ther.Res., *6,* 123–150, 1982.

21. Minuchin, S., and Fishman, H.C.: Family Therapy Techniques. Cambridge (Mass.), Harvard University Press, 1981.

22. Andolfi, M., Angelo, C., Menghi, P. et al: Behind the Family Mask. Therapeutic Change in Rigid Family Systems. New York, Brunner/Mazel, 1983.

23. van der Hart, O.: Rituals in Psychotherapy. Transition and Continuity. New York, Irvington, 1983.

24. Garfinkel, P.E., and Garner, D.M.: Anorexia Nervosa: A Multidimensional Perspective. New York, Brunner/Mazel, 1982.

25. Bloch, S., Couch, E., and Reibstein, J.: Therapeutic factors in group psychotherapy: A review. Arch.Gen. Psychiatry, *38,* 519–526, 1981.

26. Sclare, A.B.: Group therapy for specific psychosomatic problems. *In* Wittkower, E.D., and Warnes, H. (eds.): Psychosomatic Medicine. Its Clinical Applications. Hagerstown, Harper & Row, 1977.

27. Vandereycken, W.: The management of patients with anorexia nervosa and bulimia - Basic principles and general guidelines. *In* Beumont, P.J.V., Burrows, G.D., and Casper, R. (eds): Handbook of Eating Disorders. Volume 1: Anorexia Nervosa and Bulimia. Elsevier/North Holland, 1985.

28. Agras, W.S., and Kraemer, H.C.: The treatment of anorexia nervosa: Do different treatments have different outcomes? *In* Stunkard, A.J., and Stellar, E. (eds): Eating and Its Disorders. New York, Raven Press, 1984.

## Appendix 1

University Psychiatric Center
Kortenberg (Belgium)
Anorexia/Bulimia Nervosa Unit
Head: Dr. W. Vandereycken

## PROBLEM AREAS

In this list you will find a number of problems frequently encountered by patients with an eating disorder. You are asked to choose at least two problems out of each category (A, B and C). You yourself can change the formulation of the items, or add new ones, if they are not mentioned in this list. The problem areas you pick out will be a guide, both for you and the staff, to formulate your aims of therapy and the way to reach them. Therefore, you are asked to give for each problem three concrete examples (gradual steps) that indicate the way you are going to try to cope with it. This document will also serve as a basis for the evaluation of your progress.

## Problems around eating and weight

Abnormal attitude towards body shape:
> e.g., I'm constantly thinking about my weight; I'm obsessed by the wish to be slimmer.

Confusing bodily sensations:
> e.g., I don't feel when I'm hungry or when I'm satiated.

Preoccupation with food:
> e.g., I check the amount of calories of everything I eat.

Bulimia, vomiting, purging:
> e.g., I cannot stop eating; I frequently vomit or take laxatives in order to control my weight.

Hyperactivity and problems with leisure:
> e.g., I'm always busy, I constantly want to be active; I don't know what to do with my leisure time.

Lack of insight:
> e.g., I don't know why I have these eating problems; I have everything to be happy.

## Self-experience

Fear of growing up:
> e.g., To become a grown-up woman is hard to accept.

Perfectionism:
> e.g., I often think that everything I'm doing ain't good enough.

Apathy:
> e.g., I often feel empty and worthless.

Feelings of inferiority:
> e.g., I have little self-confidence; I always compare myself with others.

Emotional vagueness:
> e.g., I'm seldom sure about my own feelings; I don't know when I'm sad, anxious or angry.

Mood swings:
> e.g., I'm very unstable, now I'm satisfied, again I feel blue.

**Interactions**

Overdependence:

e.g., I cannot make decisions on my own; I wonder how I could live without my parents.

Concealment of feelings:

e.g., I seldom talk about my own feelings; I always try to hide my emotions in company with other people.

Subassertiveness:

e.g., I seldom express my personal opinion to others in order to avoid conflicts.

Problems at home:

e.g., In our family many problems remain undiscussed and unresolved.

Lack of social contacts:

e.g., I hardly know other people outside my own family; I have difficulties in making friends.

Sexual problems:

e.g., I'm not at least when thinking about sex; I'm afraid to have sexual intercourse.


**Appendix 2**

University Psychiatric Center
Kortenberg (Belgium)
Anorexia/Bulimia Nervosa Unit
Head: Dr. W. Vandereycken


# GOAL-ATTAINMENT EVALUATION: TREATMENT PLAN

Name:
Date:

Write down six problem areas (two from A, two from B, two from C) which you're going to work on during your treatment. Formulate for each problem or long-term goal at least three concrete steps by which you will try to cope with it, this means to attain short-term goals.

A. *Problems with eating and weight*
   Problem A 1:
   Step (a)
      (b)
      (c)

   Problem A 2:
   Step (a)
      (b)
      (c)

B. *Self-experience*
   Problem B 1:
   Step (a)
      (b)
      (c)
   Problem B 2:
   Step (a)
      (b)
      (c)

C. *Interactions*
   Problem C 1:
   Step (a)
      (b)
      (c)
   Problem C 2:
   Step (a)
      (b)
      (c)

*Note:* In reality, this form counts three pages with enough space for specifying details.

**Appendix 3**

University Psychiatric Center
Kortenberg (Belgium)
Anorexia/Bulimia Nervosa Unit
Head: Dr. W. Vandereycken

## GOAL-ATTAINMENT EVALUATION: PROGESS REPORT

Patient:

Judge:                                   Date:

Indicate the change in the respective problem areas since past evaluation. Keep in mind the concrete steps formulated for each problem area. Put a little cross on the line matching your impression.

| | Clearly Worse | Slightly Worse | Unchanged | Slightly Better | Clearly Better | Problem Solved |
|---|---|---|---|---|---|---|

Problem area

A1 _____

A2 _____

B1 _____

B2 _____

C1 _____

C2 _____

Remarks:

# CHAPTER 5

# Oral Manifestations of Eating Disorders

Jeffrey B. Dalin DDS

## INTRODUCTION

Anorexia Nervosa and Bulimia are disorders that affect all parts of the body, the oral cavity being no exception. The effects of eating disorders on the teeth and oral tissues have not been recognized, however, until recently. The dental manifestations—although not life threatening and not evident until the later stages of the illness—are the only manifestations of eating disorders that cannot be reversed[1]. The problems can range from slight to quite serious. All areas of the oral cavity can be affected and will be discussed separately:

1) The Teeth
   a) Perimylolysis
   b) Dental Caries
   c) Bruxism
2) The Oral Soft Tissues
   a) Periodontal Tissues, Gingival Tissues
   b) The Lining of the Mouth, Pharynx, Esophagus
   c) The Lips and Tongue
   d) The Salivary Glands

Many patients with eating disorders visit their dentists regularly. Because of this, the dentist is in a position to identify these patients and take appropriate actions. The dentist's five areas of responsibility here are: 1) Identifying the eating disorder patient, 2) Intervention, 3) Referral, 4) Coordinated treatment with the therapist, and 5) Follow-up.[2] The identification process will be discussed below, in the context of the physical effects listed above. One must, however, screen out nervous, physiological, and drug-related causes of vomiting. Patients

71

with symptoms of such non-neurotic origin will always admit their problem during a thorough medical history, since vomiting is annoying to them, while the anorectic/bulimic will try to hide his/her problem. The intervention process begins with the prevention of any further damage to the oral environment, and the referral of the patient to an appropriate therapist.

During the patient's treatment, it is important to remain informed about his or her case. This coordination with the psychiatrist or therapist will avoid medication conflicts and will also provide the basis for important follow-ups. The dentist can help make sure the patient is performing the necessary preventive procedures. Finally, the dentist must note any failures of work he has performed as well as any further deterioration of oral tissues. These clinical findings can indicate recurrence of the eating disorder and allow the dentist to get the patient back into a therapy program.

# PERIMYLOLYSIS

One of the problems that occurs in patients with eating disorders is called perimylolysis. This process differs slightly from erosion, which is defined as a loss of tooth substance by a chemical process that does not involve bacterial action. Hellstrom[3] defines perimylolysis as a loss of enamel and dentin on the lingual surfaces of the teeth as a result of chemical and mechanical effects caused mainly by regurgitation of gastric contents and activated by the movements of the tongue. The destruction can range from slight—where one notices just a smooth and polished appearance to the surface of the teeth—to extremely severe—where the dissolution of tooth structure goes through to the nerve of the tooth. In more severe cases, all surfaces of the teeth are affected by the acid erosion.

When the dentist sees a large amount of erosion or perimylolysis, other physical causes must be eliminated before bulimia is assumed to be the cause of the tooth loss. Dental erosion has been attributed to various factors, including the local accumulation of acid caused by inflammation of the gingival crevice, salivary citrates and pyrophosphates, and chronic intake of acidic carbonated beverages, citric juices, and fruits. Other studies have dealt with the oral use of medications containing hydrochloric acid, exposure to industrial acids, and chronic vomiting and regurgitation of gastric contents.[4] Perimylolysis has also been reported to develop secondary to many medical conditions such as gastric dysfunction, obstipation, hiatus hernia, duodenal and peptic ulcers, antabuse therapy for ethanol abuse, pregnancy, achlorhydria, and chronic vomiting after use of some medications such as opiates, cancer chemotherapy agents, levodopa, tetracyclines, disulfiram, etc.[5] All of the above problems should be ruled out before the patient is assumed to have an eating disorder. Again, most patients with any of these physical ailments will readily admit their problem when questioned about it, while anorectics/bulimics will generally try to hide their problem.

Perimylolysis is generally seen in the bulimic or the bulimic/anorectic patient and not in the patient exhibiting restrictive anorexia alone, since the latter does not usually vomit to purge. The chronic vomiting (sometimes five to ten or more times daily) brings the gastric acids into the oral cavity. This acid dissolves tooth structure. Enamel will not usually erode until regurgitation has occurred for two years.[6] The surfaces most commonly affected are the lingual, or tongue-side parts of the upper teeth. The other teeth are protected by the position of the tongue, lips, and cheeks. Holst and Lange[7] suggest that acidic gastric juices accumulate among the papillae of the tongue and that tongue movement continually deposits the acid on the lingual surfaces of the teeth.

Figures 1, 2, and 3 show the appearance of a bulimic/anorectic patient exhibiting the classic manifestation of moderate-to-severe perimylolysis:

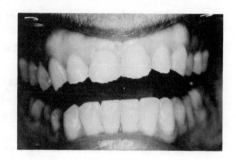

Figure 1
Front View of Upper
and Lower Teeth

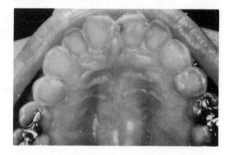

Figure 2
Tongue-side View
of Upper Teeth

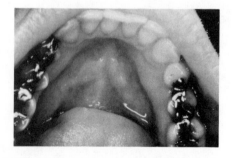

Figure 3
Tongue-side View
of Lower Teeth

According to Stege and associates[1], lingual erosion of maxillary incisors sometimes causes shortening of crown length and gives the appearance of an open bite. Lingual topography is eliminated, and dentinal exposure causes patients to report sensitivity to probing and air. In most cases, the mandibular teeth are protected. Often stains and lines are absent. The enamel defects caused by acid erosion usually have rounded margins in contrast to defects caused by abrasion, which have a sharp, notched appearance. Posterior teeth displaying occlusal erosion show loss of occlusal anatomy. Existing amalgam restorations appear to be raised above the tooth surfaces. Vertical dimension may be lost, especially if the erosion is coupled with parafunctional habits such as bruxism.

## DENTAL CARIES

Dental caries is seen in excess in patients with eating disorders. This is due to: 1)an excessive carbohydrate intake, 2)poor oral hygiene, 3)changes that occur in the saliva. Strictly defined, dental caries is a process of progressive destruction of the hard tissues of the teeth initiated by bacterially produced acids at the tooth surface. Dental decay results from the interaction of three factors (see illustration below). First, the mouth must harbor certain types of caries-producing microorganisms; second, the diet must contain carbohydrates, particularly sucrose, which the bacteria consume and ferment to acid that in turn dissolves the enamel of the tooth; third, the teeth must be susceptible to the action of the acid.

Figure 4
The Three Interacting
Factors Needed To
Produce Dental Caries

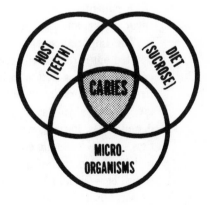

It is unlikely that any one approach will completely solve the problem of caries prevention and control. Efforts, therefore, should be directed at minimizing the effects of all of the above factors. The first circle, the host or teeth, is a factor whose role in decay can be minimized by protective measures such as topical fluorides and pit and fissure sealants. Fluorides help the tooth fight off the effects of the acid produced by the bacteria on the teeth. Sealants cover the deep grooves on the teeth to help stop the bacteria from collecting there.

The saliva is the body's natural defense in fighting decay. Its flow will wash bacteria and sugar out of the oral cavity. It has buffering capacity as well, which helps neutralize acids formed by the bacteria residing on the teeth. This neutralization helps stop decay at its inception.

The second factor, bacteria, can never be eliminated completely, but can be kept under control with proper brushing and flossing. The third factor, diet or sucrose, is the easiest to control. A proper diet is not only good for oral health but for total physical health as well.

During binge periods, huge amounts of sugar can be consumed, followed by sugar drinks, often used to relieve thirst after vomiting. Thus, bulimics tend to have higher sugar intake. The anorectic patients obviously will not get much excess sugar, since their diet is limited. These patients have to be careful when under the care of a physician, since some medications given to them, such as dextrose tablets, Meritene, and vitamin C drinks, contain sugar.

Neglect of oral hygiene can be seen in both anorectic and bulimic patients, due mainly to an upset in daily routine. Their eating habits get most of their attention. Meticulous oral hygiene is a necessity in these patients, due to excess acid present in the oral cavity, excess sugar intake, and disturbances in the saliva.

The importance of saliva in preventing dental caries has been pointed out earlier. Hellstrom[3] notes decreased salivary pH and decreased buffering action in both resting and stimulated saliva in patients with anorexia. Valentine and associates[8] have shown that the low pH of saliva has a strong relationship with the occurrence of dental caries. Patients with anorexia typically have decreased salivary flow as well. Systemic complications of the eating disorders—such as malabsorption, malnutrition, hormonal disturbances, anemia, anxiety states, etc—all add to this problem.

Michels and Schoenberg[9] state that fear and depression decrease salivary flow and affect its composition, thus potentially contributing to the formation of caries. Often this decreased flow of saliva is potentiated by the frequent misuse of laxatives and diuretics. These drugs decrease total fluid volumes and affect electrolyte balance, causing an even further diminished salivary flow. The use of such drugs should be discontinued at once. These alterations in saliva may not seem obvious, but they have a devastating effect on the oral environment.

In summary, bulimic patients are more prone to erosion and perimylolysis, due to excess hydrochloric acid in contact with tooth surfaces, but will not always exhibit severe decay problems. It has been theorized that the excess acid may be too harsh on the bacteria that cause caries. Anorectic patients on the other hand, with virtually no natural defense against caries, seem to have monumental decay problems.

# BRUXISM

Bruxism is the habitual grinding of the teeth, either during sleep or as an unconscious habit during waking hours. This term is generally applied both to the clenching habit, during which pressure is exerted on the teeth and supporting structures by actual grinding or clamping of the teeth, and also to the repeated tapping of the teeth.[10] Many causative factors have been postulated to help explain this wearing away of tooth structure. Local factors are occlusal disturbances that occur in the patient (the teeth do not fit together properly). Bruxism occurs as a way for the body to resolve this problem, though systemic factors also can come into play. Some of these are gastrointestinal disturbances, nutritional deficiencies, allergies, and endocrine problems. The most commonly described causative factors for bruxism are psychologic factors. Fear, rage, rejection, and emotional tension are often expressed through the unconscious grinding and clenching of the teeth. Some occupations seem to favor the development of this habit. Athletes, who are under a great deal of physical stress, and people who perform precise, detailed work, are particularly prone.

Once the habit is firmly established, the teeth begin to display the effects of severe wear. If the problem continues for long periods of time, one can see loss of integrity of the supporting bone, resulting in loosening or drifting of the teeth. Temporomandibular joint disturbances are often reported to occur with bruxism. The wear will be worse in bulimic patients with perimylolysis present, because the teeth are already thinner, exposing the softer dentinal layer after the enamel has been dissolved by gastric acid bathings. Treatment can only be symptomatic, to protect the teeth against further wear. A night guard will accomplish this until the psychologic causative factors are determined.

## ORAL SOFT TISSUES

Tissue health is impaired by xerostomia (dry mouth) and the resulting reduction of the saliva's membrane-lubricating effects.[11] Xerostomia can be traced to numerous etiologic factors, all of which have been discussed previously. Due to dryness and poor oral hygiene, gingivitis or inflammation of the gums is quite common in eating disorder patients. This inflammation, if left untreated, can spread into the supporting structures of the teeth, cause bone loss, and eventually result in the exfoliation of the teeth. Hellstrom[3] found that some patients with chronic vomiting had lower incidences of plaque, gingivitis, and caries. She attributed this to the alteration of bacterial plaque by the acid from gastric juices present in the mouth.

Vitamin deficiencies from poor diets have very marked effects on soft tissues. The following clinical descriptions are provided by Shafer, Hine, and Levy in their textbook on Oral Pathology[10]:

The oral effects of vitamin C deficiency occur chiefly in the gingival and periodontal tissues. The interdental and marginal gingiva are bright red with a swollen, smooth, shiny surface. In fully developed scurvy, the gingiva becomes boggy, ulcerates, and bleeds. In severe cases, one can see hemorrhage into and swelling of the periodontal membranes, followed by loss of bone and loosening of the teeth.

In riboflavin deficiency, there is glossitis (inflammation of the tongue), which begins with soreness of the tip and/or the lateral margins of the tongue. The filliform papillae become atrophic, while the fungiform papillae remain normal or become engorged and mushroom-shaped, giving the tongue surface a reddened, coarsely granular appearance. In severe cases, the tongue may become glazed and smooth owing to complete atrophy of all papillae. Paleness of the lips, especially at the angles of the mouth, but not involving the moist areas of the buccal mucosa, is the earliest sign of the deficiency disease. The pallor, which usually continues for days, is followed by cheilosis, which is evidenced by a maceration and fissuring at the angles of the mouth. The fissures may be single or multiple. The lips become unusually red and shiny because of a desquamation of the epithelium.

Nicotinic acid deficiency causes complaint of a burning sensation in the tongue, which becomes swollen and presses against the teeth, causing indentations. The tip and lateral margins of the tongue become red. In the acute stages of this deficiency, the entire mucosa become fiery red and painful. The epithelium of the entire tongue desquamates. Tenderness, pain, redness, and ulcerations begin at the interdental gingival papillae and spread rapidly.

Pyridoxine(B6) deficiency can cause symptoms similar to those caused by nicotinic acid deficiency, particularly that of angular cheilosis.

Folic acid deficiency develops into glossitis that appears initially as a swelling and redness of the tip and lateral margins of the dorsum. The papillae then disappear.

Bulimic patients may evidence abrasions of the lining of the throat due to the use of fingers or foreign objects to induce vomiting. The caustic gastric acid—brought up during the purging process—inflames esophageal, pharyngeal, and salivary gland tissues.

The presenting sign of parotid gland enlargement in patients with eating disorders is not an unusual occurrence. Buchner and Sreebny[12] have reported more than twenty-five factors which can cause salivary gland enlargement. Two explanations for this problem are: 1)irritation hyperplasia and 2)nutritional or malnutrition swelling. The high acid level of gastric contents which bathe the oral cavity irritates the salivary gland to such an extent that hypertrophy occurs. In nutritional mumps, as it is known, Batsakis and McWhirter[13] have reported an increased size of the individual acinar cells, an increase in the number of secreting granules, fatty infiltration, and mild-to-moderate fibrosis without chronic inflammatory cell infiltrate. According to DuPlessis[14], the parotid enlargement is due to a "work hypertrophy" and is reversible with the patient's return to a normal diet.

# TREATMENT AND CONCLUSION

Ideally, the best way to stop all of the previously mentioned problems is to have the patient: 1)stop vomiting, 2)begin eating a balanced diet, 3)stop abusing laxatives and diuretics, 4)perform meticulous oral hygiene procedures. These steps would reduce the high acid content present in the oral cavity, lower sugar consumption and its effects, restore normal vitamin and mineral levels in the body, restore normal salivary composition and flow, and keep the teeth clean. This may be hard to accomplish all at once, however. In these cases, treatment becomes symptomatic.

For chronic vomiting and its acid effects, rinsing with a sodium bicarbonate (baking soda) solution immediately after vomiting is advisable if the impulse to purge cannot be resisted. Rowe[15] and Stafne and Lovestadt[6] have advocated the use of sodium bicarbonate or magnesium hydroxide to neutralize gastric acid present in the oral cavity, to reduce decalcification and damage (perimylolysis) to teeth and soft tissues. Hellstrom[3] also recommends daily rinsing with sodium fluoride (.05% to .2%) or self-administration of fluoride gel in custom-made trays. This will help make the teeth more resistant to acid dissolution. Fluoride, combined with multiple daily brushing and flossing sessions to remove cavity-causing plaque from the tooth surfaces, can significantly reduce decay.

In order to stimulate salivary flow, it is important that the patient stop taking all laxatives and diuretics. The side effects of these drugs include reduction of saliva in the oral cavity. Sugar-free mints and sugar-free gum may be used to stimulate the flow, but only the return to a normal diet will restore the saliva's composition, pH, etc to its natural state. Cheese is an excellent food to eat with these disorders because it increases salivary flow, increases the pH of plaque and saliva, and increases calcium concentrations.

For those with bruxism, nightguard appliances can be constructed. They protect the teeth from further wear, particularly from grinding that occurs at night.

Application of some or all of the above treatments to the patient with an eating disorder will only stabilize the oral environment. Once the disorder has been brought under control by the patient and the therapist, more definitive work can be begun. This can range from acid-etch composite resins for minor areas of erosion and wear, to rebuilding the entire mouth with full crown coverage. See figures 5 and 6 below for an illustration of what the acid-etch composite resions can do for the appearance of teeth damaged by anorexia nervosa and bulimia. Not only does this restoration help protect the teeth from further dissolution and wear, but it improves the patient's self-esteem. It should be noted, however, that this restorative work should not be begun until the patient is in therapy and has made some progress. It would be a waste of time, money, and effort to perform the work before then, since any work performed would surely fail in an oral environment still under stress from an uncontrolled eating disorder.

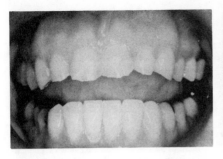 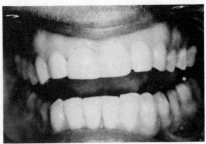

**Figure 5**
Preoperative Photograph of Anorectic/
Bulimic Patient Shown Earlier

**Figure 6**
Patient After Acid-Etched Composite
Resins Placed-Note The More
Uniform Appearance Of The Teeth

In dealing with patients with eating disorders, it is important to remember how to approach them. Hellstrom[3] points out that these patients do not respond well to negative criticism. One should explain procedures as well as the reasons behind all treatment, so they can take an active role in the entire process. The dentist must be gentle and supportive, reassuring the patient that his/hers is not a unique problem, and that others have been helped. Despite their guilt and worry over their dental problems, it will still be hard to motivate them to adhere to the above measures (cessation of vomiting, of laxative and diuretic abuse, the use of fluoride and sodium bicarbonate rinses, daily hygiene, etc).

In conclusion, the dentist is in a unique position to identify eating disorder patients and guide them to an appropriate therapist. The dentist is less psychologically threatening to these patients, and the teeth and their appearance can be a useful motivational tool. The oral complications seen with eating disorders can start out as slight sensitivity, but can progress to loss of tooth structure, pulp exposures, loss of teeth, reduced masticatory ability, and unesthetic appearance. Even though this destruction can get quite extensive and one is challenged to prevent any further tooth loss and pain involved, it must be remembered that these diseases can be potentially life-threatening and medical treatment must come before definitive dental treatment. It is important that people with eating disorders be under the care of a knowledgeable dentist so that these irreversible changes may be kept to a minimum.

# BIBLIOGRAPHY

1) Stegge, P., Visco-Dangler, L., Rye, L.: "Anorexia Nervosa: Review Including Oral and Dental Manifestations". Journal of the American Dental Association, 104:648–652, May, 1982.

2) "Tooth Sleuths Uncover Bulimia, The Hidden Disease". AGD Impact, Volume II, Number 8, Oct, 1983, pp. 4.

3) Hellstrom, I.: "Oral Complications in Anorexia Nervos". Scandinavian Journal of Dental Restorations, 85:71–86, 1977.

4) White, D., Hayes, R., Benjamin, R.: "Loss of Tooth Structure Associated With Chronic Regurgitation and Vomiting". Journal of the American Dental Association, 97:833–835, 1978.

5) Kleier, D., Aragon, S., Averbach, R.: "Dental Management of the Chronic Vomiting Patient". Journal of the American Dental Association, 108:618–621, 1984.

6) Stafne, E., and Lovestadt, S.: "Dissolution of Tooth Substances by Lemon Juices, Acid Beverages, and Other Sources". Journal of the American Dental Association, 34:586–592, 1947.

7) Holst, J. and Lange, F.: "Perimylolysis: Contribution Towards Genesis of Tooth Wasting From Non-Mechanical Causes". Acta Odont. Scand., 1:36, June 1939.

8) Valentine, A., Anderson, R., Bradnock, G.: "Salivary pH and Dental Caries". British Dental Journal, 144:195–107, 1978.

9) Michels, R. and Schoenberg, B.: Diagnosis of Diseases of the Mouth and Jaws. Lea and Febiger, Philadelphia, 1969, pp. 526–527.

10) Shafer, W., Hine, M. Levy, B.: Textbook of Oral Pathology. W.B. Saunders Company, Philadelphia, 1974, pp. 490–491, 597–603.

11) Brady, W.: "The Anorexia Nervosa Syndrome". Journal of Oral Surgery, 50:509–516, Dec, 1980.

12) Buchner, A. and Sreebny, L.: "Enlargement of Salivary Glands: Review of The Literature". Journal of Oral Surgery, 34:209–218, 1972.

13) Batsakis, J. and McWhirter, J.: "Non-Neoplastic Diseases of Salivary Galnds". American Journal of Gastroenterology, 57:238, 1972.

14) DuPlessis, D.: "Parotid Enlargement in Malnutrition". South African Medical Journal, 302:700–703, 1956.

15) Rowe, A.: "A Palliative Treatment For Severe Enamel Erosion". British Dental Journal, 133:435, 1972.

16) Hasler, J.: "Parotid Enlargement: A Presenting Sign in Anorexia Nervosa". Journal of Oral Surgery, 53:567–573, June 1982.

17) Barkmeier, W., Peterson, D., Wood, L.: "Anorexia Nervosa: Recognition and Management". Journal of Oral Medicine, 37:33–37, Apr-June, 1982.

18) Carni, J.: "The Teeth May Tell: Dealing With Eating Disorders in the Dentist's Office". Journal of the Massachusetts Dental Society, 30:80–86, 1981.

# CHAPTER 6

# Bulimia: an Evolving Concept

**Rodrigo A. Muñoz, M.D.**

In recent years there has been a veritable explosion of papers on bulimia. We do expect that future field research will bring about agreement concerning diagnostic criteria, course, differential diagnosis, and family characteristics. In the meantime, there are problems that should be solved before solid information can be shared.

Some immediate problems relate to differing definitions of bulimia in the United States and in England. Others refer to the psychopathology of binge eating, which may have been relatively common among "normal" populations throughout the history of humanity.

People with bulimia but diagnosed as suffering a different disorder have been reported for several centuries. We do not know whether "bulimia" represents the extreme of a common behavior or a disorder that can be distinguished from uncomplicated binging. We would like to establish whether biological correlates often mentioned in relation to bulimia can be applied to most bulimics or only to those who vomit. There are remaining problems in differential diagnosis, specially from affective disorders.

## PROBLEMS IN THE PATH OF AGREEMENT ON BULIMIA:

### 1. DEFINITION:

Many American psychiatrists have done research based on the DSM-III Diagnostic Criteria for Bulimia[1]. Some British investigators have followed the Diagnostic Criteria formulated by Russell[2].

Some may consider the DSM-III Criteria as "soft". A person could meet them if she has had several episodes of rapid consumption of a

83

large amount of food in a short time—specially if it was "junk" food ingested unconspicuously until she developed abdominal pain, if she considered this eating as abnormal, had fear of loss of control upon eating, felt depressed after eating, and did not suffer any other disorder.

As pointed out by Lowenkopf[3], overeating seems to have been a common practice for most of the time humans have existed. Primitive tribes dependent on hunting may go into prolonged binges for one or two days after a successful expedition and before spoilage may set in, attempting to compensate for long periods of famine. The Romans had vomiting rooms built next to their banquet halls. Hermann and Matt[4] and Hawkins and Clement[5] have speculated that social pressure has led a number of young people to diet, trying to maintain a body weight below a biologically determined "set point". This leads to episodic loss of control and "binging episodes" accompanied by guilt and loss of self-esteem. These binges may be said to have a social cause.

That binge eating is common, is exemplified by Halmi, Falk and Schwartz[6], who found that 68.1% of the women and 50.2% of the men in a college population answering a binge eating and vomiting questionnaire indicated that they had had at least one eating binge.

A separation between binge eating and bulimia may be obtained by those who follow the writings of the British author Russell[2], who proposed a "hard" definition of bulimia.

He selected patients with a history of episodes of overeating followed by self-induced vomiting, or purging, or both. The introduction of vomiting and/or purging as necessary criteria for the diagnosis of bulimia most likely made his population different from the samples studied in America. This is clearly shown by the differences in vomiting reported by American authors,[6] and by British authors[7].

## 2. BULIMIA AS AN ILLNESS:

It has become fashionable to talk about the recent increase in the incidents of bulimic behavior[8]. One problem in evaluating such an assumption is the tendency for some disorders to change names and importance even though the symptoms may be the same. Louduom[9] has addressed this issue. He has indicated that bulimia as a medical curiosity or symptom of illness was recognized in the 18th and the 19th centuries. During that time "binge-vomiting" was described as bulimia nervosa or caninus appetitus, but diagnosed as "Chlorosis", which was deemed a more important disorder at the time.

The evidence would suggest that bulimia has existed all along. Its relative importance may have increased lately, not only because of fashions in eating and in weight goals, but also because mass communications permit surveys that were not possible only a few years back.

## 3. RETICENCE AND SECRECY:

As pointed out by Fairburn and Cooper[7], it is likely that cases of bulimia will escape detection by conventional clinical methods because of extreme guilt and secrecy that are typical of binging and self-induced vomiting. Much of what we know about vomiting and purging has come from studies in which the anonymity of the respondents was kept.

Using a confidential questionnaire, Fairburn and Cooper[7-10] found large populations of bulimics who used vomiting, laxatives, or both in order to control their weight. This study would justify the incorporation of vomiting and use of laxatives as diagnostic criteria for bulimia.

To the contrary, Halmi, Falk and Schwartz[6], in a survey study of a college population in which anonymity was not kept, found among patients who met the DSM-III Criteria for Bulimia a relative small proportion who described vomiting. These authors did not feel that self-induced vomiting was a necessary symptom for diagnosis.

## 4. BIOLOGICAL CORRELATIONS:

We do not know whether there is a continuum made up of the dieter who occasionally binges on the foods he has suppressed, the recurrent binger, and the individual described by Russell as suffering bulimia. Until this is known, it would be unfair to compare the person who meets the DSM-III Criteria for bulimia but does not vomit nor uses purgatives with those who develop physiologic abnormalities associated with vomiting. As an example, Winstead and Willard[12] described gastrointestinal complaints, dental and oropharyngeal changes, and salivary gland enlargement as diagnostic clues regarding bulimia, though indicating that they are all the result of vomiting.

## 5. DIFFERENTIAL DIAGNOSIS:

Using careful and restrictive criteria, 10% of patients with bulimia report a history of anorexia nervosa[10]. Such patients should be diagnosed as suffering anorexia with secondary bulimia.

Patients with bulimia are known to display behaviors associated with other diagnoses, including use of alcohol and street drugs, stealing, suicide attempts, and self-mutilation[13]. This would indicate the need for careful discrimination and, when necessary, establishment of discrete subgroups. Work in this area has been rewarding. Hatsukami, Eckert, Mitchell and Pyle[14], reported on 108 women who met the DSM-III Criteria for bulimia and were evaluated for affective disorder and alcohol or drug abuse by means of the DSM-III Diagnostic Criteria. 43.5% had a history of affective disorder, and 18.4% had a history of alcohol or drug abuse. Approximately, 56% scored within the moderate to severe range of depression on the Beck depression inventory. Hatsukami, Eckert and Mitchell[15], have thought of anorexia nervosa and bulimia as variants of mood disorders.

## COMMENT:

Ideas about bulimia are developing rapidly, but further progress will require the concensus that can come only from clear thinking. British and American researchers have developed criteria that are not incompatible but may apply to different populations. I am here proposing restrictive criteria similar to those used by Fairburn and Cooper[11]. They are likely to render homogenous populations that may be suitable for diagnostic studies that have been so successful in other disorders.

## PROPOSED CRITERIA FOR PRIMARY BULIMIA:

a. A distorted, implacable attitude towards food, eating, or weight that leads to binge eating accompanied by induced vomiting or use of laxatives.

b. Self-induced vomiting or use of laxatives occurs on at least 4 occasions over the past four weeks, and an average of at least once a week, over the previous six months.

c. No known medical illness that could account for the binge eating or vomiting.

d. No other known psychiatric disorder with special reference to primary affective disorder and anorexia nervosa.

The definition of a binge is taken from Fairburn and Cooper: "Episodes of uncontrolled eating in which a huge amount of food is consumed, often rapidly and in secret. These episodes usually end because of stomach pain, interruption by others, running out of food supplies, or vomiting. Although the actual eating may be enjoyable, afterwards one invariably feels disgusted, guilty, and depressed"[11].

# REFERENCES

1. American Psychiatric Association: Diagnostic and Statistical Manual of Mental Disorders. Third Edition, 1980.

2. Russell, G: Bulimia Nervosa: An Ominous Variant of Anorexia Nervosa. *Psychological Medicine,* 9:429–448, 1979.

3. Lowenkopf EL: Bulimia: Concepts and Therapy. *Comprehensive Psychiatry,* 24:546–554, 1983.

4. Hermann CP and Matt B: Restrained and Unrestrained Eating. *Journal of Personality,* 43:647-660, 1975.

5. Hawkins RC and Clement PS: "Development and Construct Validation of a Self-Report Measure of Binge Eating Tendencies". *Addictive Behavior,* 5:219–226, 1980.

6. Halmi KA, Falk JR and Schwartz E: "Binge Eating and Vomiting: A Survey of A College Population". *Psychological Medicine,* 11:697–706, 1981.

7. Fairburn CG and Cooper PJ: "Self-Induced Vomiting and Bulimia Nervosa: An Undetected Problem" *British Medical Journal,* 284:1153–1155, 1982.

8. Johnson C, Lewis C and Hagman J: The Syndrome of Bulimia. *Psychiatric Clinics of North America,* 7:247–273, 1984.

9. Louduom I: The Disease Called Chlorosis. *Psychological Medicine,* 14:27–36, 1984.

10. Fairburn CG and Cooper PJ: "Binge Eating, Self-Induced Vomiting, and Laxative Abuse: A Community Study". *Psychological Medicine,* 14:401–410, 1984.

11. Fairburn CG and Cooper PJ: The Clinical Features of Bulimia Nervosa. *British Journal of Psychiatry,* 144:238–246, 1984.

12. Winstead BK and Willard SG: Bulimia: Diagnostic Clues. *Southern Medical Journal,* 76:313–315, 1983.

13. Garfinkel PE, Moldofsky H and Garner DM: The Heterogeneity of Anorexia Nervosa. *The Archives of General Psychiatry,* 37:1036–1040, 1980.

14. Hatsukami D, Eckert E, Mitchell J and Pyle R: "Affective Disorder and Substance Abuse in Women With Bulimia". *Psychological Medicine,* 14:701–704, 1984.

15. Hatsukami D, Eckert E and Mitchell J: Eating Disorders: A Variant of Mood Disorders? *Psychiatric Clinics of North America,* 7:349–365, 1984.

# CHAPTER 7

# An Overview of the Bulimia Syndrome

James E. Mitchell, M.D.

The bulimia syndrome is the focus of considerable interest. This disorder—once presumed quite unusual and only recently described in full detail—is evidently a fairly common disorder which may well be increasing in incidence. Bulimia has also been shown to be associated with significant psychological and medical sequelae. Despite our growing knowledge about the epidemiology and associated features of this disorder, little is known about the longitudinal course of bulimia or what constitutes effective treatment.

This disorder has also received considerable attention in the lay press. This exposure may have served the useful function of alerting parents, families, and health care providers to the problem. This publicity, however, conceivably may be contributing to the spread of this disorder, although there is no firm evidence to substantiate this.

The current DSM-III category of bulimia was proposed before much was known about this clinical condition. Despite this, the DSM-III Criteria have held up quite well in subsequent research. The term bulimia remains confusing, however, since the word is used in various ways by different medical authors. For example, the word bulimia has been used to describe a subgroup of patients with anorexia nervosa who binge-eat. It has also been used as a term to indicate the act of binge-eating rather than the complete syndrome as defined in DSM-III.[60] The British term of bulimia nervosa is perhaps more acceptable since it suggests a link to anorexia nervosa and differentiates the syndrome from simple binge-eating.[81] There are several other terms used in the literature to describe the same or related conditions including bulimarexia,[6] the dietary chaos syndrome,[67] and psychogenic vomiting.[25] What terminology will prevail remains to be seen.

There are two other problems which should be addressed when one considers bulimia as a diagnostic entity. First is the question as to whether bulimia represents a separate and distinct syndrome from other eating disorders. As stated before, there is a subgroup of anorexia patients who engage in bulimic behaviors, and there is evidence that these patients in some ways are similar to patients of normal weight with bulimic symptoms.[9] Although these anorexia nervosa patients with bulimic symptoms are specifically excluded from a bulimic diagnosis by the DSM-III Criteria since they meet weight criteria for anorexia, this differentiation is not always easy to make clinically. It is not uncommon to see patients of low weight who are not yet sufficiently emaciated to meet weight criteria for anorexia yet who have the same attitudes toward their weight and the same body image distortion as anorectics.

At the other end of the spectrum, the DSM-III Criteria do not always eliminate overweight patients who binge-eat but do not engage in self-induce vomiting or laxative abuse, although such patients usually are different from normal weight bulimic patients.[87] Therefore, bulimia as a symptom can be seen across a spectrum of eating disorders and the limits of the bulimia syndrome within this spectrum are unclear.

A second problem relates to the need to differentiate clinically significant bulimic symptoms from normal eating behavior. As will be seen, it is not uncommon for individuals in the general population to report binge-eating sporadically without obvious social or medical consequences.[73] The DSM-III Criteria—which lack chronicity and frequency parameters—do not always screen out these normal individuals if the Criteria are interpreted broadly. Therefore, the boundaries between bulimia and other eating disorders and between bulimia and normal eating behavior are not always clear.

## Epidemiology

Beginning with Hawkins and Clement's[29] 1980 survey of a college student population, several large survey studies have been reported which have attempted to delineate the prevalence of bulimic behaviors. Most studies have involved surveys of college students[11,24,48,64,71,73,83] while a few surveys have sampled other populations including clinic patients,[13] high school students,[8,43,71] and shopping mall visitors.[69] These surveys have varied widely as to the size of the populations surveyed and the percent response to the instruments used. Perhaps most importantly, the instruments have varied widely in terms of their definitions of the behaviors of interest, in particular the definition of binge-eating.

The results of these studies are summarized in Table 1. As can be seen, many members of the populations surveyed admitted to binge-eating, depending on how the question was asked. Several investigators have attempted to use modifications of the DSM-III Criteria to determine the prevalence of bulimia rather than binge-eating. These studies suggest that between 3.9% and 19% of women and between 0% and 6.1% of men meet DSM-III Criteria for bulimia. Using more stringent criteria, several authors have attempted to identify those individuals most likely to be having bulimic behaviors at a clinically significant level. Using the criteria of weekly binge-eating (minimum) coupled with either weekly (minimum) self-induced vomiting or laxative abuse, the prevalence of bulimia in females appears to be between 1.0 and 3.0%.[43,69,73]

Taken together, these facts suggest that binge-eating as a symptom is common in young men and women, and that the criteria for bulimia —when broadly interpreted based on questionnaire responses—identify a surprisingly high percentage of females (and a lower percentage of males). When more rigid criteria are used, however, the prevalence of bulimia appears to be much lower, although an overall prevalence of 1-3% of women in the college age group suggests that bulimia is a common condition.

## General Description

Several series of patients with bulimia have been reported in the literature. These studies suggest that bulimia is seen almost exclusively in females, with less than 10% of the reported cases being in males.[1,3,15,19,20,30,31,32,44,62,72,81] A typical patient with bulimia first develops the bulimic symptoms between the ages of 16 and 19 and has bulimic symptoms, on average, for about six years before seeking care.[1,15,19,20,62,72] The disorder appears to be uncommon in minority groups.

Why certain individuals develop bulimia remains unknown although several potential risk factors have been noted. Some patients who develop bulimia have a period of being overweight prior to the onset of the disorder[16] and the onset of the illness may coincide with a period of dieting.[72] Usually binge-eating begins before vomiting or the two behaviors begin at about the same time, although some patients will first develop vomiting after normal meals and only later develop eating binges.[63] Chiodo and Latimer[10] found that the majority of bulimic patients could specify incidents associated with the onset of vomiting and that most developed the problem after hearing about the behavior from someone else or after reading an article or seeing a TV program which dealt with eating disorders.

The cardinal feature of bulimia is binge-eating. Although many individuals in the general population admit to binge-eating, the eating binges of most non-bulimic individuals are small relative to the amounts eaten during binge-eating episodes by patients who meet DSM-III Criteria for bulimia. Russell first noted that patients with bulimia not uncommonly consumed 5,000 to 20,000 calories during eating binges.[81] This was subsequently substantiated.[59,61] Bulimic individuals tend to consume large amounts of food in a fairly short period of time, usually an hour or less, and to feel a distressing lack of control over their eating.[1,59] Many describe entering an altered state while they are ingesting food. Patients with bulimia cite several moods or cognitions which may precede individual binges which include tension,[1,63,72] craving certain foods,[63,72] unhappiness,[63,72] uncontrolled appetite,[63,72] and insomnia.[63,72] Although certain antecedents are commonly cited, most patients end up institutionalizing the bulimic eating pattern into their everyday routine. They will binge-eat and then vomit at certain times, frequently upon returning to their residence after work or school. Late afternoon and early evening are the most common times for binge-eating.[63] The foods most commonly ingested are those high in fat and/or carbohydrate which can be easily ingested and do not require much preparation such as ice cream, doughnuts and candy.[59] Immediately after binge-eating, most bulimic individuals self-induce vomiting. They then feel a strong sense of guilt and dysphoria.[63,72]

Although binge-eating is the cardinal feature of the disorder, most bulimic individuals also engage in a variety of other abnormal eating-related behaviors and weight control techniques.[18,44,62,63,72] These are summarized in Table 2. Vomiting is often induced by mechanical stimulation of the gag reflex, using the fingers or a utensil. Many patients eventually teach themselves to vomit reflexly without stimulation.

A fairly high percentage also abuse laxatives and/or diuretics as weight control techniques. The laxative abuse problem usually involves the ingestion of large amounts of laxatives—often many times the recommended daily amount—in hopes of inducing diarrhea and losing calories through this method. Recent research by Lacey and Gibson suggests that laxative abuse is relatively ineffective as a weight-control technique. The laxatives most commonly used are stimulant-type laxatives which can lead to a variety of gastrointestinal and metabolic problems.[4]

As Table 2 indicates, bulimia should not be seen merely as a disorder of binge-eating and self-induced vomiting. It must also be regarded as a syndrome characterized by a variety of types of abnormal eating-related behaviors and weight management techniques. It must be remembered that bulimic behaviors are not superimposed on an ongoing normal eating pattern. Most patients with bulimia eventually experience a crowding out of normal eating behavior and rarely, if ever, eat normal meals.[63] These individuals, as reflected in the DSM-III Criteria, also have significant weight fluctuations owing to overeating and to the use of the various purging and dehydrating behaviors.[16,17,62,72]

## Associated Features

Several problems have been described in association with bulimia. The two which have received the most attention are depression and drug abuse.

The relationship between bulimia and depression is a complicated one and is a matter of considerable controversy. Depression is commonly seen in patients with bulimia. It is unclear, however, whether depression develops secondary to the social problems which accompany bulimia or whether bulimia may actually represent a variant of affective disorder—disordered eating may reflect an underlying depressive change. These models are, of course, not mutually exclusive.

Regardless of the sequence, there is considerable evidence of a significant association between depression and bulimia. First, patients with bulimia are usually depressed when they are first evaluated or respond to questionnaires. Johnson has reported that the majority of a series of 316 individuals with bulimia indicate they are "always or often depressed,"[44] and Hatsukami et al.[16] have reported that 45.6%

of a series of 108 patients with bulimia score in a moderate to severe range of depression on the Beck Depression Inventory. Johnson et al.[42] have also shown that not only depression and dysphoria but problems of mood fluctuation are reported by bulimic individuals.

Many patients with bulimia also receive affective disorder diagnoses. The frequencies of such diagnosis vary considerably among studies—a range of 35.2% to 77.8% of patients received such diagnoses, as recently reviewed by Hatsukami et al.[23,26,27,30,31,34,70] Using the Diagnostic Interview Schedule, Hudson et al.[35] found that in a series of 70 patients with bulimia, 80% met criteria for a major affective disorder (66% major depressive disorder, 14% bipolar affective disorder), and an additional 10% met criteria for minor affective disorder. Taken together, these studies suggest a high prevalence of affective disorder symptoms in these patients. This finding, of course, does not answer the question of temporal association or causality—a question which is not particularly relevant in using the DSM-III Criteria.

Researchers have also used family history methods. Several authors have noted a high rate of depression in the first-degree relatives of patients with bulimia:[20,26,27,35,72] between 34% and 60% of bulimic patients will report a history of depression in a first-degree relative.[26] Hudson et al.[35,37] reported a family history study involving 55 bulimic subjects. Relatives were diagnosed using DSM-III Criteria. Overall, 54.5% of bulimic subjects had a first-degree relative with an affective disorder and 16% of the relatives received a diagnosis of major affective disorder with an additional 1% diagnosed as minor affective disorder. This was significantly higher than the rate in control populations of patients with schizophrenia and borderline personality disorder, but not significantly different from the rate for affective disorder controls. However, a study by Stern et al.[84] found no excess of affective disorder in the relatives of bulimics compared to controls. These authors compared 27 bulimic subjects to 27 normal controls and found the rate of affective disorder in first-degree relatives of the bulimics to be 9% and for controls 10%, a nonsignificant difference. Eight of the 27 controls, however, also met criteria for major depressive disorder, a high rate for women in this age group. Clearly, further work needs to be done in examining the depression/bulimia association and further family studies are indicated.

Another major associated problem of bulimia is drug abuse. In early reports of bulimic patients and patients with bulimia nervosa it was noted that there is a high rate of chemical dependency problems. Pyle et al.,[72] reported that eight of 34 patients with bulimia had a history of chemical dependency treatment. In our series of 275 patients with bulimia, 17.7% were found to have a history of chemical dependency treatment, 23% a history of alcohol or drug abuse sufficient to satisfy research criteria, and 34.4% a history of "problems" with alcohol or other drugs.[63] This suggests a significant relationship between these two disorders—particularly in view of the fact that most individuals with bulimia are not through the high-risk age for developing drug abuse problems.

Hatsukami et al.[28] have commented on the similarities between drug abuse behaviors and bulimia—including the secretiveness of the behavior, that the behavior results in a mind altered state, that the patient becomes preoccupied with usage, that engaging in the secretive behavior tends to isolate the individual from those around them. The notion that bulimia can be regarded as a "substance abuse" disorder which is analogous to abuse of alcohol or other drugs (as substances) appears to be a useful construct for understanding some of the features of bulimia. The presence of drug abuse problems should be screened for in all these patients.

Overall, there is also evidence of considerable social impairment associated with this disorder. In our series, over half of the patients reported significant problems in intimate and interpersonal relationships. Family problems and financial problems were also related to the behavior.[63] Johnson and Berndt[40] demonstrated that the overall social adjustment of bulimic individuals were significantly poorer than a normal control group. Norman and Herzog[66] demonstrated that social impairment persisted one year after evaluation despite many of the patients having undergone treatment. This suggests that there may be ongoing social adjustment problems in these patients which must be considered in treatment planning and follow-up care.

## Personality Variables

Several authors have examined the personality characteristics of patients with bulimia. This research addresses the characteristics of patients who are actively bulimic and seeking treatment for the disorder or symptomatic volunteers. To what extent these characteristics reflect the effects of the illness rather than representing preexisting or predisposing factors is unknown.

Weiss and Ebert[89] reported a study comparing 15 bulimic subjects to 15 controls matched by age, sex, socioeconomic status, and IQ. A variety of instruments were administered and several important findings emerged. As indicated on the SCL-90, the bulimic subjects evidenced more pathology on all nine symptom dimensions. Marked differences were shown in several areas including obsessive-compulsive traits, feelings of inadequacy and inferiority, and depression. Bulimics had considerably lower self-esteem, were more impulsive, more likely to report stealing behavior, and reported a higher frequency of previous suicide attempts. They also reported more menstrual difficulties and more episodes of amenorrhea compared to the controls.

Katzman and Wolchik[47] reported a comparison between 30 bulimics, 22 binge-eaters who did not meet criteria for bulimia, and 28 normal controls. As would be predicted from the Weiss and Ebert study,[89] many significant differences were shown between bulimics and controls in the expected direction. The comparison between the bulimics and the binge-eaters, however, also revealed lower self-esteem, poorer body attitude, and a greater level of depression in the bulimics. This supports the idea that the DSM-III category of bulimia is distinct from simple binge-eating.

Two studies have reported MMPI results in bulimic patients. Hatsukami et al.[28] reported that the profiles of a group of bulimic women resembled the MMPI's of women undergoing treatment for chemical dependency. Norman and Herzog[65] compared the MMPI's of restricting anorectics, bulimic anorectics and normal weight bulimics and found similar profiles among the bulimics, with scale 4 elevations.

## Medical Aspects

The disruption of eating behavior evidenced by patients with bulimia can have significant physical consequences—some of which are apparently benign, and some of which can be serious.[54] These medical problems will be discussed by examining each organ system and are summarized in Table 3.

The most common type of abnormality seen in patients with bulimia are fluid and electrolyte abnormalities.[62] Self-induced vomiting and laxative abuse promote fluid loss, volume contraction, and the loss of several electrolytes. Gastric fluid is rich in hydrogen ion and chloride, both of which are lost in large quantities during vomiting.

Potassium is also lost through vomiting. Further loss of potassium through the kidney is promoted by the secondary hyperaldosteronism which results from the volume contraction. The use of laxatives results in the production of diarrhea rich in electrolytes. This promotes further loss. The net overall effect of bulimic behavior is a hypochloremic, hypokalemic alkolosis or some variant of this picture with acidosis in some laxative abusers. Overall, nearly 50% of patients with bulimia will manifest at least mild electrolyte abnormalities. In a small percentage of cases, the electrolyte abnormalities, particularly hypokalemia, may require hospitalization.[62]

Several gastrointestinal problems can also develop.[54] Particularly common is sialodenosis or swelling of the salivary glands, most evident in the parotid glands. Patients may report "puffy cheeks" to indicate this problem. This swelling at times can be seen on physical examination. A modest elevation in serum amylase is also found on serum chemistry analysis. The other gastrointestinal problem of particular concern is gastric dilatation.[82] The pathophysiology of this problem is unclear but it appears to relate to binge-eating behavior. For reasons that are not understood, the gastroesophageal junction obstructs. Due to the continued secretion of gastric fluid into the lumen of the stomach there is a risk of gastric rupture. There have been over 60 cases of spontaneous rupture of the stomach reported.[82] Several of these have developed in anorexia nervosa patients undergoing refeeding and at least two appear to have resulted from binge-eating episodes in patients with bulimia. It is possible that other cases of gastric dilatation or rupture may have resulted from binge-eating episodes but that it was not suspected as the cause.

One of the most potentially expensive complications of bulimia is dental erosion.[54] Vomiting exposes the surface of the teeth to the highly acid gastric contents. This causes enamel erosion. The pattern is characteristic and can be diagnosed by dentists or other health care professionals who are familiar with the pattern. The effects of acid are most pronounced on the lingual, palatal and posterior occlusal surfaces of the teeth. An examination of the restorations also proves useful diagnostically since the restorations are relatively resistent to the acid and end up projecting above the surface of the teeth.

Irregular menses has been reported by patients with bulimia, but the profound amenorrhea associated with anorexia nervosa is rarely seen if patients are of normal weight.[89]

The endocrine system is being studied in some detail in patients with bulimia. Researchers wish to examine the consequences of bulimic behavior on this organ system and also to examine neuroendocrine control mechanisms as a way of evaluating hypothalamic functioning in patients with bulimia. These studies are analogous to the efforts devoted to delineating hypothalamic dysfunction in anorexia nervosa.[54,55,79] Such research indirectly examines the hypothesis that eating disorders (both anorexia nervosa and bulimia) might be attributable to primary CNS dysfunction in at least a subgroup of patients.

The evaluation of the endocrine system has focused on several parameters which have also been studied in anorexia and affective disorders. The dexamethasone suppression test has been shown to be positive (nonsuppression) in both major depressive disorder and anorexia. Hudson et al.[34] demonstrated that five of nine bulimic patients were nonsuppressors. These same authors[36] subsequently reported a larger study of 47 subjects in which 47% were nonsuppressors. Gwirtsman et al.[23] reported a nonsuppression rate of 66.7% in a series of 18 patients with bulimia and our group[56] reported a nonsuppression rate of 50% in a series of 28 patients.

Two groups of investigators have reported data on TSH responsiveness to TRH in bulimia patients. Gwirtsman et al.[23] reported a blunted response in 8 of 10 subjects. Our own group reported blunting in only 1 of 6 subjects.[55]

Other reports indicate abnormalities in the neuroregulation of growth hormone secretion in patients with bulimia,[23,55] but few subjects have been studied.

Katz et al.[46] studied sleep physiology in the normal controls and in 20 anorexia nervosa subjects, 17 of whom had bulimic symptoms and four of whom were 85% or more above ideal body weight when tested. These researchers demonstrated a significant decrease in REM latency and an increase in urinary free cortisol excretion in the patients. These changes were reminiscent of changes reported in depression.

Another approach to examining the possibility of primary neurological dysfunction has been pursued by Rau, Green, and their colleagues. These authors have described a possible association between eating disorders and EEG abnormalities.[22,75] A review article by this group summarized their data on 59 patients, many of whom had been previously reported in their other series.[76] Abnormal EEGs were seen in 64.4% of the series. The most common abnormal findings were paroxysmal dysrhythmias.[22,75,76] However, it is unclear whether or not the abnormalities described are associated with significant behavioral abnormalities.[21,53,77,86]

Our own group evaluated EEG's in a series of 25 normal weight patients with bulimia using sleep deprived EEG's and nasopharyngeal leads.[58] Four of these patients were found to have abnormalities while the other 21 records were read as normal. All records were examined by two independent raters blind to diagnosis. The question of EEG abnormalities in bulimia requires further work, but at this point there is no compelling evidence that most patients with bulimia have such abnormalities.

On first evaluation, patients with bulimia also may report symptoms suggestive of the behavior's physical consequences. These include weakness (83.6%), feeling "bloated" (75.2%), "stomach pains" (63.1%) and "puffy cheeks" (50.0%), as well as "dental problems (36.5%).[63]

The published studies suggest that patients with bulimia need to be screened medically at the time of evaluation. Of particular concern are fluid and electrolyte abnormalities. Patients may also need periodic monitoring of their electrolytes while they are undergoing treatment. Also, research into the neuroendocrine and neurophysiological functioning of these patients may prove fruitful. While such studies may not demonstrate primary hypothalamic dysfunction as a cause of bulimia, they may well delineate secondary physiological changes which may be perpetuating the behavior.

## Treatment

The treatment literature on bulimia remains limited but has grown dramatically in the last 5 years. Researchers have not treated sufficient numbers of patients with bulimia or followed them for long enough periods of time to adequately assess treatment efficacy and long-term follow-up results. Much of treatment literature remains descriptive, with the exception of the psychopharmacological studies, which indicate that anti-depressants represent a promising therapy alternative.

Three major therapeutic approaches have been discussed: (1) individual psychotherapy, most commonly using a behavioral approach —either cognitive-behavioral or exposure and response prevention[15,17,52,78] (2) group therapy, again often using behavioral techniques, particularly cognitive-behavioral techniques as well as more traditional dynamic therapies[5,6,14,41,49,50,74,80,91] and (3) pharmacotherapy,[45] using traditional anti-depressant drugs such as the tricyclics and the MAO inhibitors[7,38,39,57,68,70,85,88] as well as antiepileptic drugs[76,90] and lithium.[33] Pharmacotherapy of bulimia is to be covered in a separate chapter and will not be discussed further here.

Beginning with Boskind-Lodahl and White's report of a group therapy approach in 1978,[6] a variety of group strategies have been developed and described.[5,14,41,49,50,74,80,90] These groups have assumed a variety of theoretical orientations and formats. Most reports, however, detail treatment of only a small number of patients. The outcome and follow-up data reported suggest that several of these treatment approaches are promising and are deserving of further large scale studies. Although superficially different, many of these programs have several elements in common and, awaiting controlled trials, these elements may be presumed to be important in successful group treatment of bulimia. These include the following observations/techniques: (1) the behavior needs to be dealt with directly in the group. The expectation that most patients will normalize their eating pattern if their psychological problems are addressed appears unfounded—most programs have implemented specific techniques for reducing binge-eating behavior such as goal contracting[6] and the expectation of group cessation of bulimic behavior.[74] (2) There is considerable emphasis on instituting normal eating patterns. Techniques employed include the use of structured meal planning,[74] the use of food diaries,[80] and an emphasis on eating regular meals.[74] (3) Most programs incorporate a specific educational component which may include counseling on nutritional issues as well as education about bulimic behavior. (4) Many programs include a cognitive behavioral component[41,74] to address underlying cognitions which may be involved in eating behavior.

Individual behavioral therapy and a combined individual/group therapy have also been described.[2,15-17,49,50,52,78] The approach of Lacey which combines dynamic and behavioral principles is encouraging in terms of treatment outcome.[49,50] Fairburn has focused on the use of cognitive behavioral techniques in an individual therapy context with apparent success. Rosen, Leitenberg[52,78] and their colleagues have employed exposure and response prevention to treat bulimia. The focus is on the vomiting behavior as an "escape" mechanism. Patients are exposed to feared foods, and then are prevented from vomiting. Although few patients have been studied, the few results that do exist are promising.

Overall, the strongest evidence of efficacy has been found for pharmacotherapy. Several controlled, double-blind studies of tricyclics or MAO inhibitors have been done also.[38,57,70,88] Group and individual therapy studies involving randomization to treatment have not yet been reported with the exception of the work by Lacey.[49,50] Also, the various treatment options have not yet been compared. Treatment outcome and comparison studies are the next logical step in research on this disorder.

## REFERENCES

1. Abraham, S.F., and Beumont, P.J.V.: How patients describe bulimia or binge-eating. Psychol. Med., 12:625–635, 1982.
2. Abraham, S.F., Mira, M., and Llewellyn-Jones, D.: Bulimia: A study of outcome. International Journal of Eating Disorders, 2:175–180, 1983.
3. Anderson, A.E.: Anorexia nervosa and bulimia: A spectrum of eating disorders. Journal of Adolescent Health Care, 4:15–21, 1983.
4. Bo-Linn, G.W., Santa Ana, C.A., Morawski, S.G., et al.: Purging and calorie absorption in bulimic patients and normal women. Ann. Int. Med., 99:14–17, 1983.
5. Boskind-Lodahl, M.: Cinderella's step-sisters: A feminist perspective on anorexia nervosa and bulimia. Journal of Women in Culture and Society, 2:342–356, 1976.
6. Boskind-Lodahl, M., and White, W.C.: The definition and treatment of bulimarexia in college women: A pilot study. JACHA, 27:84–86, 1978.
7. Brotman, A.W., Herzog, D.B., and Woods, S.W.: Antidepressant treatment of bulimia: The relationship between binging and depressive symptomatology. J. Clin. Psychiatry, 45:7–9, 1984.
8. Carter, J.A., and Duncan, P.A.: Binge-eating and vomiting: A survey of a high school population. Psychology in the Schools, 21:198-203, 1984.
9. Casper, R.C., Eckert, E.D., Halmi, K.A., et al.: Bulimia—Its incidence and clinical importance in patients with anorexia nervosa. Arch. Gen. Psychiatry, 37:1030–1040, 1980.
10. Chiodo, J., and Latimer, P.R.: Vomiting as a learned weight-control technique in bulimia. Journal of Behavior Therapy and Experimental Psychiatry, 14:131–135, 1983.
11. Clark, M.G., and Palmer, R.G.: Eating attitudes and neurotic symptoms in university students. Br. J. Psychiatry, 142:399–404, 1983.
12. Connors, M.E., Johnson, C.L., and Stuckey, M.K.: Treatment of bulimia with brief psychoeducational group therapy. Am. J. Psychiatry, 141:1512–1516, 1984.
13. Cooper, P.J., and Fairburn, C.G.: Binge-eating and self-induced vomiting in the community—a preliminary study. Br. J. Psychiatry, 142:139–144, 1983.
14. Dixon, K.N., and Kiecolt-Glaser, J.: Group therapy for bulimia. Paper presented at the American Psychiatric Association annual meeting, May, 1981.
15. Fairburn, C.G: A cognitive behavioral approach to the treatment of bulimia. Psychol. Med., 11:707–711, 1981.
16. Fairburn, C.G.: Binge-eating and bulimia nervosa. SK & F Publications, 1:1-20, 1982.
17. Fairburn, C.G.: Binge-eating and its management. Brit. J. Psychiatry, 141:631–633, 1982.
18. Fairburn, C.G., and Cooper, P.J.: Rumination in bulimia nervosa. Br. Med. J., 288:826–827, 1984.
19. Fairburn, C.G., and Cooper, P.J.: Self-in-

duced vomiting and bulimia nervosa: An undetected problem. Br. Med. J., 284:1153–1155, 1982.

20. Fairburn, C.G., and Cooper, P.J.: The features of bulimia nervosa. Br. J. Psychiatry, 144:238–247, 1984.

21. Gibbs, E.L., and Gibbs, F.A.: Electroencephalographic evidence of thalamic and hypothalamic epilepsy. Neurology, 1:136–144, 1951.

22. Green, R.S., and Rau, J.H.: Treatment of compulsive eating disturbances with anticonvulsant medications. Am. J. Psychiatry, 131:428–432, 1974.

23. Gwirtsman, H.E., Roy-Byrne, P., Yager, J., et al.: Neuroendocrine abnormalities in bulimia. Am. J. Psychiatry, 140:559–563, 1983.

24. Halmi, K.A., Falk, J.R., and Schwartz, E.: Binge-eating and vomiting: A survey of a college population. Psychol. Med., 11:697–706, 1981.

25. Hill, O.W.: Psychogenic vomiting. GUT, 9:348–352, 1968.

26. Hatsukami, D.K., Eckert, E., Mitchell, J.E., et al: Affective disorders and substance abuse in women with bulimia. Psychol. Med. (in press).

27. Hatsukami, D.K., Mitchell, J.E., and Eckert, E.D.: Eating disorders: A variant of mood disorders? Psychiatr. Clin. North Am., 7:349–365, 1984.

28. Hatsukami, D., Owen, P., Pyle, R., et al.: Similarities and differences on the MMPI between women with bulimia and women with alcohol or drug abuse problems. Addictive Behaviors, 7:435–439, 1982.

29. Hawkins II, R.C., and Clement, P.F.: Development and construct validation of a self-report measure of binge-eating tendencies. Addictive Behaviors, 5:219–226, 1980.

30. Herzog, D.B.: Bulimia in the adolescent. Am. J. Dis. Child, 136:985–989, 1982.

31. Herzog, D.B.: Bulimia: The secretive syndrome. Psychosomatics, 23:481–487, 1982.

32. Herzog, D.B., Norman, D.K., Gordon, C., et al.: Sexual conflict and eating disorders in 27 males. Am. J. Psychiatry, 141(8):989–990, 1984.

33. Hsu, L.K.G.: Treatment of bulimia with lithium. Am. J. Psychiatry, 141:1260–1262, 1984.

34. Hudson, J.I., Laffer, P.S., and Pope, H.G.: Bulimia related to affective disorder by family history and response to the dexamethasone suppression test. Am. J. Psychiatry, 139:685–687, 1982.

35. Hudson, J.I., Pope, H.G., and Jonas, J.M.: Bulimia: A form of affective disorder? Presented at the American Psychiatric Association Annual Meeting, May, 1983.

36. Hudson, J.I., Pope, H.G., Jonas, J.M., et al.: Hypothalamic-pituitary-adrenal axis: Hyperactivity in bulimia. Psychiatry Res., 8:111–117, 1983.

37. Hudson, J.I., Pope, H.G., Jonas, J.M., et al.: Family history study of anorexia nervosa and bulimia. Brit. J. Psychiatry, 142:133–138, 1983.

38. Hughes, P.L., Wells, L.A., Cunningham, C.J., et al.: Treating bulimia with desipramine: A double-blind placebo-controlled study. Paper presented at the American Psychiatric Association annual meeting, May, 1984.

39. Jonas, J.M., Hudson, J.I., and Pope, H.G.: Treatment of bulimia with MAO inhibitors. J. Clin. Psychopharmacology, 3:59–60, 1983.

40. Johnson, C., and Berndt, D.J.: Preliminary investigation of bulimia and life adjustment. Am. J. Psychiatry, 140:774–777, 1983.

41. Johnson, C.L., Connors, M., and Stuckey, M.K: Short-term group treatment of bulimia, A preliminary report. International Journal of Eating Disorders, 2:199–207, 1983.

42. Johnson, C.L, and Larson, R.: Bulimia: An analysis of moods and behavior. Psychosom. Med., 44:341–351, 1982.

43. Johnson, C.L, Lewis, C., Love, S., et al.: Incidence and correlates of bulimic behavior in a female high school population. Journal of Youth and Adolescence, 13:15–26, 1984.

44. Johnson, C.L., Stuckey, M.K., Lewis, L.D., et al.: Bulimia: A descriptive survey of 316 cases. International Journal of Eating Disorders, 2:321–326, 1982.

45. Johnson, C.L, Stuckey, M.K, and Mitchell, J.E: Psychopharmacological treatment of

anorexia nervosa and bulimia—review and synthesis. J. Nerv. Ment. Dis., 171:524–534, 1983.

46. Katz, J.L., Kuperberg, A., Pollack, C.P., et al.: Is there a relationship between eating disorder and affective disorder? New evidence from sleep recordings. Am. J. Psychiatry, 14:753–759, 1984.

47. Katzman, M.A., and Wolchik, S.A.: Bulimia and binge-eating in college women: A comparison of personality and behavioral characteristics. J. Consult. Clin. Psychol., 52:423–428, 1984.

48. Katzman, M.A., Wolchik, S.A., and Brauer, S.L.: The prevalence of frequent binge-eating and bulimia in a non-clinical college sample. International Journal of Eating Disorders, 3:53–62, 1984.

49. Lacey, J.H.: An outpatient treatment program for bulimia nervosa. International Journal of Eating Disorders, 2:209–214, 1983.

50. Lacey, J.H.: Bulimia nervosa, binge-eating, and psychogenic vomiting: A controlled treatment study and long-term outcome. Br. Med. J., 286:1609–1613, 1983.

51. Lacey, J.H., and Gibson, E.: Does laxative abuse control weight? A comparative study of purging and vomiting bulimics. Applied Nutrition, 39A:36–42, 1985.

52. Leitenberg, H., Gross, J., Peterson, J., et. al.: Analysis of an anxiety model and the process of change during exposure plus response prevention treatment of bulimia nervosa. Behavior Therapy, 15:13–20, 1984.

53. Maulsby, R.L.: EEG patterns of uncertain diagnostic significance. In Klass, D.W., and Daly, D.D. (eds.): Current Practice of Clinical Electroencephalography. New York, Raven Press, 1979.

54. Mitchell, J.E.: Medical complications of anorexia nervosa and bulimia. Psychiatric Medicine, 1:229–255, 1984.

55. Mitchell, J.E., and Bantle, J.P.: Metabolic and endocrine investigations in women of normal weight with the bulimia syndrome. Biol. Psychiatry, 18:355–365, 1983.

56. Mitchell, J.E., Boutacoff, L., Pyle, R.L., et al.: The dexamethasone suppression test in patients with bulimia. J. Clin. Psychiatry (in press).

57. Mitchell, J.E., and Groat. R.: A placebo-controlled, double-blind trial of amitriptyline in bulimia. J. Clin. Psychopharmacology, 4:186–193, 1984.

58. Mitchell, J.E., Hosfield, W., and Pyle, R.L.: EEG findings in patients with the bulimia syndrome. International Journal of Eating Disorders, 3:17–23, 1983.

59. Mitchell, J.E., and Laine, D.C.: Monitored binge-eating behavior in patients of normal weight with bulimia. International Journal of Eating Disorders, 4:177-183, 1985.

60. Mitchell, J.E., and Pyle, R.L.: The bulimia syndrome in normal weight individuals: A review. International Journal of Eating Disorders, 1:61–73, 1982.

61. Mitchell, J.E., Pyle, R.L., and Eckert, E.D.: Frequency and duration of binge-eating episodes in patients with bulimia. Am. J. Psychiatry, 138:835–836, 1981.

62. Mitchell, J.E., Pyle, R.L., Eckert, E.D., et al.: Electrolyte and other physiological abnormalities in patients with bulimia. Psychol. Med., 13:273–278, 1983.

63. Mitchell, J.E., Pyle, R.L., Eckert, E.D., et al: The Characteristics of 275 patients with bulimia. Am. J. Psychiatry, 142:482-485, 1985.

64. Nagelberg, D.B., Hale, S.L., and Ware, S.L.: The assessment of bulimic symptoms and personality correlates in female college students. J. Clin. Psychology, 40:440–445, 1984.

65. Norman, D.K., and Herzog, D.B.: Bulimia, anorexia nervosa, and anorexia nervosa with bulimia: A comparative analysis of MMPI profiles. International Journal of Eating Disorders, 2:43–52, 1983.

66. Norman, D.K., and Herzog, D.B. Persistent social maladjustment in bulimia: A one-year follow-up. Am. J. Psychiatry, 141:444–446, 1984.

67. Palmer, R.L.: The dietary chaos syndrome: A useful new term? Br. J. Med. Psychol. 52:187–190, 1979.

68. Pope, H.G., Hudson, J.I., and Jonas, J.M.: Antidepressant treatment of bulimia: Preliminary experience and practical recommendations. J. Clin. Psychopharmacology, 3:274–281, 1983.

69. Pope, H.G., Hudson, J.I. and Yurgelun-Todd, D: Anorexia nervosa and bulimia among 300 suburban women shoppers. Am. J. Psychiatry, 141:292–294, 1984.

70. Pope, H.G., Hudson, J.I., Jonas, J.M., et al.: Bulimia treated with imipramine: A placebo-controlled double-blind study. Am. J. Psychiatry, 140:554,558, 1983.

71. Pope, H.G., Hudson, J.I., Yurgelun-Todd, D., et al.: Prevalence of anorexia nervosa and bulimia in three student populations. International Journal of Eating Disorders, 3:45-51, 1984.

72. Pyle, R.L., Mitchell, J.E., and Eckert, E.D.: Bulimia: A report of 34 cases. J. Clin. Psychiatry, 42:60–64, 1981.

73. Pyle, R.L., Mitchell, J.E., Eckert, E.D., et al.: The incidence of bulimia in freshman college students. International Journal of Eating Disorders, 2:75–85, 1983.

74. Pyle, R.L., Mitchell, J.E., Eckert, E.D., et al.: The interruption of bulimic behaviors. Psychiatr. Clin. North Am., 7:275–286, 1984.

75. Rau, J.H., and Green, R.S.: Brief communication: soft neurological correlates and compulsive eaters. J. Nerv. Ment. Dis., 166:435–437, 1978.

76. Rau, J.H., Struve, F.A., and Green, R.S.: Electroencephalographic correlates of compulsive eating. Clin. Electroencephalogr., 10:180–187, 1979.

77. Reiher, J., Ham, O., and Klass, D.W.: EEG characteristics and clinical significance of small sharp spikes—a reappraisal. Electroencephalogr. Clin. Neurophysiol., 26:360–636, 1969.

78. Rosen, J.C., and Leitenberg, H.: Bulimia nervosa: Treatment with exposure and response prevention. Behavior Therapy, 13:117–124, 1982.

79. Roy-Byrne, P., Gwirtsman, H., Yager, J., et al.: Neuroendocrine tests in bulimia. Paper presented at the American Psychiatric Association annual meeting, May, 1982.

80. Roy-Byrne, P., Lee-Benner, K., and Yager, J.: Group therapy for bulimia: A year's experience. International Journal of Eating Disorders, 3:97–116, 1984.

81. Russell, G.: Bulimia nervosa: An ominous variant of anorexia nervosa. Psychol. Med., 9:429–448, 1979.

82. Saul, S.H., Dekkar, A., and Watson, C.G.: Acute gastric dilatation with infarction and perforation. GUT, 22:978–983, 1981.

83. Sinoway, C.G.: The incidence and characteristics of bulimarexia in Penn State students. Paper presented at the American Psychological Association annual meeting, August, 1982.

84. Stern, S.L., Dixon, K.N., Nemzer, E., et al.: Affective disorder in the families of women with normal weight bulimia. Am. J. Psychiatry, 141:1224–1226, 1984.

85. Stewart, J.W., Walsh, B.T., Wright, L., et al.: An open trial of MAO inhibitors in bulimia. J. Clin. Psychiatry, 45:217–219, 1984.

86. Struve, F.A., and Ramsey, P.P.: Concerning the 14 & 6 per second positive spike cases in post-traumatic medical-legal EEGs reported by Gibbs and Gibbs: A statistical commentary. Clin. Electroencephalogr., 8:203–205, 1977.

87. Stunkard, A.J.: Eating patterns and obesity. Psych. Quart., 33:284–295, 1959.

88. Walsh, B.T., Stewart, J.W., Roose, S.P., et al.: Treatment of bulimia with phenelzine. A double-blind placebo-controlled study. Arch. Gen. Psychiatry, 41:1105–1109, 1984.

89. Weiss, S.R., and Ebert, M.H.: Psychological and behavioral characteristics of normal weight bulimics and normal weight controls. Psychosom. Med., 45:293–303, 1983.

90. Wermuth, B.M., Davis, K.L., Hollister, L.E., et al: Phenytoin treatment of the binge-eating syndrome. Am. J. Psychiatry, 134:1249–1253, 1977.

91. White, W.C., and Boskind-White, M.: An experimental-behavioral approach to the treatment of bulimarexia. Psychotherapy: Theory, Research and Practice, 18:501–507, 1981.

TABLE 1. Epidemiology of Bulimia and Bulimia Nervosa

| | College Students (9 studies) N=4,827 | H.S. Students (3 studies) N=1,999 | Clinic Patients (1 study) N=369 | Other (1 study) N=300 |
|---|---|---|---|---|
| **Binge-Eat** | | | | |
| Females | 46.2% – 79.0% | 57.0% | 26.4% | — |
| Males | 38.0% – 60.2% | — | — | — |
| **Bulimia** | | | | |
| Females | 3.9% – 19.0% | 6.5% – 8.3% | — | 10.3% |
| Males | 0 – 6.1% | 0% | — | — |
| **Rigid Criteria*** | | | | |
| Females | 1.1% | 1.0% | 1.9%** | 3.0% |
| Males | 0% | — | — | — |

*Weekly binge-eating and weekly vomiting and/or laxative abuse (minimum)
**Bulimia Nervosa

TABLE 2. Eating, Fating-Related, and Weight Reduction Behaviors in Bulimic Patients

| Behavior | % Reporting* | Behavior | % Reporting |
|---|---|---|---|
| Binge-eating | 100% | Laxatives | 61% |
| Fasting | 92% | Diet Pills | 50% |
| Exercise | 91% | Ruminate | 33% |
| Vomiting | 88% | Diuretics | 33% |
| Chew and Spit | 65% | Saunas | 12% |

* During course of the illness – not necessarily at time of evaluation.

TABLE 3. Medical Considerations in Patients with Bulimia

**Fluid and Electrolytes**
Dehydration
Alkalosis
Hypochloremia
Hypokalemia
Acidosis
Edema

**Gastrointestinal**
Salivary gland swelling
Amylase elevation
Gastric dilatation
Gastric rupture
Pancreatitis

**Neurological**
EEG abnormalities

**Endocrine**
DST positive
Blunted TSH response
GH regulation abnormalities

**Dental**
Enamel erosion

**Hematologic**
Bleeding diathesis

CHAPTER 8

# Bulimia—Towards a Rational Approach to Diagnosis and Treatment

J. Hubert Lacey, M.B., Ch.B., M.Phil., F.R.C.Psych.
A. Harte, Dip.C.O.T.,
S.A. Birtchnell, M.B., B.S., M.R.C.Psych.

## Bulimia - the uneasy diagnosis

In recent years the pattern of clinical presentation of eating disorders has changed. Abnormal eating behavior—such as binge-eating or self-induced vomiting—which used to be associated with the weight disorders of anorexia nervosa or obesity is now being reported at normal body weight. Towards the end of the seventies, a number of clinicians delineated a normal body weight binge-eating syndrome which Russell[21] called bulimia nervosa. This term is perhaps unfortunate because by so labelling it, the condition has become too closely tied to anorexia nervosa—it could be argued that on certain demographic grounds and aspects of behavior, the majority of bulimic patients resemble a successful but maladaptive response to potential obesity than to failed anorexia nervosa.

Whatever its etiology—and more of this later—the original descriptions of bulimia describe it as a disorder characterized by powerful urges to binge-eat, particularly with carbohydrate foods. The fatness and weight gain that would ordinarily result are prevented by intermittent periods of starvation, purgation and self-induced vomiting such that the patient's body weight remains within a normal range. Depression, anger and guilt are common concomitants.

Two sets of diagnostic criteria—those of DSM-III[1] and Russell's[2]—have been established and both have major imperfections.

107

The American Psychiatric Association sets out three criteria of diagnosis apart from binge-eating itself and a clause to exclude anorexia nervosa. These are: that the patient is aware that the eating pattern is abnormal and has a fear of it; that she experiences an associated depressed mood with depreciatory thoughts; and that she demonstrates three of a list of five behaviors associated or caused by binge-eating. These behaviors are in no way pathonomonic of bulimia but occur whenever binge-eating is done, irrespective of the primary diagnosis. This does not minimize their relevance, but it does reduce their importance in clarifying the diagnosis. What is not stated in these criteria and which is perhaps more important than the extent of binge-eating, is the sense these patients describe of being out of control. This lack of control—which contrasts dramatically with the controlled behavior of the anorectic—is perhaps the most disturbing feature of the condition. It transcends food abuse and is additionally appreciated by the patient as the hallmark of her interpersonal relationships. Again, however, this cannot be said to be pathonomonic of bulimia: bulimic anorectics and the obese both describe such feelings.

The presence or absence of a weight disorder has major diagnostic and prognostic implications. Everything in the last two paragraphs (with the exception of the reference to body weight) can be applied to the bulimic anorectic or the bulimic obese. As the bulimic anorectic and the obese need a different treatment approach (and, in particular, the bulimic anorectic usually needs inpatient help) the clinician must first establish the definitive diagnosis. Merely saying that the patient has bulimia without reference to the underlying etiology is as unhelpful (at least, in terms of treatment) as saying that a patient has a temperature while having no idea of the underlying pathogen.

In his original description[21] and at a recent conference[23] Russell made it clear that bulimia nervosa was a form of anorexia nervosa and that all bulimia nervosa patients must have had a period of anorexia nervosa. He emphasizes this by making a morbid fear of fatness a diagnostic criterion of bulimia nervosa just as it is a criterion of anorexia nervosa.[21] He thus merges the concept of the bulimic anorectic with bulimia occurring at normal body weight. Such a view denies the differing treatment responses of the two patient groups. It also denies a diagnostic label of the 60% of normal body weight bulimics who have no previous history of anorexia nervosa. This is particularly unfortunate. This is the group that most easily responds to treatment. The diagnostic situation becomes more confusing because according to DSM-III a history of anorexia nervosa precludes a diagnosis of bulimia!

While all this is unfortunate, within the diversity of symptoms offered by patients it would be surprising if clinical descriptions were identical. Boskind-Lodahl's Bulimorexia[3], Lacey's Bulimic Syndrome[10,13], and Palmer's Dietary Chaos Syndrome[20] all vary in their emphasis—an indication of the heterogenous nature of the clinical presentation. An effective diagnostic structure must recognize these differences in clinical presentation. In particular it is important whether the effects of binge-eating are controlled by self-induced vomiting or by purgation[16]. Even more important is whether the loss of control affects only food or whether binge-eating forms a pivot for other maladaptive impulses such as binge-drinking, drug abuse, stealing or sexual disinhibition.[15] We will return to the relevance of these later.

## From Diagnosis to Treatment

From this confusion it is essential to develop a system of diagnosis. We feel the system should be strict and relevant to the psychopathology such that it will give a strong indication of response to treatment. Further, it is necessary that the diagnosis should be capable of clinical division into subgroups indicative of different etiology and treatment response.

To achieve these aims we must first return to the diagnosis of anorexia nervosa. All major writers have referred to a central psychological core, whether it be a "pursuit of thinness"[4], a "morbid fear of fatness"[22], or whatever. Crisp, in his writing[6], has referred to the "phobia of normal body weight" central to the diagnosis of anorexia nervosa. In fact, he has taken it further by stating the pathonomonic feature of anorexia nervosa (that is the feature that separates anorexia nervosa from all other syndromes) is the presence of a weight phobia. If the patient expresses this, even though her weight is within a normal range, then she is anorectic: her temporary "normal" weight being due to binge-eating. This is what Crisp means by abnormal/normal weight control[5]. If the symptom-cluster surrounding the binge-eating of the anorectic is the only target for treatment, then the patient will "fight" against her treatment: her desire to lose weight overcomes treatment and leads her to "diet," thereby encouraging binge-eating. If control is gained over her eating, her weight will fall in line with the underlying phobic psychopathology and classical anorexia nervosa will reoccur. Thus, if the patient expresses either overtly or covertly a weight phobia on initial consultation, then she should be diagnosed as having the bulimic variant of anorexia nervosa and appropriate treatment recommended[7,14,15,22]. Only if there is no weight phobia and lack of food control is the main complaint should the diagnosis of bulimia be considered.

If these two concepts are added to the criteria for diagnosis of bulimia as established by the American Psychiatric Association[1] along with the fifth diagnostic statement of DSM-III—"bulimic episodes are not caused by anorexia nervosa"—then the diagnosis of bulimia becomes firm: it can be separated from bulimic anorexia nervosa and from binge-eating which is common in normal populations[18] and in morbid conditions such as depression.

Our criteria for diagnosis is thus:

(1) Current episodes of distressful binge-eating within a normal range of body weight ($-15\%$ to $+20\%$ mean matched population weight)[16]

(2) The absence of an irrational fear of normal body weight must be confirmed—while the patient may wish to lose weight her desired target weight is within a normal range.

(3) A sense that eating patterns are out of control: a feeling that may transcend food abuse and be appreciated in other areas of the patient's life.

(4) While the bulimic episodes may have developed within the context of anorexia nervosa, massive obesity or physical illness, they are not maintained by these pathologies.

(5) Depressed mood and self-depreciatory thoughts may or may not be associated with eating binges and the removal of binge-eating does not necessarily lead to a normal mood state.

(6) Behaviors often associated with binge-eating will be present: the eating of large amounts of food, secret binge-eating, frequent attempts to lose weight (though within a normal range), fluctuation of body weight, control of the effects of binge-eating by intermittent periods of starvation, purgation or self-induced vomiting.

These criteria lead us to emphasize the need to categorize bulimia further into three etiological types which are important for treatment outcome. These are:

(a) Type I Bulimia: In this neither the patient nor her family describe a history of previous anorexia nervosa, weight phobia or massive weight loss although weight fluctuation is common. This has been referred to as the Bulimic Syndrome[10] and its prognosis with treatment, is good.[11]

(b) Type II Bulimia: In this the previous anorexia nervosa patient has "recovered" to normal body weight. This is somewhat similar to the concept of bulimia nervosa. The patient no longer expresses a fear of normal body weight. Prognosis is not as good as Type I Bulimia.[11]

(c) Type III Bulimia: These patients enter bulimia from massive obesity and, as such, give a history of being at least 60% above mean matched population weight in the past. They are usually in excess of 10% above mean matched population weight on presentation. Long-term prognosis is poor.

## The Theoretical Base of Treatment

It would be logical before devising a treatment for bulimia to examine the principles of those programs which have been successful in treating anorexia nervosa. The classical treatments for anorexia nervosa have a consistent structure which falls into two stages: first, weight and eating are controlled within a nursing program and second, therapy by whatever approach attempts to deal with the emotional difficulties generated by such control. Generally, treatments which have used such principles have been successful. Before we rush to replicate this structure, however, we must caution ourselves. Similar treatment models used in massive obesity—where binge-eating is common— have not been as successful. Also anorexia nervosa treatments tend to be less successful when applied to bulimic anorectics than when applied to those who abstain. In other words, impulsive behavior as opposed to behavior which is over-controlled may not respond easily to such a model.

Additionally, the syndrome bulimia is more than a behavioral problem surrounding a single impulsive problem. It is a complex syndrome whose most obvious symptom, binge-eating, dominates but only superficially. Beneath, as we have indicated, there is a mixed affective state and a subjective feeling of lack of control. The patient's fear that this lack of control may break out into other maladaptive behaviors of a social or sexual kind must be dealt with by any successful treatment program. Further, treatment must recognize the total syndrome has its roots in and is driven by a complex dynamic conflict vested in the social, psychological and sexual roles which are imposed on women by our society.

To expect any one treatment (or even one psychological orientation) to deal with what is literally "chaos" is courting failure. And so it was when we attempted the initial trial[9]. The patients found dynamic therapies did not stop the overt eating problem. Behavioral techniques also failed to deal with the underlying, unresolved tensions. The patients themselves were polled to determine what aspects of the various types of treatment seemed effective to them. A close supportive relationship with the therapist was felt to be essential. Also deemed important was a formal structure of disciplined help aimed at symptom removal. They also requested a forum in which they could examine the emotions released when eating is brought under control.

The theoretical basis of our treatment is, thus, shown in Table 1. The eating disorder and the emotion and social problems attendant on it need to be dealt with by different approaches, in different settings but by the same therapist. This latter point is important because consistency of the therapist rather than therapy was highly rated by patients and without it treatment could disintegrate. We found we could control the eating disorder itself by simple behavioral means in one-to-one therapy. But as emotional and interpersonal difficulties become exposed, the therapy needs to change to insight-directed psychotherapy. The movement from behavioral to insight therapy should be determined by the patient and her progress. Patients who are slow to give up symptoms need more counseling and behavioral help while those who are able to give it up can move quickly on to psychodynamic therapy. Undoubtedly the latter can be a reward for eliminating the bulimic behavior and in a sense of dynamic, therapy can be seen as a part of behavioral treatment.

We believe that insight-directed therapy should be provided not only in individual sessions but also in a psychotherapy group. The reason for this will be discussed later but the cost-effectiveness of conducting psychotherapy within a group setting cannot be overemphasized when the number of women seeking treatment is formidable. Any treatment program devised must not only be effective, but also short-term and capable of handling a number of patients at a time.

When faced with such a large scale problem there would appear to be little advantage in developing treaments which are long-term, expensive and only capable of being conducted by charismatic, sophisticated —and hence rare—psychotherapists. To emphasize this point it should be noted that in my own clinic where referral is untrammeled by the need for direct payment, the median social class is Social Class III (semi-skilled). Such women would in Europe seek help from the public health sector and in the United States would in all probability have less than luxurious health insurance.

## The Treatment Programs

Three treatment programs have been devised, details of which are published elsewhere[9]. Two treatment programs—one using both individual and group techniques, the other using only individual sessions —are set in the outpatient department and are time-limited, ten and twelve week treatments respectively. These outpatient programs are aimed at the majority of bulimic patients. When the condition is more complicated, however, and the patient presents with multiple impulse disorder embracing alcohol or drug dependence, sexual promiscuity, stealing or self-harm, the third program—inpatient treatment—is preferred[9].

The first program we developed is a time-limited, individual group treatment suitable for general psychiatric outpatients. It takes place on one-half day a week thereby allowing the patient to continue in employment. Five patients are treated in each program by two therapists. The design of each afternoon's therapy is that the patient will attend a half-hour individual therapy session before joining the four other patients and two therapists in a psychotherapy group. It is important the group session takes place after the individual session such that they are linked.

The important initial control of eating is effected by behavioral self-monitoring in which the intake of food, the incidence of binge-eating and vomiting are recorded temporarily. Thoughts, feelings and behavior which the patient believes may be associated with her abnormal eating are written down as they occur and the patient is required to explain them. Patient education and counseling focuses in developing an adaptive eating pattern. All this is attempted using a dietary diary which the patient carries on her person at all times and completes as she eats.

In addition, the patient enters a contract which is graduated and becomes more controlling as the treatment progresses[9]. The contract is modified according to the treatment response. The patient always contracts to attend all ten sessions and their related groups, and to maintain her presenting body weight throughout the program. She also contracts to eat a prescribed diet of three meals a day at set times each with adequate carbohydrates. From the beginning of treatment the patient is encouraged to reduce and then to stop binge-eating. Each stage is marked by its incorporation into the contract. The patient is encouraged, then contracted to eat the next prescribed meal regardless of the proximity of the previous binge.

Individual therapy has two distinct stages of treatment, both done by the same therapist. This is summarized in Table II. It should be emphasized that the amount of insight-directed therapy provided is sufficient to allow the average patient to deal herself with emotional and relationship problems which may be exposed during treatment. At worst, it should allow her to seek help from the general psychiatric services without being encumbered by an eating disorder.

## How Effective is Treatment?

In treating bulimia, it cannot be claimed that an immediate cessation of symptoms following therapeutic intervention is an indication of permanent change. Any treatment must be monitored in a controlled study and outcome measured over at least two years. This was done[11] for our combined group and individual program. This treatment proved effective at stopping bulimic behavior. The effect of the treatment on the binge-eating and self-induced vomiting of thirty patients is shown in Table III. All patients reduced the frequency of their bulimia and twenty-four of the thirty had stopped their binge-eating by the end of treatment and twenty-six had stopped self-induced vomiting.

Thus, the immediate effect of treatment is good. In fact, the results are sufficiently good that, despite being tested in a controlled study, they deserve replication. This has now been done on fifteen more patients and is awaiting assessment of longer term outcome. We can confirm, however, that, as before, 80% initially stop their binge-eating and vomiting at the end of treatment or, roughly, four out of every five patients treated. Similar results of the initial impact of treatment are reported by other centers[8,19]. These treatments, like our own, have a heavy reliance on behavioral techniques and, interestingly, one of them[19] reinforces these techniques by group pressure and lasts for a similar period of time.

The success of the initial impact of treatment begs the question: what of the longer term results? To determine this our original thirty patients were followed up for two years. Although one patient refused follow-up and one needed inpatient admission, the remaining twenty-eight patients judged the treatment a success. Twenty had no bulimic episodes while the remainder had occasional episodes, roughly three or four times a year.

The patients had follow-up appointments at one month, three months and thereafter three-monthly intervals over a two-year period. Table V indicates the reported incidence of disordered eating over the preceeding three months at each of the follow-up appointments for the two-year period. At the end of the treatment twenty-four had stopped binge-eating and thereafter between twenty-two and twenty-seven patients were not binge-eating in any three-month period. It is these longer term results, rather than the initial results, which mark out our treatment program.

## How Does the Treatment Work?

The results of our treatment program and the work of others demonstrates that a disordered eating pattern can be interrupted by behavioral self-monitoring. It is important to recognize, however, that it is only an interruption and symptoms will most likely reappear. The aim therefore must be to achieve a period of stability during which time other therapies can attempt a more permanent resolution of the patient's problem.

A patient who is duly motivated can usually stop her binge-eating between the fourth and sixth week of treatment. No longer hindered by food manipulation, underlying emotional issues become exposed and depression and anger are more appropriately felt. In other words, although the patient's eating pattern achieves stability, the converse is true of her emotional state. It appears logical to us, therefore, that successful treatment—by which we mean a clinical behavioral change which is permanent, tested against a control, and not deviated into other neurotic behaviors—requires a forum to examine these emotional feelings and their underlying conflicts.

An example of this is shown in Fig. 1: analogue scale scores of depression increase at just that point—week six—the eating disorder comes under control: a visual representation of the translation of the eating problem into emotional terms. The period of two weeks—

usually in the middle of our ten-week treatment program and during which the patients tend to give up their disturbed eating behavior—is associated with major and fluctuating emotional feelings. They feel more humiliated, guilty, frightened, anxious and isolated. These feelings which are significant and measured in a study presently in preparation are temporary and it is essential that the treatment emphasizes their temporary nature. By tackling the underlying problems psychotherapeutically, relief can be attained, however.

The treatment's power to alter within psychotherapy entrenched and core symptoms has been further shown in a recent study[2] on the disturbed body perception of these patients. Bruch[4] was the first to claim that body image disturbance was an essential characteristic of weight disorders. She considered its correction as a "precondition to recovery". Many clinicians treating anorectics have felt it important to address the distortion of body image during treatment. But direct attempts at modification tend to be unproductive. Generally it has been noted that the patients' body image eventually "self-corrects" once more fundamental emotional issues are faced.

Prior to treatment the normal body weight bulimic over-estimates various (usually emotionally charged) areas of her body.[2] This over-estimation is significantly more than normal weight control and similar to that shown in anorectic populations. (Table VI) We examined twenty-nine bulimic patients before and after their ten-week outpatient treatment program using the same body image perception apparatus in the same room. The decrease in over-estimation of body width would appear to be an effect of treatment. No similar reduction in body image distortion was reported in control subjects. We would thus argue that emotional conflict—particularly conflict concerning role, femininity, or problems associated with interpersonal relationships—which are ordinarily displaced are re-channelled by psychodynamic psychotherapy. This leads to a retreat from the over-estimation towards the norm. Further we believe these results show group psychotherapy sessions in conjunction with individual therapy sessions provide an efficient means of exploiting the control of eating gained by behavioral techniques.

Apart from this, though, is the group component of treatment important? Could our structured but eclectic treatment work using individual sessions only? To examine this we repeated our treatment on sixteen further patients. But this time we did so without the group component. We increased the individual sessions in length so patients had the same therapy time as in our original study. We kept the same philosophy of using behavioral therapy to control symptoms, then shifting later to psychodynamic treatment. Table VII shows the preliminary results. In our original study twenty-four of the thirty patients were not binging at the end of treatment. There were no drop-outs. Without the group component, three of the sixteen patients dropped out of treatment. It thus appears that the group component prevents the drop-out rate which is commonly reported in this condition, probably by means of mutual support and other effects of group psychotherapy. Of the thirteen patients who remained in treatment eleven stopped binge-eating—85%—which compares well with the 80% who stopped binge-eating with the combined group and individual treatment program.

We have already suggested it is our long-term results over the two years of follow-up rather than the immediate results of treatment which distinguish this treatment program. We believe these results show the way deeper issues are tackled by insight therapy and that this form of therapy is more appropriate than cognitive and behavioral restructuring. There is another possibility, however: the follow-up appointments consisted of a formal interview using a standard format which could in themselves, if only partly, be curative. Certainly the patients would discuss how they had been "getting along" in the three months between appointments. In no sense was this psychodynamic in the way the treatment program was attempted. But it was supportive. The question therefore arises whether these appointments themselves influenced our results.

To test this we continued our study on the twenty-eight patients who remained in the outpatient clinic two years after their time-limited individual treatment program had finished (Table IV). The population was divided into two groups of fourteen patients: one group was followed up at three monthly intervals in exactly the same way as they had been followed up in the previous two years. The other fourteen patients had no follow-up. The results are shown in Table VIII. Of the fourteen who continued their follow-up appointments, nine had no bulimic attacks and five had occasional episodes. This was similar to the reported incidence of food manipulation in their first two years of follow-up. However, in those who had no follow-up appointment, two developed severe bulimia, six had occasional bulimic episodes and only six remained clear of dietary abuse. In other words, some of those patients who had maintained their improvement over two years significantly deteriorated in their third year when they had no follow-up appointments. Those who continued to have only minimal contact—in some cases by letter alone—maintained their improvement. It is, however, important to note that despite this, most who had no follow-ups still either had no bulimic episodes or only minor episodes of binge-eating. Thus the really important issue is to detect those patients who need follow-up appointments and those who do not.

## How to Determine Who Will Benefit from Treatment

It is now possible to determine within-group prognostic indicators for longer term outcome in bulimia. Motivation is central for any psychological treatment and one must make no apologies for making it the most important reason for improvement. However, it is important to remember that as psychiatrists it is our responsibility to engender within the patient motivational forces which can allow her to make the best use of her treatment. Similarly, failure to engage in psychotherapy or to find alternative behaviors to binge-eating leads to a poorer response. Perhaps somewhat surprisingly, severity of symptoms and length of illness appear to be less important than one would imagine. Apart from motivation, however, there appear to be two important prognostic indicators which should be determined on the initial interview.

Six of the thirty patients originally treated reported alcohol abuse (Table IX). Of these six patients, five reported mild or severe bulimia during the first two years of follow-ups. Of the twenty-six patients who reported no alcohol abuse, nineteen had no bulimic episodes over the two years of follow-up.

The combination of binge-eating and alcohol abuse may encompass, additionally, drug abuse, stealing and perhaps sexual disinhibition. We have called this the personality disordered form of bulimia[10]. About 18% of our clinic sample fit into this pattern. We believe that this group needs longer and more intensive treatment than that given in our published treatment program. In fact, we now recommend inpatient help for these patients[9].

On the other hand, patients who tend to be hard-working, yet whose impulsivity is unimodal and focused on food alone, tend to do well. These are some 80% of the clinic sample. Their predominant clinical symptoms—apart from their eating disorder—are sadness and anger and the prognosis of this group is good. For clinical details see[10] and for treatment see[9,11].

Another factor which influences outcome—although less so than with alcohol abuse—is the presence or absence of a previous weight disorder. We have discussed our subdivisions into Type I, Type II and Type III at the beginning of the chapter. In our controlled study of our treatment program six patients reported a previous history of anorexia nervosa and five of these developed either mild or severe bulimic episodes during the first two years of follow-up (Table X). Of the twenty-four patients who had no previous history of anorexia nervosa (Type I Bulimia) none developed severe bulimia, nineteen had no bulimic episodes at all and five only mild bulimic episodes. In fact, of the twenty patients who had no bulimic episodes during follow-up, nineteen gave no previous history of anorexia nervosa.

A similar pattern of response is seen in these patients who are described as being markedly overweight (Type III Bulimia) and who reduce their body weight to the norm usually by enthusiastic vomiting. In an uncontrolled study of seven severely disturbed obese bulimics who reduced body weight to the norm under treatment, all initially stopped their binge-eating. But then they relapsed during the follow-up period.

The efficient harnessing of motivational forces may be helped by the sex of the therapist. Initially, we used a male and female therapist —although later we used two female therapists working together. We can detect no difference in outcome as measured by binge-eating and vomiting, but patients seems to feel that being treated by women therapists only is more helpful.[9].

## Conclusion

Unfortunately, of the apparently successful treatment programs published to date, only our own has been subjected to a controlled study. Certain common features of the various treatments, however, appear to be important for treatment outcome. All[8, 9, 11, 19] emphasize an outpatient setting. They all attempt to make the patient responsible for her own progress. All have a high expectation of success which would engender motivation. All emphasize that disordered eating must be interrupted to give a period of stability during which time other therapies are brought to bear. All use behavioral self-monitoring and emphasize the importance of maintaining body weight and the development of healthy eating behavior. Counseling and re-education are a feature of all of them.

In addition, there are features of our own program which separate it from the others. We believe that the eclectic nature of the treatment is important. In particular, the emphasis on insight-directed therapy is especially so. Treatment should be time-limited—nothing concentrates a patient's mind more than the realization that she has only ten weeks in which to alter her behavior. We have shown evidence to support the efficacy of the group component to treatment.

This chapter makes four major points. First, that behavioral methods can effectively interrupt binge-eating. Second, that it is essential that underlying conflicts be dealt with or the symptoms will recur (this is one of the reasons for the poorer results reported by some authors). Third, that drop-out can be contained by the use of group techniques. Fourth, long-term success can also be maintained by infrequent supportive appointments. These appointments, however, are only needed for a subgroup of the bulimic population and the features of this population have been described above.

The forthcoming years of research into the eating disorders field will be exciting. The response of bulimia to treatment is encouraging. So much so, that, it warrants a maximum effort on all our parts—for untreated bulimia remains to its sufferers a highly disturbing psychosomatic condition.

## REFERENCES

1. American Psychiatric Association: Task force on nomenclature and statistics. Diagnostic and statistical manual of mental disorders. Edition III. Washington DC 1980

2. Birtchnell, S.A., Lacey, J.H., Harte A.: Body image distortion in Bulimia Nervosa. Brit.J. Psychiat, 1985, 147, 408–412.

3. Boskind-Lodahl, M. Cinderella's stepsisters: A feminist perspective on anorexia nervosa and bulimia. J.Women Cul.Soc., 2; 342–356, 1976.

4. Bruch, H.: Eating Disorders: Obesity, Anorexia Nervosa, and the Person Within. New York, Basic Books, 1973.

5. Crisp, A.H.: Anorexia Nervosa at normal body weight! The abnormal normal weight control syndrome. Int.J.Psychiat.Med., 11 (3), 203–33.

6. Crisp, A.H.: Anorexia Nervosa: Let Me Be. London. Academic Press, 1980.

7. Crisp, A.H.: A treatment regime for anorexia nervosa. Brit.J. Psychiatry, 112, 505–512 (1966).

8. Fairburn, C.G.: A cognitive behavioral approach to the treatment of bulimia. Psychol.Med., 11, 707–711, 1981.

9. Lacey, J.H.: Time-Limited Individual and Group Treatment for Bulimia. In Garner, D.M. and Garfinkel P.E. (Eds) Handbook of Psychotherapy for Anorexia Nervosa and Bulimia, New York, Guilford Press, 1984.

10. Lacey, J.H.: The Bulimic Syndrome. In

Fergusson A (Ed): Advanced Medicine - 20 London Royal College of Physicians/Pitman, 1984.

11. Lacey, J.H.: Bulimia nervosa, binge-eating and psychogenic vomiting: A controlled treatment study and long term outcome. Br.Med.J., *286* 1609–1613, 1983.

12. Lacey J.H.: The bulimic syndrome at normal body weight: Reflections on pathogenesis and clinical features. Int.J. Eating Disorders, *2:* 59–66, 1982.

13. Lacey, J.H.: The Bulimic Syndrome. Proceedings 13th European Conference on Psychosomatic Research, Istanbul, (1980).

14. Lacey, J.H.: Anorexia nervosa. Nursing Times, *72*(11) 407–8 (1976).

15. Lacey, J.H., Birtchnell, S.A.: The Eating Disorders. *In* The Psychosomatic Approach (Ed. Christie, M) John Libbey, Chichester, (1985).

16. Lacey, J.H., Gibson, E.: Does laxative abuse control body weight? A comparative study of purging and vomiting bulimics. Human Nutrition: Applied Nutrition, 39A 53–59, 1985.

17. Lacey, J.H., Coker, S., Birtchnell, S.A.: Factors associated with the onset and maintenance of bulimia nervosa. In.J. of Eating Disorders (in press), 1985.

18. Lacey, J.H., Chadbund, C., Crisp, A.H., Whitehead, J., Stordy, J.: Variation in energy intake of adolescent girls. J.Human Nutr. *32*, 419–426 (1978).

19. Mitchell, J.E., Hatsukami, D., Goff, G., et al.: An intensive outpatient group treatment program for bulimia, *In* Garner, D.M. & Garfinkel, P.E. (Eds): A Handbook of Psychotherapy for Anorexia Nervosa and Bulimia, New York, Guilford Press, 1984.

20. Palmer, R.L: The dietary chaos syndrome: A useful new term? Br.J. Med. Psychol., *52:* 187–190, 1979.

21. Russell, G.F.M.: Bulimia nervosa: An ominous varient of anorexia nervosa. Psychol. Med., *9:* 429–448, 1979.

22. Russell, G.F.M.: Anorexia nervosa -its identity as an illness and its treatment. *In* Modern Trends in Psychological Medicine (Ed. J.H. Price) Vol.2., pp 131–64. Butterworth, London, 1972.

23. Russell, G.F.M.: Clinical Features of Bulimia Nervosa. Presentation 15th European Conference of Psychosomatic Research, London, 1984.

**FIGURE 1:** Mean Analogue Scale Scores For Depression And Anger During Each Week Of Treatment

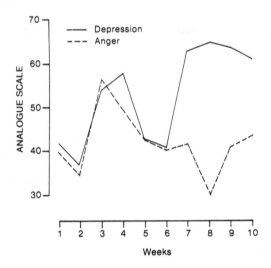

**TABLE I:** Theoretical Basis Of Treatment

| Problem | Treatment | Setting |
| --- | --- | --- |
| Eating disorder | Simple behavioral therapy counseling | Early individual sessions |
| Emotional conflicts | Insight-directed therapy | Later individual sessions and the Group |
| Social problems | Counseling Insight-directed therapy | Individual sessions and the Group |

**TABLE II:** The Stages Of Individual Therapy

| | Orientation | Methods |
| --- | --- | --- |
| STAGE 1 | Behavioral/Counseling | Food Dairy Prescribed Diet Weight Maintenance Contract |
| STAGE 2 | Insight-directed | Relief of anger and depression New ways of coping Re-education Redefinition of symptoms in terms of underlying conflicts |

**TABLE III:** Incidence of dietary abuse in each of 30 patients over 14 days before and after treatment.

| Case No. | Bulimia | | Vomiting | |
|---|---|---|---|---|
| | Before Treatment | After Treatment | Before Treatment | After Treatment |
| 1 | 120 | 28 | 136 | 36 |
| 2 | 45 | 0 | 54 | 0 |
| 3 | 31 | 0 | 39 | 0 |
| 4 | 34 | 0 | 41 | 0 |
| 5 | 27 | 0 | 35 | 0 |
| 6 | 50 | 0 | 52 | 0 |
| 7 | 48 | 0 | 55 | 0 |
| 8 | 22 | 0 | 31 | 0 |
| 9 | 50 | 13 | 52 | 13 |
| 10 | 73 | 0 | 94 | 0 |
| 11 | 56 | 0 | 56 | 0 |
| 12 | 50 | 0 | 51 | 0 |
| 13 | 29 | 0 | 31 | 0 |
| 14 | 67 | 0 | 82 | 0 |
| 15 | 15 | 0 | 24 | 0 |
| 16 | 99 | 26 | 92 | 15 |
| 17 | 42 | 0 | 52 | 0 |
| 18 | 29 | 0 | 34 | 0 |
| 19 | 49 | 1 | 56 | 0 |
| 20 | 25 | 0 | 29 | 0 |
| 21 | 41 | 0 | 46 | 0 |
| 22 | 43 | 0 | 55 | 0 |
| 23 | 45 | 0 | 52 | 0 |
| 24 | 59 | 0 | 51 | 0 |
| 25 | 48 | 0 | 48 | 0 |
| 26 | 38 | 1 | 47 | 1 |
| 27 | 56 | 2 | 60 | 0 |
| 28 | 31 | 0 | 37 | 0 |
| 29 | 43 | 0 | 52 | 0 |
| 30 | 38 | 0 | 46 | 0 |
| Mean | 46.6 | 2.36 | 53 | 2.17 |

**TABLE IV:** Outcome Over 2 Years of 30 Treated Bulimic Patients

| OUTCOME GROUP | N |
|---|---|
| No bulimic episodes | 20 |
| Mild occasional episodes | 8 |
| Needed further treatment | 1 |
| Refused follow-up | 1 |
| TOTAL | 30 |

**TABLE V:** Number Of Asymptomatic Patient During 2 Years Of Follow-Up

| | At The End Of Treatment | Months Of Follow-Up | | | | | | |
|---|---|---|---|---|---|---|---|---|
| | | 1 | 3 | 6 | 9 | 12 | 18 | 24 |
| Total Sample | 30 | 28 | 28 | 28 | 28 | 28 | 28 | 28 |
| Patients With No Vomiting | 27 | 27 | 25 | 25 | 23 | 24 | 26 | 26 |
| Patients With No Binge Eating | 24 | 27 | 25 | 24 | 22 | 24 | 25 | 26 |

**TABLE VI:** Body Image Perception Indices (%)* Of Bulimics
Pre and Post Treatment

|  | Pre-Treatment (n=29) | | Post Treatment (n=29) | | |
|  | mean | S.D. | mean | S.D. | |
| --- | --- | --- | --- | --- | --- |
| Chest | 124.8 | 23.82 | 114.6 | 18.18 | NS |
| Waist | 131.1 | 21.39 | 118.6 | 19.83 | 0.05 |
| Hips | 121.7 | 22.86 | 106.5 | 16.87 | 0.01 |
| Object | 101.1 | 14.83 | 99.4 | 12.85 | NS |

*Perceived Width/Real Width $\times$ 100

**TABLE VII:** The Effect On Binge-Eating And Drop-Out Rate Of Adding Group Therapy To The Treatment Of Bulimia

| Type of Therapy | N | Not Bingeing | Reduced Bingeing | Dropouts |
| --- | --- | --- | --- | --- |
| Individual/Group | 30 | 24 | 6 | 0 |
| Individual Only | 16 | 11 | 2 | 3 |

**TABLE VIII:** Effect Of Follow-Up Appointments On Longer Term Follow-Up

| 1ST TWO YEARS | | | 3RD YEAR | | | Follow Up |
|---|---|---|---|---|---|---|
| No Binging | Occasional Binging | Severe Binging | No Binging | Occasional Binging | Severe Binging | |
| 10 | 4 | 0 | 9 | 5 | 0 | YES |
| 10 | 4 | 0 | 6 | 6 | 2 | NO |

(No Binging: braced 20; Occasional Binging: braced 8; Severe Binging: braced 0)

**TABLE IX:** Outcome Over 2 Years After Treatment Of 30 Bulimic Patients With And Without A History Of Alcohol Abuse

| Outcome Group | No Alcohol Abuse | Alcohol Abuse |
|---|---|---|
| No bulimic episodes | 19 | 1 |
| Mild bulimic episodes | 4 | 4 |
| Severe bulimia | 1 | 1 |
| TOTAL | 26 | 6 |

**TABLE X:** Outcome Over 2 Years After Treatment Of Bulimic Patients Categorized According To History Of Anorexia Nervosa

| | Type I Bulimia (no previous anorexia) | Type II Bulimia (previous anorexia) |
|---|---|---|
| No bulimic episodes | 19 | 1 |
| Mild bulimic episodes | 5 | 3 |
| Severe bulimic episodes | 0 | 2 |
| TOTAL | 24 | 6 |

## CHAPTER 9

# An Intermediate Care Model for the Treatment of Eating Disorders: THE BASHsm APPROACH

Félix E. F. Larocca, M.D., F.A.P.A.

Since the description of anorexia nervosa by Morton,[22] Gull,[11] and others, most authors have recommended the outpatient model of treatment for anorectic patients. But as cases became more recognized and literature more abundant, a trend towards inpatient methods developed for treatment of cases that were refractory, chronic, or had intercurrent life-threatening complications. I have developed such an inpatient program and have described it in the 1984 June issue of *Psychiatric Clinics of North America*[14] and in the 1984 December issue of *Missouri Medicine*.[19]

Yet, to date, no outpatient or intermediate day care program has been outlined in print that significantly depends on an inpatient program which emphasizes self-help. Only BASHsm has proposed such a format.[16] This paper will review some existing programs that utilize outpatient methods, and introduce a model that blends both outpatient treatment and intermediate care.

Any such model should take an holistic approach. This approach should include: family involvement, support from other patients, informational meetings, weekly sessions with the Medical Director of the program, and supplementary methods such as training selected patients for the job of group leader (facilitator). Taking this kind of approach will result in the optimum enhancement of significant contacts thus making treatment considerably more effective.

Any such model should also take into account that anorectics are not the only individuals afflicted with an eating disorder. Since Russell's momentous description of bulimia nervosa,[24] other eating disorders have been defined. As Garfinkel et al.[10] have proposed, a heterogeneity of subgroups exists in an area that needs clarification, understanding, restraint from spectacular claims of success, and scientific scrutiny.

# REVIEW OF LITERATURE

On page 33 in his excellent monograph, "Anorexia Nervosa," Thomä quotes Freud:

> Psychoanalysis should not be attempted when the speedy removal of dangerous symptoms is required as, for example, in the case of hysterical anorexia.

And on page 33, Thomä makes an interesting conclusion: "On only one aspect of treatment is agreement unanimous, patients must be removed from their home environment."

Hilde Bruch[2] is one such proponent of nonpsychoanalytical methods. Bruch has criticized behaviorism and has clearly dispensed with psychoanalysis as a reliable method of treatment for anorexia. Thus Bruch has treated anorexia utilizing interpersonal therapy which is not based on the above methods. To Bruch, Bulimia or "Bulimarexia" are terms (particularly the latter) to be regarded as a "nomenclature atrocity."

Selvini-Palazzoli[25] of the Milan school on the other hand has developed group therapeutic efforts conforming to psychoanalytical theory and individual and family dynamics. Selvini-Palazzoli, Prata, and other members of the Italian school have proposed an outpatient model for treatment. But they have thus far contributed little to the management of the bulimia syndrome. Perhaps this is because their contributions preceded the formal description of bulimia as a distinct entity and its ultimate inclusion in the DSM III.[6]

In a more recent theoretical formulation, Minuchin, Rossman, Baker,[21] and their associates at the Philadelphia Child Guidance Clinic have developed their own outpatient approach of structural family therapy. Vandereycken's *Anorexia Nervosa: A Clinician's Guide to Treatment*[27] provides an excellent review of the literature on this subject. It contrasts the various schools and renders a critique of their merits and shortcomings.

New developments in the treatment of bulimic patients have resulted in the emergence of three different methods which are similar in structure if not in philosophy. Fairburn[8,9] in Great Britain utilizes cognitive therapy and record keeping of the bulimic episode from trigger event to resolution. Pyle, Mitchell,[23] et al. in Minnesota have developed a method that involves intensive intervention with cognitive therapy, exposure to fear foods, the supervision of meals, and lectures aimed at the important systematic knowledge of the possible life threatening factors of eating disorders. They encourage patients and their families to seek self-help from existing groups in the community, endorsing "Bulimia Anonymous." Finally, Lacey[12] et al. rely primarily on an eclectic blending of the various approaches, utilizing group therapy as the main tool of treatment. At this time, Lacey does not place strong emphasis on self-help though he is known to have recognized its importance and has participated in meetings sponsored by self-help organizations.

Yet all the methods above seem to skirt the issue of self-help. In my opinion, self-help should go beyond the formation of an association to provide information to those seeking help. It should not be a clearing house for the mailing of literature nor a depository of therapists' names and addresses. It should not be a referral service. It is clearly an integral part of the process of overall therapeutic involvement. For this reason it, too, requires independent validation, theoretical underpinnings, and scientific formulation along with a set of explicit guidelines for its delivery. BASH[sm] (Bulimia Anorexia Self-Help, Inc.) from its inception in 1981 has set its aim to fulfill these requirements.

# DESCRIPTION OF BASH[sm]

BASH[sm] formed around the need of my patients for a more flexible method of treatment. By blending the less restrictive nature of outpatient care with the tighter controlled inpatient approach, I hoped to develop a flexible intermediate program that would suit the needs of each individual patient. The building block I hoped to use to build such a program with was self-help. The BASH[sm,c,17] format was born from the idea that self-help was the key factor in the treatment of eating disorders.

In addition to providing patients with its unique format of intermediate care (described in detail with an example case in two upcoming sections), BASH[sm] publishes a newsletter. The newsletter summarizes the monthly meetings and announces schedules for informational and regular meetings. It provides editorials pertinent to the needs of those suffering from eating disorders. It provides a bibliography and synopsis and updates letters to the editor. It also has an important section of book reviews. John Adams Atchley, President of Bulimia Anorexia Nervosa Association of Teaneck, New Jersey, has said of this newsletter, "It is the most comprehensive newsletter of this field."[1]

A *Public Primer*[c,15] on eating disorders may also be obtained from the BASH[sm] office, along with BASH/PAK[c,13]—a rather comprehensive and systematic educational tool for understanding and treatment of eating disorders.

Finally, BASH[sm] stimulated the development of an inpatient program. (BASH Treatment and Research Center). Due to recognition BASH[sm] had received from public and private sectors, the James S. McDonnell Foundation donated $300,000 for a grant that would provide funds for a public awareness campaign, a crisis center (the only center of its kind in the community), and a hot-line serving those seeking information or relief in a time of need. This center—The Mary Anne Richardson Memorial BASH[sm] Assistance and Information—was dedicated and named after the late daughter of Mrs. Agnes Cavelero, President of Bulimia Anorexia Foundation Association of Everett, Washington.

# REVIEW OF THE PREDECESSORS OF THE INTERMEDIATE CARE APPROACH

Intermediate care or partial hospitalization has been used by doctors throughout the past. In 1946 T.F. Main[20] was the first person to use the concept of "Therapeutic Community." He stressed the importance of redirecting the patient's dependence on the doctor to the outside world. He changed the traditional authoritarian role to a less directive role of "treatment facilitator." By rejecting the idea of the hospital as a refuge from society, he was able to develop the concept of "mutual treatment responsibility."

The development of partial hospitalization (intermediate care) can be traced back as far as 1933 when Dzhagarov[7] in Moscow instituted the first "hospital without beds" due to the lack of funds. In 1946, Cameron[3] in Canada offered his program to complement full first-time hospitalization and to reduce the need for twenty-four hour care. By

1952 several major centers in the U.S. had opened programs to ease the transition from the hospital to the community.

Many old concepts were being challenged by these new programs. In 1947, Cameron[4] structured his program on the rejection of various premises that had been used in the existing medical model. Cameron stresses: 1) de-emphasizing the importance of the hospital bed 2) including the family in the treatment program and 3) recognizing the bulk of the work would be done upon discharge from the hospital through partial hospitalization.

In his review of partial hospitalization, DiBella[5] stresses crisis intervention as an important function of partial hospitalization. He recognizes no comprehensive program can be developed without blending other theoretical treatment possibilities. He defines partial hospitalization as "a treatment program of eight or more waking hours per week, designed for improvement of a group of six or more ambulatory patients, provided by two or more multi-disciplinary clinical staff."[5,p.11] Partial hospitalization is recognized by DiBella as a cost effective and practical alternative for patient care. It is also of interest that DiBella and his co-workers stress the use of groups as the most effective tool for treatment in partial hospitalization.

# THE BASHsm MODEL OF INTERMEDIATE CARE

The BASHsm Intermediate Care Program has been adapted from existing programs by utilizing the philosophies of the programs that have proven most practical. The emphasis of the format is placed on:

1. The necessity for educating the patient and their families
2. The crucial role of groups
3. The importance of having specially trained professionals (therapists, nurses, facilitators, etc.)
4. The flexibility of therapeutic involvement.

The BASHsm format stresses self-help as the key tool in providing the flexibility needed in the treatment program. In addition, the intermediate care program has had great impact on the already established inpatient and outpatient programs.

Patients come to the program after they have been formally screened for appropriateness and suitability. Since there are no explicit rules for screening patients, those accepted comprise a wide range. Each patient's individual needs is, therefore, stressed.

Once a patient has been accepted, she may be assigned to one of two categories: morning day treatment or afternoon day treatment. Morning day treatment patients arrive at 7:30 AM and leave the unit at 5:00 PM (after eating the evening meal). Afternoon day treatment patients arrive by 11:30 AM and leave by 8:00 PM. Though emphasis is not placed on gaining weight, this may be an issue. For this reason the patients are weighed at the end of the day rather than at the beginning. Some patients are not weighed at all. Any patient may find out her weight measurement upon request, but in keeping with the philosophy of this program, nondisclosure of weight measurements is recommended whenever possible.

Depending on the need for intensive care, patients may be assigned to attend Monday through Friday, Monday-Wednesday-Friday, or Monday and Friday. The principal components of the program, adapted from other programs, are designed to fulfill the premises stated at the beginning of this section. They include (for hourly breakdown see table 2 at end of paper):

1. Daily visits with the Medical Director.
2. BASHsm meetings: a monthly meeting that offers an informational lecture followed by self-help groups led by facilitators (explicit guidelines for this process can be found in the *Facilitator's Manual.* )[18]
3. Nutritional classes: a weekly session directed by a dietician whose aim is to educate the patients in the *facts* of nutrition. The dietician also offers assistance with menu selection emphasizing each patient's individual needs.
4. As much individual therapy as deemed necessary.
5. Group therapy facilitated by the nursing staff.
6. BRUNCH:sm a noon meal attended by inpatients, outpatients, intermediate care patients, the Medical Director, nursing staff, and dietician. A speaker is chosen from among the patients by the Medical Director and discusses, informally, a personal aspect of her involvement with eating disorders (i.e. guilt feelings suffered after binging).
7. Community meetings:sm a weekly group meeting between the patients and the Medical Director to discuss the various workings of the program.
8. B/ANsm meetings: a weekly outpatient group meeting centered around smaller self-help groups arranged according to age.

9. Informational meetings:sm meetings similar in nature to BASHsm meetings. But unlike the lecture topics BASHsm meetings, the lecture topics of the informational meetingssm tend to be personal rather than academic.

10. Family meetings: weekly meetings designed to provide information and support for family and friends of patients from the various programs.

11. Therapeutic Breakfast:sm a weekly breakfast attended by patients and the Medical Director who lectures while the patients are eating.

12. Facilitators training: training for selected patients who are or will be group leaders.

The Intermediate Care Program of BASHsm is unique in many ways. It provides a program that is flexible enough to treat a wide range of patients, each with a different need. It creates a powerful partnership with the already established inpatient and outpatient programs, making each substantially more effective. And it uses self-help as the key tool in treating eating disorder patients. The following illustration shows the interaction of the intermediate care program with the existing programs:

TABLE I: 1 Program Interactions

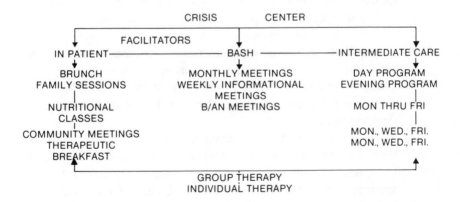

# CASE PRESENTATION

The following case illustrates the interaction of the various aspects of the treatment programs, stressing the relevance of intermediate care.

J.B. was 28 years of age when she came to my attention. She was single and worked as a senior researcher for a major international corporation. She had attained distinction in her scientific career, but it was not enough to mitigate her feelings of inferiority and low self-esteem.

She was admittedly bulimic at the time of the initial visit and had suffered from anorexia nervosa while in college. Her height was 170.18 cm. and her weight was 45.5 kg. She feared meal times at work. She managed to avoid them by assigning herself extra work. She exercised on a stationary bicycle at home as an excuse for not keeping social contacts. She admitted to feelings of depression and self-hatred. She suffered from many spells of lost self-control—she was unable to stop vomiting at least four to five times a day. Because the patient lacked the motivation for treatment, because her history showed she was unable to control her symptoms, and because there existed the possibility of her resorting to suicide, she was admitted to the eating disorders department.

During the early part of her hospital stay she became progressively withdrawn and gave additional history she had withheld. Twice within the past three years she had taken an overdose of sleeping pills, surviving both attempts with no treatment. Only a close friend knew of these incidents. Routine blood chemistry and lab examinations appeared normal with the one exception of Potassium, which was 3.0 mEq/1.

The patient was treated utilizing comprehensive approaches including daily individual psychotherapeutic sessions with emphasis placed on issues of her expressions of anger, awareness of her fears of losing control, and how to deal with her depression. To aid the treatment of depression she was also placed on Phenelzine Sulfate 15mg. three times a day.

After three weeks in the program, J.B. was released to attend weekly sessions at the office along with bimonthly group psychotherapeutic sessions and group support systems. She returned to her apartment and work but soon discovered some of the old patterns beginning to reappear. She began to count calories while reducing and restricting food intake. She ran no less than five miles a day, and vomited most of the meals she managed to eat. On her own initiative she contacted the BASH<sup>sm</sup> Crisis Center and after several sessions of support via telephone conversations with one of the facilitators, she agreed to check in at the Center for several days in order to escape the loneliness and lack of support of her apartment—she lived alone in the company of her pet.

During her stay at the Center, J.B. became aware that she was productive enough to return to the bulk of her scientific work, but not stable enough to be discharged from the hospital. Thus a day treatment program was devised for her: attendance Monday through Friday the first week, Monday-Wednesday-Friday the subsequent two weeks, and Monday and Friday the final three weeks.

Symptom remission resulted at the end of the fourth week of intermediate care. Currently, the patient necessitates only once a week individual therapy, bimonthly group therapy and rigorous attendance to the support systems such as facilitators training and supervision.

## DISCUSSION AND CONCLUSION

I have managed to outline in detail an intermediate care program that utilizes a comprehensive interdependence on several known aspects of the management of eating disorders. The key areas blended from both inpatient and outpatient care are: individual psychotherapy, family psychotherapy, group psychotherapy, attendance to various kinds of meetings thus promoting social interaction among patients and staff alike, facilitators training, and in the case of J.B. the use of medication.

The advantage of my multi-model approach is that all aspects of treatment can be made to fit each patient's individual needs. The BASH<sup>sm</sup> format, using the available resources, creates a flexibility that makes treatment of eating disorders more effective. It maintains this flexibility by relying on self-help as its center—self-help from which management emanates and to which everything returns when treatment is completed. Thus the patient, having played a large role in her own treatment, has a better chance of taking responsibility for her life and maintaining self-control.

To my knowledge, such a multi-model program does not exist elsewhere. It has among its many merits and advantages the soundness of its principles—it designates with specificity not only what aspect of treatment would best fit a patient's needs, but also to what degree. Finally, self-help as utilized by this program, becomes the most cost effective element and may be used in any aspect of treatment.

**TABLE 2:** Hourly Breakdown Of Patient And Family Involvement

| Therapeutic Tools | Time Involved |
| --- | --- |
| Visits with the Medical Director | 30 minutes/day |
| Scheduled Group Therapy | one hour/day |
| Nutritional class | one hour/week |
| BRUNCH<sup>SM</sup> | one hour/week |
| Community meetings | one hour/week |
| BA/N<sup>SM</sup> meetings | one hour/week |
| Informational meetings | one and one-half hours/week |
| Family meetings | one and one-half hours/week |
| Therapeutic Breakfast | one and one-half hours/week |
| BASH<sup>SM</sup> meetings | three hours once/month |
| Facilitators Training | one and one-half hours twice/month |

NOTE: In a five day period from Monday through Friday, the projected hours of Therapeutic involvement for 1) a patient would be 14.5 hours, 2) a family member would be 3.0 hours. The week of BASH$^{sm}$ a patient's involvement could be 17.5 to 20.5 hours. A family member's involvement could increase to 6.0 to 9.0 hours. The variance in each case is dependent on involvement in the Facilitator Training program.

## BIBLIOGRAPHY

1 Atchley, J.A.: Personal communication to Dr. F.E. Larocca. Nov. 1984.

2 Bruch, Hilda: Eating Disorders: Obesity, Anorexia Nervosa and the Person Within. New York, Basic Books, 1973.

3 Cameron, D.E.: The day hospital. In: A.E. Bennett, E.A. Hargrove and B. Engle (Eds.), The Practice of Psychiatry in General Hospitals. Berkeley, CA: University of California press, 1956.

4 Cameron, D.E.: The day hospital: Experimental forms of hospitalization for patients. Modern Hospital, 69(3): 60–62, 1947.

5 DiBella, G., Weitz, G., Poynter-Berg, D., Yurmark, J.: Handbook of Partial Hospitalization. New York, Brunner/Mazel, 1982.

6 DSM III.: Diagnostic and Statistical Manual of Mental Disorders. Edition 3. Washington, D.C., American Psychiatric Association, 1980.

7 Dzhagarov, M.: (Experience in organizing a half hospital for mental patients). Neuropathologia Psikhatria, 6:137–147, 1937.

8 Fairburn, C.C.: Binge eating and its management. Brit. J. Psychiatry, 141:631–633, 1982.

9 Fairburn, C.G.: Bulimia: Its Epidemiology and Management. In: Stunkard, A.J., and Sellers, E., (Eds.): Eating and Its Disorders. New York, Raven Press, 1983.

10 Garfinkel, P.E. et al.: The heterogeneity of anorexia nervosa: Bulimia as a distinct subgroup. Archives of General Psychiatry, 37(9):1036–40, 1980.

11 Gull, W.W.: The address in medicine delivered before the annual meeting of the BMA at Oxford. Lancet, 2:171, 1868.

12 Lacey, H.J.: Bulimia nervosa, binge-eating, and psychogenic vomiting: A controlled treatment study and long-term outcome. BR. Med. J., 286:1609–13, 1983.

13 Larocca, F.E.F.: Anorexia nervosa: The role of educating the patient and the family for a successful treatment outcome. A paper read at the *Tenth International Congress of the Association for Child and Adolescent Psychiatry and Allied Professions.* Dublin, Irish Republic, July 25–30, 1982.

14 Larocca, F.E.F.: An inpatient model for the treatment of eating disorders. Psychiatric Clinics of North America, 7(2): 287–298, June 1984.

15 Larocca, F.E.F.: A Public Primer on Eating Disorders: The BASHsm Approach. St. Louis, MIssouri, BASHsm Inc., 1984.

16 larocca, F.E.F.: The relevance of self-help in the management of anorexia nervosa and bulimia. Res Medica, 1:16–19, 1983.

17 Larocca, F.E.F.: Self-help on anorexia and bulimia. *15th Conference of Psychosomatic Research.* Sept. 14–17, 1984, London.

18 Larocca, F.E.F., Kolodny, H.J.: A Facilitators Training Manual, A Primer: The BASH sm Approach. St. Louis, Missouri, Midwest Medical Publications, 1983.

19 Larocca, F.E.F., Stern, J.: Eating disorders: Self-help treatment in Missouri. Missouri Medicine, 81(12):764–769, December 1984.

20 Main, T.F.: The hospital as a therapeutic institution. Bulletin of the Menniger Clinic, 10:66–70, 1946.

21 Minuchin, S., Rossman, B.L., and Baker, L.: Psychosomatic Families: Anorexia Nervosa in Context. Cambridge, Harvard University Press, 1978.

22 Norton, R.: Phthisiologica: Or a Treatise of Consumptions. London, Sam Smith and Benjamin Walford, 1689.

23 Pyle, R.L., Michell, J.E. et al.: The interruption of bulimic behaviors: A review of three treatment programs. Psychiatric Clinics of North America, 7(2):275–286, June 1984.

24 Russel, G.F.: Bulimia nervosa: An ominous variant of anorexia nervosa. Psychological Medicine, 9(3):429–448, 1979.

25 Slevini-Palazzoli, M.: Self-Starvation: From Individual to Family Therapy in the Treatment of Anorexia Nervosa. New York, Jason Aronson, 1978.

26 Thomä, Helmut: Anorexia Nervosa, translated by Gillian Brydone. New York, International Universities Press, 1979.

27 Vandereycken, W., Meermann, R.: Anorexia Nervosa: A Clinician's Guide to Treatment. Berlin, New York, deGruyter, 1984.

## CHAPTER 10

# Eating Disorders and Dissociative States

by
Moshe S. Torem, M.D.

## Introduction

Anorexia nervosa and bulimia with the variant of bulimia nervosa are the main eating disorders in the U.S.A. Although these conditions have been studied extensively[1-6], their etiology remains an enigma and their treatment less than satisfactory. In fact, the mortality rate of anorexia nervosa may be as high as 21.5%[7]. The purpose of this article is to shed some light on a subgroup of patients with eating disorders who have been shown to have a previously unmentioned mechanism of ego-dissociation as part of the psychodynamic etiology responsible for the abnormal eating behavior.

This author has studied 60 eating disorders patients and found twelve who had dissociated ego states that were in disharmony with one another. In some of these patients, it was difficult to fit the DSM-III diagnostic criteria for a multiple personality disorder[8]. In others, it was a matter of milder conditions that would not fit the DSM-III diagnostic criteria for multiple personality disorder but would still fit the concept of the abnormal eating behavior originating from a different ego state. Compared to the patient's host ego state, this other ego state was sometimes hidden from the patient's host ego state. Other times, the patient had full awareness of it but felt helpless to change the behavior once she switched into the "bulimic" or "anorectic" ego state. Since dissociation is the underlying mechanism of switching from one ego state to another, there is a need to discuss and review in detail the dissociation concept.

## Dissociation and Dissociative States

Pierre Janet[9] was the first to coin the term "dissociation." He claimed that dissociation represented a basic mechanism responsible for many psychopathological conditions: somnambulism, fugue states, psychogenic amnesia and multiple personality. To Janet's understanding, the healthy individual does not have a subconscious—all mental functions are integrated together in a unified personality dominated by the ego. When dissociation takes place, however, certain mental events that are ordinarily within conscious awareness escape the ego's control and become subconscious. Janet thought that the tendency to dissociate was genetic in origin. Certain individuals are predisposed by heredity. When such persons are exposed to trauma, their weakness is manifested. They cannot hold and bind events (i.e. perceptions) into a unified stream of consciousness. Instead, they dissociate. In Janet's model, the patient is the victim of heredity.

Breuer and Freud[10] claimed dissociation occurs as a result of an active process of the ego. The ego rejects ideas, thoughts, feelings, and memories from conscious awareness that are incompatible with the rest of the ego. Freud called this process "repression."

Following these and other formulations, dissociation as an important concept disappeared in psychoanalytical literature. Recently, with the increased interest in hypnosis and its application to clinical medicine and psychiatry, there has been a renewed interest in dissociation.

Some claim that all hypnosis is in fact a controlled state of dissociation[11,12], Hilgard[13, 14] has developed a neodissociation theory to explain dissociative phenomena—such as "hidden observers" seen in mentally healthy individuals[15,16]. In addition, recent interest in the condition of multiple personality has invoked an interest in its underlying mechanism of dissociation[17].

In a recent publication by Ludwig[18], dissociation is defined as "a process whereby certain mental functions which are ordinarily integrated with other functions presumably operate in a more compartmentalized or automatic way usually outside the sphere of conscious awareness or memory recall." Ludwig states that not only is dissociation an underlying mechanism for such states as conversion hysteria, hypnotic trance, fugue states, spirit possession states, and multiple personality, but also has a great survival value. He goes on to mention how under certain conditions, dissociation serves to facilitate the following functions:

1. automatization of certain behaviors
2. the efficiency and economy of effort
3. the resolution of irreconcilable conflicts
4. escape from the constraints of reality
5. the isolation of catastrophic experiences
6. the cathartic discharge of certain feelings
7. the enhancement of herd sense

Watkins[12] describes the separation of ego states as a kind of relative dissociation determined by the degree of rigidity and permeability of the boundaries between them. Watkins and Watkins[19,20] claim that dissociation lies on a continuum. In healthy dissociation, we see the individual who in one ego state crawls on the floor with his baby son making baby talk and playing "peek-a-boo." Ten seconds later he is on the phone giving sophisticated instructions to an emergency room nurse on how to manage a medical crisis. On the other end of Watkins' continuum, we see the patient with a multiple personality disorder in whom the various ego states may become unaware of one another's existence. These are referred to by some as alter personalities[21]. In between there is a wide range of personality organization and structures that may exist. Ego states can be hypnotically activated, under hypnosis, the source of otherwise unexplained psychopathology are revealed: binge-eating, self-induced vomiting, body image distortion, laxative abuse, self-starvation, etc. These psychopathological behaviors may become manifested as a result of one ill ego state. Often, however, they are a result of disharmony and internal fighting among the various states.

## Clinical Case Examples:

*Case 1:* "The Woman with Internal Commands"

The patient was a 28-year-old Caucasian single woman who was hospitalized on a medical unit for the diagnosis and treatment of severe weight loss. At the time of admission, her weight was 84 pounds and her height, 5'10." She was diagnosed as suffering from anorexia nervosa and all attempts to convince her to eat had not succeeded. A psychiatric consultation was requested.

The patient looked emaciated. She reported being tense, frustrated, and worried. Commenting on her eating habits, she said, "I really am hungry and sometimes I want to eat but any time the food is brought before me, I have this thought in my head saying, 'Don't you dare touch this food.". When asked to elaborate on this thought's source, she responded, "I don't know . . . I wish I knew more."

Since the patient complained of being tense and anxious, I asked her whether she would be interested in learning self-hypnosis as a way to relax. She agreed and I used the Hypnotic Induction Profile to clinically assess her capacity for hypnosis. The results showed a hypnotizable subject. She learned self-hypnosis and reported an immediate relief of inner tension. She was instructed to practice relaxation using self-hypnosis.

She reported success in creating internal calmness by using self-hypnosis on her own. She agreed to use her newly discovered skill of hypnosis to explore any underlying tensions or conflicts regarding anorexia. She was guided into a hypnotic state. It was discovered that this patient had a hidden ego state named Kelly, age 12, who was responsible for the thoughts experienced by Marla, as, "Don't you dare touch this food."

The exploration under hypnosis revealed this patient's anorexia was the result of an internal dissociated ego state fighting for its survival with the patient's host personality. The following is a segment of the conversation with this hidden ego state:

Dr.: "Is there another part of Marla that knows more about anorexia?"

Pt.: Signals "yes" through ideomotor signaling.

Dr.: Is it O.K. to talk to that part of Marla about anorexia?"

Pt.: Signals "yes."

Dr.: "In a little while, I am going to touch your left eyebrow. As I do this, your eyes will open and that part of Marla who knows more about anorexia will come out to talk to me. Later, when I touch your left hand, your eyes will close and you again will go into a deep, relaxed state. Is that understood?"

Pt.: Signals "yes."

Dr.: Touches patient's eyebrow giving the hypnotic suggestion. The patient's eyes open.

Pt.: "Hi."

Dr.: "Hi. Who am I talking to?"

Pt. K: "My name is Kelly," (in a very quiet and different voice from Marla).

Dr.: "Kelly, I am Dr. Torem. I am glad you came out to talk to me. How old are you?"

Pt. K: "I am 12-years-old."

Dr.: "How do you feel about Marla?"

Pt. K: "I hate her! She wants to grow up and live on her own, but I don't want her to . . ."

Dr.: "Why not?"

Pt. K: "Because if she grows up, she won't need me anymore and she'll get rid of me."

Dr.: "So, Kelly, you don't want to be ignored. You want to be part of her life?"

Pt. K: "Yes. We used to play a lot and I was good to her. I kept her company. We used to be good friends."

Dr.: "How old was Marla then?"

Pt. K: "Eight."

Dr.: "So you want to be a good friend to Marla?"

Pt. K: "Yes. I don't want her to grow up. I am afraid she won't need me anymore. I want her to be like me. I don't want her to eat and be big and grown up."

Dr.: "What do you do to keep her little?"

Pt. K: "I tell her not to eat."

Dr.: "Does she listen to you?"

Pt. K: "Yes. She must. She doesn't know about me. She thinks these are her own thoughts."

The above segment demonstrates how hidden dissociated ego states may be the underlying cause of self-starvation. Often the hidden state attempts to control the host personality. The following segment shows how the therapist can become a mediator to help resolve the internal conflict:

Dr.: "Kelly, you said you wanted to be friends with Marla and to be a part of her life."

Pt. K: "Yes."

Dr.: "Kelly, you know Marla is in the hospital because her body is sick and weak. It is too skinny. It is starving for food."

Pt. K: "I know she is in the hospital."

Dr.: "Do you know Marla and you share the same body and this is why you are in the hospital, too?"

The therapist is confronting the delusion of separateness which is common in patients with a multiple personality disorder.

Pt. K: "I think so."

Dr.: "If something happens to Marla's body and she dies, you, Kelly, will also die."

145

Pt. K: "Now, I know."

Dr.: "Kelly, do you want to live?"

Pt. K: "Yes!"

Dr.: "Then we must save Marla's body. Do you want to help?"

Pt. K: "Yes, I want to."

Dr.: "Are you willing to give your promise and word of honor to stop fighting Marla and combine your forces with hers by feeding the body that both of you share?"

Pt. K: "I agree only if she agrees to like me and promises not to throw me away."

Dr.: "Kelly, is Marla listening to our conversation?"

Pt. K: "Yes, she is."

Dr.: "Can we turn to Marla for a moment to ask for her opinion and then I'll come back to you?"

Pt. K: "Yes."

Dr.: "All right. Let Marla come out now."

The patient closes her eyes. Her eyelids flutter for 10 seconds. Then her eyes open and the patient's voice changes again.

Pt. M: "Hi, Dr. Torem."

Dr.: "Hi, Marla. Have you heard what Kelly is agreeing to?"

Pt. M: "Yes."

Dr.: "Do you give your promise and word of honor to abide by this agreement?"

Pt. M: "Yes, I do."

Dr.: "Do you agree to have an open internal dialogue with her and resolve disputes peacefully?"

Pt. M: "Yes, I do."

Dr.: "Let's shake hands on the agreement." (Patient and doctor shake hands.) "Now, please tell me if Kelly has been listening to our conversation."

Pt. M: "Yes, she has."

Dr.: "And what is she saying?"

Pt. M: "She agrees."

Dr.: "Would you allow her to come out and sign the agreement with a hand shake?"

Pt. M: "Yes."

Dr.: "You may stay in the background and listen as I talk to Kelly."

Dr. M: "O.K. I will."

Dr.: "All right, Kelly, please come back out." (Patient again closes her eyes. Her eyelids flutter and open again.)

Pt. K: "Hi."

Dr.: "Am I talking to Kelly now?"

Pt. K: "Yes."

Dr.: "Well, Kelly, did you hear what Marla has agreed to?"

Pt. K: "Yes, I did."

Dr.: "Do you give your promise and word of honor to abide by this agreement to save the life of Marla's body which you share too?"

Pt. K: "Yes."

Dr.: "And you agree to have an open dialogue and resolve disagreements with Marla peacefully?"

Pt. K: "Yes."

Dr.: "Let us shake hands on this agreement like I did with Marla." (Patient and doctor shake hands.) "This is to affirm your commitment, Kelly, to work together with Marla to supply the body which you both share with three wholesome meals a day and move forward to a full recovery."

Pt. K: "I give my word."

Dr.: "Is Marla listening?"

Pt. K: "Yes."

Dr.: "What does she say?"

Pt. K: "She is relaxed and hopeful."

Dr.: "Kelly, are there any questions you want to ask me now?"

Pt. K: "Will you talk to me again?"

Dr.: "Yes, I will. Good-bye, for now." (Doctor touches the patient's left hand. The patient's eyes close and she takes a deep breath.) "That's right. Calm and relaxed and now at your own pace, simply count back from 3 to 1." Her eyes open. "You will be fully alert and awake and the calmness will stay with you."

The patient opens her eyes and comes out of the formal hypnotic trance with the host personality, Marla. She reported feeling calm and relaxed.

That same day, the patient resumed normal eating and ate all her meals. A steady weight gain followed and she was discharged from the hospital four weeks later. She weighed 96 pounds.

*Case 2:* "The College Girl Who Would Not Stop Binging"

The patient was a 22-year-old single college student who was seen as an outpatient for bulimia. She suffered from episodes of binge-eating followed by self-induced vomiting for more than six years. She had made many attempts to resolve this condition through participation in support groups, behavior modification, and by various doctors who used anti-depressants and minor tranquilizers. When asked about the binge-eating episodes, she reported them to be as frequent as 3–4 times a day and other times as infrequently as once a week.

"When I start binging," she said, "it feels like I am not myself, as if I am in a daze and it is not me doing it." This statement and others alerted the author to further exploration under hypnosis. The interview revealed this patient had a hidden ego state that was responsible for the binging.

This ego state had split off when the patient was 7-years-old—her father had left her mother, never to be seen again. The patient was abused as a child by both parents, physically and emotionally. The pain and hurt were encapsulated in this one ego state which had no specific name except, the "Angry One."

This ego state punished the patient and didn't allow her to succeed in life. So the binge-eating and vomiting episodes would increase following successful attempts by the patient to move forward with her life towards more independence and self-reliance.

The treatment focused on conscious awareness and acceptance of the hidden ego state. Next the focus was on restructuring and reframing to help alleviate the guilt and the constant need for punishment. The hidden ego state was brought out. Through controlled dissociation—using self-hypnosis—this ego state was encouraged in prescribed constructive activities. Behavior modification methods with the "Angry One" were also used: renaming the hidden ego state the "Assertive One," teaching the value of anger as an emotion and its constructive use in relationship to self and others. Concomitantly, the bingeing-vomiting episodes significantly reduced in frequency, creating a sense of self-mastery.

### Discussion:

The importance of identifying dissociative states as the underlying dynamic in the patient with an eating disorder cannot be overstated. Not only does it allow for further exploration with the use of hypnosis, but it also opens the door on an effective treatment approach termed "ego state therapy" by Watkins and Watkins[20]. This therapy is the application of the various techniques known from group and family therapy for internal conflict resolution within a single individual. Using the ego-states concept, the individual's psyche is viewed as made up of various parts that have different functions and constitute the whole. The therapist acts as guide, teacher, mediator, negotiator and physician. It is important to listen to the patient for clues of the existence of an underlying dissociative state. Watch for such statements by the patients as:

- "I don't know why I do it. I am so confused. It is not like me."
- "A part of me wants to binge and then throw up and another part of me hates it and is just plain disgusted."
- "Whenever food is put in front of me, I automatically become frightened like a little kid. I know I need to eat, but it's like the Devil gets into me."
- "When I binge, it feels so strange, as if I am in a daze. I don't know what comes over me."

These clues should be viewed as invitations by the patient to have the therapist explore the situation in more depth. It may prove wise to evaluate all new patients with eating disorders for hypnotizability. If a particular case needs it, then explore for the possible existence of an underlying dissociative state. Naturally, this will require a clinician who is trained and skilled in the use of hypnosis.

**Summary:**

This written presentation focuses on dissociation—a rather overlooked and not uncommon mechanism underlying the psychopathology of many patients including those with eating disorders. Dissociation and dissociative states were discussed and defined and clinical examples were given demonstrating how the concept of ego states is used in developing a new understanding regarding the psychopathology of eating disorders. Moreover, a treatment approach is discussed and demonstrated by case examples. Suggestions are made on how to improve early detection of such cases and the need to include hypnosis and hypnoanalytic, explorative techniques as a routine part of the diagnostic assessment of new patients with eating disorders.

**REFERENCES**

1. Halmi, K.A.: Anorexia Nervosa and Bulimia, Psychosomatics, 2:111–129, 1983.
2. Larocca, F.E.: Symposium on Eating Disorders (Editor) Psychiatric Clinics of North America, 7:199–407, 1984.
3. Larocca, F.E.: An Inpatient Model for the

Treatment of Eating Disorders, Psychiatric Clinics of North America, 7:287–298, 1984.

4. Herzog, D.B.: Bulimia: The Secretive Syndrome, Psychosomatics, 23:481–487, 1982.

5. Gross, M.: (Ed.) Anorexia Nervosa, A Comprehensive Approach, Lexington, Massachusetts, The Collamore Press, 1982.

6. Palazzoli, M.S.: Self Starvation, New York, Jason Aronson, 1974.

7. Halmi, K.A., Broadland, G., Rigas, C.: A Follow Up Study of 79 Patients with Anorexia Nervosa: An Evaluation of Prognostic Factors and Diagnostic Criteria, in Wirt R, Winokur, G, Roff, M. (eds): Life History Research and Psychopathology, University of Minnesota Press, 1975, pp. 290–301.

8. APA: Diagnostic and Statistical Manual III, Washington, D.C., American Psychiatric Association Press, 1980.

9. Janet, P.: The Major Symptoms of Hysteria, New York, Basic Books, 1924.

10. Breuer, J. and Freud, S.: Studies on Hysteria, in J. Stranchey (ed.), the standard edition of "The Complete Psychological Works of S. Freud" (Vol. 2, London, Hogarth Press, 1955 [1985]), New York, Basic Books, 1975.

11. Beahrs, J.O.: Unity and Multiplicity, New York, Brunner/Mazel, 1982.

12. Watkins, J.G.: The Therapeutic Self, New York, Human Sciences Press, 1978.

13. Hilgard, E.R.: Divided Consciousness: Multiple Controls in Human Thought and Action, New York, Wiley, 1977.

14. Hilgard, E.R.: Dissociation Revisited. In M. Henle, J. Jaynes, and J. Sullivan (Eds.), Historical Conceptions of Psychology, New York, Springer, 1973, pp. 205–219.

15. Wilson, I.: All in the Mind, Garden City, New York, Doubleday and Company, 1982, pp. 151–163.

16. Hilgard, E.R. and Hilgard, J.R.: Hypnosis in the Relief of Pain, Los Altos, California, William Kaufman, Inc., 1975, pp. 166–187.

17. Braun, B.G.: Symposium on Multiple Personality, The Psychiatric Clinics of North America, 7:1–198, 1984.

18. Ludwig, A.M.: The Psychobiological Functions of Dissociation, Am J of Clin Hypnosis, 26:93–99, 1983.

19. Watkins, J.G., and Watkins, H.H.: Ego States and Hidden Observers, J Alt States of Consciousness, 5:3–18, 1979–80.

20. Watkins, J.G. and Watkins, H.H.: Ego-State Therapy, In Abt. L.E. and Stuart, J.R. (Eds.): The Newer Therapies: A Sourcebook, New York, Von Nostrand Reinhold, 1982, pp. 136–155.

21. Kluft, R.P.: Varieties of Hypnotic Interventions in the Treatment of Multiple Personality, Am J Clin. Hypnosis, 24:230–240, 1982.

# CHAPTER 11

# Treatment of Bulimia with Thymoleptic Medications
# Theoretical Background and Current Findings

Harrison G. Pope Jr. M.D.
James I. Hudson M.D.
Jeffrey M. Jonas M.D.

Several different therapeutic techniques, including individual psychotherapy, group therapy, family therapy, and behavioral therapy, have been proposed for the treatment of bulimia. All have been reported to produce benefit in uncontrolled trials. At the time of this writing, however, none of these techniques has been shown effective in a *controlled* study—a study in which one group of bulimic patients received a "placebo" treatment while a second, matched group, run in parallel, received the actual therapy. Given that bulimia may often improve spontaneously,[1] it is critical for studies of any therapeutic technique to include a parallel control group in order to show that the proposed therapy is more effective than what would be expected by the "placebo effect" alone.

In fact, even if we expand our criteria to include uncontrolled studies of psychological treatments in bulimia, the number remains small. There is, to our knowledge, no study of individual psychotherapy in bulimia beyond the level of anecdotal case reports. Cognitive behavioral therapy has been reported effective in two uncontrolled studies with bulimic patients[2,3] and also in several reports of individual patients. Although controlled studies of behavior therapy in bulimia are now underway at various centers, none has as yet been completed and published.

Several uncontrolled studies of group psychotherapy have now appeared.[4–8] Most find that a majority of bulimic patients show a marked decrease in their frequency of binge-eating with treatment. In addition to being uncontrolled, however, many of these studies used only the index of binge-eating frequency to measure the outcome of therapy. This one index may be too simple a measure to indicate overall improvement in the patient. For example, in the most successful group therapy study—in which two thirds of the patients developed a remission of binge-eating—depression was found to *rise* by about 50% over the course of treatment.[7] Thus, although the subjects studied were improved in eating behavior, it would seem difficult to argue that they were improved in a more general sense.

Of course, not all studies of group therapy have reported such increases in depression. One more recent study, for example, reported improvement in both eating behavior and depression ratings.[9] In this as in all uncontrolled studies, however, it is difficult to ascertain to what degree the observed improvement represented an actual therapy effect, and to what degree it was due to placebo factors, since none of these studies used a parallel group of patients receiving "placebo" therapy for comparison purposes.

In summary, given the current lack of controlled data to support the effectiveness of psychological techniques in bulimia, a new therapeutic technique, demonstrably effective in placebo-controlled trials, would be welcome. Recently, a series of studies in several centers have suggested that thymoleptic medications—medications effective in the treatment of major depression or bipolar disorder—may offer such an alternative.

### Background: The Relationship of Bulimia to Major Affective Disorder.

The rationale for use of thymoleptic medications in treating bulimia rests largely on evidence that bulimia may be closely related to major affective disorder—the family of psychiatric illnesses that includes major depression and bipolar disorder (manic depressive illness). This evidence stems primarily from three types of research: phenomenologic studies, family studies, and biological tests.

Several *phenomenologic studies* have described cohorts of bulimic patients, seeking treatment, who were administered structured diagnostic interviews, such as the National Institute of Mental Health Diagnostic Interview Schedule (DIS),[10–12] or the Schedule for Affective Disorders and Schizophrenia (SADS).[13] These studies have found that bulimic patients display an elevated prevalence of both current and past major depression and bipolar disorder in their personal histories. The high prevalence of major affective disorder in the histories of bulimic patients suggest that the two disorders may be related, or indeed that they might even be two different symptomatic expressions of some common underlying abnormality.

These findings are affected by several methodological limitations, however. First, most studies examined samples of bulimic patients who sought treatment. It might be argued that these patients are more likely to have a history of major affective disorder than those who do not seek treatment. If so, studies of such patients may find exaggerated rates of major affective disorder in their cohorts as compared to what might be found in the population of bulimic patients as a whole.

In an attempt to deal with this limitation, Hudson et al. recently performed a study using the DIS to interview a sample of remitted bulimic subjects.[14] They used newspaper advertisements to recruit 20 subjects who had a past history of bulimia, but who had been free of bulimic symptoms for at least six months. When this remitted bulimic group was administered the DIS, their lifetime prevalence of major affective disorder was found to be virtually identical to that of a comparison group of actively bulimic patients. This preliminary finding suggests that the high prevalence of major affective disorder observed in bulimic patients is not an artifact caused by patients self-selecting themselves for treatment. More detailed studies will be necessary, however, to address this question thoroughly.

A second criticism of available phenomenologic studies has been that the depression observed in bulimic patients might be secondary to their eating disorder, rather than a "primary" depression. This appears unlikely, however; one study has found that major depression occurred at least one year prior to the onset of bulimia in nearly 50% of the patients interviewed.[12] In addition, several studies have reported bulimic patients with bipolar disorder as opposed to major depression. It would seem difficult to argue that bipolar symptoms are secondary to the eating disorder.

Tentatively, then, the elevated prevalence of current and past major affective disorder reported in bulimic patients appears to be a real phenomenon, not explainable by methodologic artifacts. These findings are reinforced by a second line of evidence: studies of family history in bulimia.

Several studies have assessed the prevalence of major affective disorder and other psychiatric disorders in the first-degree relatives of bulimic patients.[14-17] Most found that the prevalence of major affective disorder in the relatives of bulimic subjects was substantially higher than would be expected in a normal population. One study, however, failed to find such a difference—but in this study, an unusually high prevalence of major affective disorder was also found in the relatives of controls.[17] For example, in this study, 10 (37%) of the 27 control probands' mothers (virtually the only first-degree relatives personally interviewed) were found to display current or past major affective disorder. This would correspond to a morbid risk for major affective disorder in the mothers of over 50%—a figure which suggests that the control group may not have been representative of the general population.

The family studies also suffer from certain methodological limitations. First, most of the studies were performed on bulimic patients who sought treatment, and thus might be subject to the same bias discussed above. In the Hudson et al. study of remitted bulimic patients described earlier,[14] however, the morbid risk of major affective disorder in the first-degree relatives of the remitted patients was found to be 38%. This was slightly higher than the 25% morbid risk of major affective disorder in the first-degree relatives of an age- and sex-matched group of 20 control patients with current or past major depression. The family histories of these groups of patients were obtained by investigators blind to the diagnosis of the proband, suggesting that investigator bias was unlikely to influence the finding.

A second deficiency of available family studies in bulimia is that most[14-16] have used the family history method—in which information about first-degree relatives is sought primarily from the proband—as opposed to the family interview method, in which the first-degree relatives are interviewed by a separate investigator who is blind to proband diagnosis. Also, the only study which did use the family interview method generally utilized interviews of only one relative in each family.[17] The family history method may not represent a serious limitation, however, since previous studies have suggested that it tends to underestimate the prevalence of psychiatric disorders in relatives as compared to what would be found with the family interview method— a not surprising finding.[18-19] Thus, it might be expected that available family history studies of bulimic patients would understate the prevalence of major affective disorder in first-degree relatives.

A third line of evidence, also possibly suggesting a relationship between bulimia and major affective disorder, is from studies using biological tests. For example, several studies have applied the dexamethasone suppression test (DST) to bulimic patients.[16,20,21] In this test, 1 mg of dexamethasone is administered at 11 P.M. on day one and plasma cortisol is measured at 4 P.M. on day two. It has been shown that in cohorts of patients with major depression, approximately 50% will display elevated plasma cortisol levels (a level of greater than 5.0 ug/ml is generally considered positive).[22,23] However, normal individuals display a much lower prevalence of positive tests—typically 5–15%.[22,23] Studies with bulimic patients have consistently found that they display an increased prevalence of nonsuppression of cortisol on the DST, comparable to that reported in studies of depressed patients.

This finding would seem consistent with the phenomenologic and family history findings discussed earlier. Various factors, however, such as recent weight loss, have been shown to generate "false positive" DST's in some individuals.[24] Thus it is possible that the binge-eating and vomiting of bulimic patients might also contribute to false positives findings. On the other hand, preliminary evidence suggests that this may not be the case. For example, in one study, the prevalence of positive DST's in hospitalized patients who were prevented from binge-eating was the same as that in outpatients who were actively binge-eating and vomiting.[20] Similarly, in another center, DST's were found to be positive in bulimic patients even after they had achieved abstinence from binge-eating as a result of milieu therapy.[25] Nevertheless, the DST findings in bulimic patients must be regarded as only a tentative line of evidence in support of a possible relationship between bulimia and major affective disorder.

A second biological test, the thyrotropin releasing hormone stimulation test (TRH stimulation test) has also been found to be more frequently positive in patients with major depression than in controls.[26] This test has been found to be positive in a comparable percentage of bulimic patients, too.[16] Again, the possibility of false positives due to binge-eating and purging behavior, however, must be considered.

Finally, several aspects of sleep architecture—as assessed by the all-night sleep EEG—have been shown to differ in depressed patients as compared to normal controls.[27] Perhaps most characteristically, patients with major depression display a decreased REM latency (time from sleep onset until the beginning of the first rapid eye movement period of the night). Recently, Hudson et al. reported a similar decrease in REM latency in a group of eight bulimic patients.[28] This finding again would seem to favor a relationship between bulimia and major affective disorder, and seems unlikely to have been influenced by such factors as binge-eating, purging, or weight loss.

In summary, then, three lines of evidence—phenomenological, genetic, and biological—all would seem to suggest a relationship between bulimia and major affective disorder. These findings would be largely of only theoretical interest, however, were it not for the possibility that bulimia might respond to the medications customarily used in the treatment of major affective disorder—particularly anti-depressants, lithium carbonate, carbamazepine, and sodium valproate. In the next section, we review the accumulated data suggesting that these various agents may be effective in treating the bulimic syndrome.

## Thymoleptic Treatment of Bulimia: The Evidence

Between 1977 and 1982, three anecdotal reports suggested that bulimic patients might show improvement in both their depression and their binge-eating behavior when treated with tricyclic anti-depressants[29] or monoamine oxidase inhibitors.[30-31] Subsequently, in late 1982, two centers reported series of bulimic patients treated with tricyclic anti-depressants[32] and monoamine oxidase inhibitors respectively.[33] Pope et al.[32] found that six of eight bulimic patients—most of whom received imipramine or desipramine—showed a reduced frequency of binge-eating. Three of these patients showed at least a 90% reduction, or a complete remission of their symptoms. This improvement was maintained for follow-up periods of 2–7 months.

Similarly, Walsh et al.,[33] treating six bulimic patients with monoamine oxidase inhibitors, observed a complete remission of binge-eating in four patients and marked improvement in the other two. These initial reports, however, are of course subject to the same criticisms as are other uncontrolled studies of various therapeutic techniques in bulimia—namely that it is impossible to rule out a placebo effect. However, several placebo-controlled double-blind studies, using various anti-depressant agents in bulimic patients, have now appeared.

In the first of these, Sabine et al.[34] administered mianserin vs placebo to a group of fifty bulimic patients. No minimum frequency of binge-eating or vomiting, or minimum period of illness, was required for entry into this study. Some relatively mild cases may have been included. The patients were randomized to mianserin (N = 20) or placebo (N = 30). Fourteen mianserin subjects and 22 placebo subjects completed the eight-week protocol.

Somewhat surprisingly, both the patients receiving mianserin and those receiving placebo improved on a number of different measures, including Hamilton Rating Scale (HRS) scores for anxiety[35] and depression,[36] and on a "bulimia rating scale" of the authors' design. Neither of the two groups, however, improved in the frequency of their binge eating behavior.

How should these findings be interpreted? First, the marked improvement in the placebo group seems difficult to attribute to contact with the investigators, since the investigators saw the patients only for brief office visits and, by their own account, did not perform any sort of formal psychotherapy. Many of the subjects, however, were seeking treatment for the first time. As a result, they may have been "primed" to try to improve their symptoms at just the time that they entered the study. This "placebo response," as the authors point out, underlines the need for controlled studies in assessing any proposed treatment for bulimia.

Nevertheless, the fact remains that mianserin was ineffective for the frequency of eating binges. A likely explanation of this, however, may be that the dose of mianserin was inadequate. The investigators used a maximum of 60 mg per day of mianserin in their patients—a dose far below the 150 mg per day that has been reported necessary to produce an antidepressant effect in another study.[37] This problem is further compounded by the fact that most of the bulimic subjects were probably engaging in purging behavior (vomiting or laxative abuse) and may have failed to absorb some of the mianserin which they were ingesting. As a result, the plasma levels of mianserin in these subjects may have been inadequate. This speculation is further supported by the observation that mianserin—despite its recognized efficacy as an anti-depressant—was not superior to placebo even on measures of depression. To resolve these questions, it would be desirable to repeat this study, using a larger dose of mianserin and documenting the plasma levels of mianserin in each subject. Pending such an investigation, it may be premature to conclude whether or not mianserin is effective in treating bulimia.

Also in 1983, a second double-blind study was performed by Pope et al., in which a cohort of 22 bulimic subjects were randomized to imipramine—at a maximum dose of 200 mg per day—or placebo.[38] For this study the authors recruited a relatively chronic and refractory group of bulimic subjects for treatment. The 22 subjects had been ill for an average of about seven years, and were binge-eating an average of more than nine times per week. Three had been hospitalized at some time in the past for symptoms of eating disorders, and most had failed to respond to one or more previous courses of psychotherapy.

Three patients dropped out during the six-week course of the study. Two developed rashes and were found, upon breaking the blind, to be taking imipramine. The third became frustrated with her lack of improvement and took an overdose of all of the pills that had been given to her. Fortunately she experienced no ill effects. She proved to be taking placebo.

At the conclusion of the study, imipramine was found to be significantly superior to placebo on most measures. The patients receiving imipramine experienced an average decrease of approximately 70% in their frequency of binge-eating, as compared to virtually no change in the placebo patients. In addition, the imipramine subjects improved by about 50% on the HRS; the placebo patients showed almost no improvement on this measure. Both the decrease in binge-eating and the change in HRS scores were statistically significant ($p < .01$ and $p < .02$ respectively). The study also found improvement on several subjective measures of eating behaviors as well: the patients receiving imipramine experienced a significant reduction in their preoccupation with food, and showed more self-control with relation to food. In addition they displayed a highly significant ($p < .001$) change in a rating of subjective global improvement. This suggests that imipramine was effective not merely for the symptom of binge-eating, but produced a more general benefit.

Recently, Pope et al. conducted a long-term follow-up of twenty of the subjects who participated in this study.[39] At the time of the last follow-up (over two years in 11 patients, over one year in four additional patients, and less than one year in the remaining five patients), 50% of patients were free of binge-eating. An additional 45% showed a marked (greater than 75%) or moderate (greater than 50%) reduction in binge-eating, and only one patient was unimproved. The unimproved patient had discontinued her anti-depressant treatment against medical advice and had promptly relapsed to her original binge-eating level. These promising results, however, were mitigated by the observation that time-consuming and difficult experimentation was often necessary in order to achieve an optimal anti-depressant response in many subjects.

In 1984, three further placebo-controlled, double-blind studies appeared; all produced positive results. In the first, Walsh et al. compared the monoamine oxidase inhibitor phenelzine (Nardil) with placebo in a cohort of twenty-five subjects.[40] These subjects displayed a frequency of binge-eating and duration of illness comparable to those in the Pope et al. study described above. Thirteen subjects were randomized to phenelzine and 12 to placebo. There were four dropouts in the phenelzine group and one in the placebo group, yielding nine and 11 "completers" in the two groups, respectively.

At the end of the eight-week study period, phenelzine proved significantly superior to placebo on both frequency of binge-eating and on the Eating Attitudes Test (EAT).[41] In fact, five of the nine phenelzine subjects showed a complete remission of their binge-eating, and three of the remaining four subjects improved by at least 50%. HRS scores did not differ significantly between the two groups, but this appeared partially due to the fact that some Hamilton items (for example, insomnia) were influenced by the side-effects of phenelzine. When these items were removed, the difference between phenelzine and placebo became significant in favor of phenelzine.

It might be asked whether a monoamine oxidase inhibitor is a safe treatment to administer to bulimic patients, given that such individuals might binge on foods that would be dangerous when ingested in conjunction with these drugs. Walsh and colleagues did not report any problem with this. They noted, however, that their sample was a selected one. Clearly, patients with bulimia must be reliably able to abstain—even when binge-eating—from such foods as aged cheeses, sour cream, and the like if they are to be treated with monoamine oxidase inhibitors.

In another placebo-controlled double-blind study, Hughes et al. administered desipramine (Norpramine) vs placebo to a cohort of 22 subjects.[42] These subjects displayed a similar time period and severity of bulimia to those in the previous two studies. Unlike the previous two groups of investigators, however, Hughes and colleagues selected exclusively bulimic patients who did not display current major depression. At first, it might seem that this selection procedure would tend to bias the results against desipramine. However, the findings of the study were actually slightly stronger than those of the previous two groups: 15 (68%) of the 22 subjects experienced a remission of their bulimic symptoms within ten weeks, and 19 (86%) of the subjects experienced at least marked improvement.

Another important finding to emerge from the Hughes et al. study was the need for assessing plasma levels of the drug in order to ensure that subjects were receiving therapeutic doses. When these investigators tested plasma levels on 20 of their subjects, they found that ten had levels that were too low and four had levels that were too high by the standards of the Mayo Clinic Laboratory (the therapeutic range in this laboratory is quoted as 125–275 ug/ml).

Of the ten subjects whose levels were found to be too low, four were already in remission and therefore did not have their dosages increased. When dosage was corrected in the remaining six subjects in order to bring their plasma levels to within the therapeutic range, however, four went on to achieve remission. Overall, these six subjects achieved a 51% further decrease in their frequency of binge-eating as a result of the dosage adjustment.

One patient required a dose of 350 mg of desipramine a day in order to achieve therapeutic levels. This finding strongly argues that plasma levels are critical when treating bulimic patients with antidepressant medications. Had the authors not assessed plasma levels of the drug, they might have considerably underestimated the efficacy of desipramine in bulimia. It is to be noted, in this connection, that Pope et al.,[18] using a similar dose (200mg) of imipramine, failed to assess plasma levels. Possibly the somewhat weaker (albeit positive) findings of the Pope et al. study are attributable to inadequate drug levels in some subjects.

Finally, in another recent placebo-controlled double-blind study, Mitchell and Groat used amitriptyline (Elavil) vs placebo in a sample of thirty-two bulimic subjects.[43] This study also assessed plasma levels on eight of the sixteen patients who had been assigned to amitriptyline. Of these eight patients, one had an amitriptyline plus nortriptyline level of zero (in other words, she may not have been taking her medication at all), and three others had levels of less than 75 ug/ml—well below what is generally considered to be the therapeutic range for amitriptyline in most studies.[44–46] Thus, as the authors themselves point out, as many as half of the subjects receiving amitriptyline in this study may have been inadequately treated.

Since the investigators measured plasma levels toward the end of the study, they were unable to correct the dosage in the manner of Hughes et al. This is a potentially important limitation, and one which may have seriously compromised the apparent efficacy of amitriptyline in the study results. Nevertheless, amitriptyline still proved to be significantly superior to placebo in this study on the HRS, and was also superior to placebo on all of the four measures of eating behavior. These latter four differences, however, did not reach statistical significance, although two of them approached significance ($P < .10$) in favor of an amitriptyline effect.

In summary, of the five available placebo-controlled double-blind studies using antidepressants to treat bulimia, three have produced positive findings, one a weaker though still positive finding, and one a negative finding. As indicated above, however, considerable evidence suggests that subjects in the latter two studies may have received inadequate does of medication.

Two other double-blind studies of thymoleptic agents in treating bulimia have also appeared. In the first of these, Ong et al. administered intravenous methamphetamine, 15 mg, to a group of eight bulimic patients.[47] On a separate day, one week apart, they were administered intravenous placebo. Methamphetamine proved significantly superior to placebo in terms of reduced caloric consumption and reduced binge-eating. Obviously, this is a finding which does not have direct practical implications, since intravenous methamphetamine is unlikely to become a clinical treatment for bulimia. It is of theoretical interest, however. One possibility is that methamphetamine worked because of its anorexigenic effects, but the authors point out this possibility runs counter to the statements of many bulimic patients that they do not actually feel hungry at the time of their binges. The alternative possibility is that the stimulant (i.e. antidepressant) effects of methamphetamine may have been primarily responsible.

In another recent double-blind study, Kaplan et al.[48] described results with six bulimic subjects treated with carbamazepine—an anticonvulsant also known to be effective in some cases of affective disorder.[49] All of the six subjects had normal EEG's. Five showed virtually no response to carbamazepine, but the sixth showed a striking remission of her bulimia—together with a remission of her cyclothymic mood symptoms—while receiving the drug. She relapsed when she was blindly switched from carbamazepine to placebo. This suggests that carbamazepine may be effective in at least occasional bulimic patients—particularly, perhaps, those with bipolar symptoms.

In addition to the above double-blind studies, there have been a number of uncontrolled reports using various other antidepressant agents. These will be briefly summarized below.

*Trazodone* was found in one study to produce a "marked" response in eight bulimic patients,[50] but has also been reported to be associated with delirium in three patients.[51] Another report described an increase in depressive and bulimic symptoms in three bulimic patients who had previously been maintained on tricyclic antidepressants or lithium carbonate and who were then switched to trazodone.[52] When these patients were switched back to their original medications, they improved. These observations suggest that trazodone may be a less satisfactory drug in the treatment of bulimia than some other antidepressant agents.

*Lithium carbonate* has been found effective in one recent uncontrolled study of fourteen bulimic women.[53] These women were binging as frequently as seventy times per week and had been ill for as long as ten years. Eight of the fourteen patients were receiving behavior therapy simultaneously with lithium administration, but the other six had either failed a course of behavior therapy or had temporarily responded to behavior therapy and then relapsed. With lithium administration, all eight of the patients receiving lithium plus behavior therapy experienced a 75% to 100% reduction in their frequency of binge-eating. Four of the six patients who had failed behavior therapy experienced a comparable improvement. Improvement was maintained for follow-up periods of six to sixteen months. During the course of the follow-up period, seven patients were able to eventually discontinue lithium carbonate without relapse.

In another report, Chevlen described seven bulimic patients who had failed to respond, or had shown an incomplete response, to various anti-depressant medications.[54] When he added lithium carbonate to the existing anti-depressant in these patients, one achieved a complete remission and two others experienced about 50% improvement. The remaining four patients apparently did not respond.

It should be noted that caution should be exercised when administering lithium to patients with bulimia, particularly if they engage in extensive vomiting. In 1980, a "normal volunteer" in a study of sleep at the National Institute of Health abruptly died in her sleep while taking lithium and alpha-methyl-para-tyrosine. When her history was investigated after her death, it was found that this "normal" volunteer had not revealed to the researchers that she had a longstanding history of anorexia nervosa and self-induced vomiting.[55] She had experienced two previous cardiac arrests, presumably attributable to reduced intracellular potassium from her vomiting. It seems possible that the ingestion of lithium during the study at NIH may have exacerbated this effect, leading to a possible cardiac arrest and her death. This experience would indicate the importance of monitoring serum electrolytes before initiating a trial of lithium in patients with bulimia.

*Nomifensine* is a new anti-depressant which has just been approved for commercial use in the United States. It appears to be quite free of side effects. Most studies indicate that it possesses fewer anticholinergic, hypotensive, and sedative properties than standard anti-depressants.[56] Pope et al. used doses of nomifensine, 150 mg to 300mg per day, in a cohort of twelve consecutive bulimic patients.[57] Two of these patients developed fevers after approximately two weeks of treatment (a side effect previously described with nomifensine) and were immediately withdrawn from the drug. Of the remaining ten patients, however, six achieved a remission of their binge-eating episodes, two a marked improvement (greater than 75% decrease in frequency of binge-eating) and two a moderate improvement (greater than 50% decrease). During a follow-up period of one to four months, two of the remitted patients relapsed, one completely and one partially. The other eight patients maintained their improvement.

All of the patients who were maintained on nomifensine found the drug to be virtually free of side effects. Two patients, however, experienced weight loss—about five pounds in one case and about twenty-five pounds in another. In bulimic patients, this side effect is rarely considered unwelcome.

Another investigational antidepressant, also relativley free of anticholinergic, hypotensive, and sedative side effects, is *bupropion*. Bupropion has not yet been approved for commercial use in the United States, but has already been subjected to study. In one report,[58] seventeen patients with bulimia and major depression—all of whom had failed to respond to previous antidepressant agents—were assigned to bupropion. After one month of treatment, 41% of the patients were described as having obtained a complete remission of their bulimia, and another 47% had experienced at least a 50% decrease in their frequency of binge-eating. Over the course of the next six months, four patients dropped out of the study, but the remaining ones maintained their degree of improvement while on the medication. Like nomifensine, bupropion was also associated with weight loss in some patients. In fact seven of the seventeen patients lost more than ten pounds during the time that they were taking the drug. Other side effects were described as minimal.

Another group (J. Ferguson, Personal Communication, February 1985) experienced less satisfactory results with bupropion. They treated seven patients who had previously failed tricyclic anti-depressants or monoamine oxidase inhibitors, and found that only three showed even a slight decrease (approximately 25%) in frequency of binge-eating. Given that these patients had been refractory to previous anti-depressants, however, this finding is not unduly disappointing. It would be of great interest to try bupropion in a sample of patients who had not previously failed other drugs.

Finally, a recent case report describes success in using *sodium valproate*—a drug previously shown effective in some cases of bipolar disorder[59,60]—in the treatment of a woman who had both bulimic symptoms and rapid cycling bipolar disorder.[61] This patient had failed to respond to neuroleptics, lithium carbonate, or carbamazepine, but experienced a prompt remission of bulimic and affective symptoms with valproate. During the course of follow-up, her valproate level fell below 50 ug/ml on two occasions. On each of these occasions, she experienced a partial relapse of her bulimic and affective symptoms, then promptly remitted again when drug levels were raised.

In summary, a number of other individual anti-depressant drugs, and one anticonvulsant drug known to be effective in major affective disorder, also tentatively appear effective in bulimia. These impressions are based on uncontrolled studies, however, and require replication in double-blind investigations.

Finally, two other reports have described series of bulimic patients who were treated with any of several different anti-depressant drugs. The first study presented 65 consecutive patients treated with tricyclic anti-depressants, monoamine oxidase inhibitors, trazodone, and in occasional cases, other thymoleptic agents.[62] The authors found that about half of their patients showed either a marked response (greater than 75% decrease in frequency of binge eating) of a remission with tricyclic anti-depressants. Of the patients who failed to respond to tricyclic anti-depressants, about two thirds responded to monoamine oxidase inhibitors with either a marked response or a remission. Overall, when patients were scored for their ultimate response to the most successful anti-depressant, it was found that 22 (33.8%) of the 65 patients had achieved remission, 25 (38.5%) had achieved marked improvement, 12 (18.5%) had achieved moderate improvement, and six (9.2%) showed no improvement.

This study stressed the importance of obtaining plasma levels for tricyclic anti-depressants and platelet monoamine oxidase levels in the case of patients treated with monoamine oxidase inhibitors. The investigators found that unusually large doses of tricyclics or monoamine oxidase inhibitors were required for some bulimic patients. In many cases, when blood levels were measured, "nonresponders" were simply found to be undertreated.

In the other study, Brotman et al. presented retrospective findings on 22 patients with bulimia treated at their center with tricyclic anti-depressants, monoamine oxidase inhibitors, or trazodone.[63] The results of this study were discouraging: only five (23%) of the patients were considered by the authors to be "true responders" who displayed a remission of bulimia and maintained this throughout a six-month follow-up period. These results may be attributable to a number of methodological problems, however: the authors used doses of anti-depressants which were likely inadequate on the basis of previous studies with bulimic patients, they failed to obtain anti-depressant plasma levels or platelet monoamine oxidase levels on any of their subjects, and they generally failed to try a second or third anti-depressant when a first was unsuccessful.

For example, a dose of 125 mg per day of a tricyclic anti-depressant was rated as an "adequate" trial by these investigators. By contrast, Hughes et al., in the double-blind study of desipramine cited earlier,[42] found that a dose of even 200 mg of desipramine produced *inadequate* plasma levels in fully 50% of the patients treated, and that one bulimic patient needed 350 mg per day of desipramine in order to achieve remission. Thus, Brotman et al.'s definition of an "adequate" dose of tricyclic anti-depressants may have been too low in some patients by as much as a factor of three. These several methodological limitations render the study results highly suspect. Another investigator[64] has published similar criticisms of the Brotman et al. report.

Finally, we should mention the literature on phenytoin, a drug not normally classed as a thymoleptic, but one felt to be effective in some cases of bulimia. Several uncontrolled studies from the 1970's suggested that bulimic patients (usually diagnosed at that time as patients with "compulsive eating disorders") had an unusually high frequency of abnormal EEG's, and would sometimes experience considerable relief of their binge-eating with phenytoin.[65-70]

As a result, phenytoin was subjected to a controlled trial in 1977.[71] In this trial, ten subjects were assigned to six weeks of phenytoin and then crossed over to six weeks of placebo, while ten others were first given placebo and then phenytoin. In the ten subjects who first received phenytoin, there was a significant decrease in the frequency of their binge-eating upon using the drug. When they were crossed over to placebo, however, this improvement continued, yielding no significant difference between the phenytoin period and the subsequent placebo period. Of the ten subjects who began with placebo, no initial improvement was seen, but a 39% average decrease in frequency of binge-eating was documented upon switching to phenytoin. The authors suggested that the subjects in the first group were experiencing a "carryover" effect even after phenytoin was discontinued.

Looking at individual response rates, only six of the subjects experienced a "marked" decrease in their frequency of binge-eating (greater than 75%) with phenytoin. Furthermore, of the four "marked" responders who continued to take phenytoin long-term, two relapsed despite continuing to take the drug. Thus, although the study did find some significant differences, the overall benefit of pheytoin appears to be modest.

It was also of interest that in this study no correlation was found between response to phenytoin and the presence of EEG abnormalities. This argues that phenytoin, when it is effective in treating bulimia, may not be working via its anticonvulsant action. The authors themselves raise this possibility, indicating that phenytoin has a wide variety of properties, and that something other than its anticonvulsant action may be responsible. We might add here that among these other properties, phenytoin has been claimed to have a thymoleptic effect of its own,[72-74] although this effect is certainly not as clear-cut as with carbamazepine[49] or sodium valproate.[59,60]

Before concluding, we should reiterate that most of the studies described in the latter section of this review—with the exception of the placebo-controlled double-blind study of phenytoin[71]—were uncontrolled. Given the observation that bulimia may improve substantially with placebo alone[34,43] —especially when the study subjects are patients who have spontaneously come seeking treatment—caution is advisable in interpreting the results of all uncontrolled reports.

*Conclusions:*

At the present state of the evidence, several preliminary conclusions may be drawn.

1. *Thymoleptic agents are clearly effective for many bulimic patients.* At present, only the tricyclic anti-depressants and monoamine oxidase inhibitors have been shown effective in placebo-controlled trials,[38,40,42,43] although many other thymoleptic agents tentatively appear effective on the basis of uncontrolled data or preliminary controlled data. Mianserin, an anti-depressant not available in the United States, has been the only thymoleptic agent which has failed to show a beneficial effect in a controlled study.[34] The low dose of mianserin used in this study, however, limits interpretation of its conclusions.

Phenytoin is the only agent not traditionally classed as a thymoleptic to be extensively studied in treating bulimia. The one controlled study of phenytoin suggests that it has at best only weak anti-bulimic properties.[71] Furthermore, evidence suggests that the anti-bulimic properties of phenytoin—when they do appear—may be unrelated to the drug's anticonvulsant effects. Whether phenytoin is itself acting as a weak thymoleptic—as some data would suggest[72-74]—or affects bulimia via another mechanism, remains unknown.

2. *The effect of thymoleptic agents is not confined to any known subgroup of bulimic patients.* Although it might be assumed that thymoleptic agents would be particularly effective for bulimic patients with concomitant major affective disorder—or with other features, such as a past history of major affective disorder, a family history of major affective disorder, or a positive dexamethasone suppression test—there is no data to support such conjectives. In fact, in the one double-blind study which specifically selected bulimic patients without major depression,[42] the outcome was actually slightly better than that of other studies. Thus, anti-depressants should clearly *not* be reserved only for bulimic patients with concurrent depression.

3. *Adequate doses of medication must be used.* Monitoring of plasma levels (in the case of tricyclic antidepressants, lithium, carbamazepine, and sodium valproate) or platelet monoamine oxidase levels (in

the case of monoamine oxidase inhibitors), whenever possible, appears critical in the treatment of many bulimic patients. Perhaps because bulimic patients tend to be younger than many patients with major depression, or perhaps because self-induced vomiting or laxative abuse may interfere with drug absorption, it is often necessary to use unusually large doses of thymoleptic agents in order to reach the therapeutic range. At least two reports[42,62] have found that many putative "nonresponders" to antidepressants were simply undertreated—and that many of these patients achieved a marked improvement or a remission of their bulimic symptoms when dosage was corrected. Furthermore, studies which probably used inadequate doses of antidepressants in many subjects,[34,43,63] or which failed to document plasma levels,[34,63] have produced much less satisfactory results than studies which have used larger dosages, or tested plasma levels.[40,42,62]

4. Although their mechanism of action in treating bulimia is as yet unknown, *thymoleptic medications very likely benefit bulimia via the same mechanism of action by which they benefit major affective disorder.* In other words, thymoleptic medications probably benefit bulimia because they are thymoleptics, and rather than because of an independent "anti-bulimic" property which they happen to share.

This final conclusion has been questioned by some observers who note, for example, that antidepressants may benefit bulima but not depression in some patients and depression but not bulimia in others.[63] This finding does not exclude, however, the possibility that the mechanism of the two effects is the same: digitalis, for example, may benefit dyspnea but not peripheral edema in some patients with congestive heart failure, and benefit primarily edema, but not dyspnea, in others. Yet the mechanism of action of digitalis is the same in both cases.

In favor of the hypothesis that thymoleptics benefit both bulimia and major affective disorder by the same mechanism, there are several lines of evidence: 1) the dose and plasma levels of antidepressants required to treat bulimia appear the same as those required to treat major depression;[42,62] 2) the time course of the antidepressant effect and the antibulimic effect appears approximately the same;[38,40,42,43] 3) in at least one study, a highly significant correlation was found between improvement in bulimia and improvement in depression;[38] 4) bulimia responds to a wide range of thymoleptic medications—medications of very different chemical structures which share little in common other than the fact that they are thymoleptics; and 5) conversely, there is little evidence that bulimia responds consistently to any non-thymoleptic medication (with the partial, and uncertain exception of phenytoin). To these findings we must add indirect evidence from the studies presented in the introduction to this chapter, which suggest that bulimia may be related to major affective disorder on the basis of 6) phenomenologic observations; 7) family history data; 8) DST findings; 9) TRH stimulation test findings; and 10) studies of sleep architecture.

The simplest hypothesis to explain these observations would seem to be that the symptons of bulimia and the symptoms of major affective disorder are caused—at least in part—by the same underlying abnormality, and that thymoleptic medications benefit both types of symptoms via their effect on this abnormality rather than by two independent effects. Although alternate hypotheses can be advanced to account for each of the above ten findings individually, it would seem difficult to construct an alternate, reasonably parsimonious hypothesis to account for *all* of the above findings collectively.

## REFERENCES

1. Pope HG, Jr, Hudson JI: New Hope for Binge Eaters: Advances in the Understanding and Treatment of Bulimia. New York: Harper and Row, 1984.
2. Fairburn C: A cognitive behavioral approach to the treatment of bulimia. *Psychol Med* 11:707–711, 1981.
3. Schneider JA, Agras WS: A cognitive behavioral group treatment of bulimia. *Br J Psychiatry* 146:66–69, 1985.
4. Boskind-Lodahl M, White WC: The definition and treatment of bulimarexia in college women - a pilot study. *J Am Coll Health Assoc* 27:85–86, 1978.
5. White WC, Boskind-White M: An experiental-behavioral approach to the treatment of bulimarexia. *Psychotherapy: Theory, Research, and Practice* 4:501–507, 1981.
6. Johnson CL, Connors M, Stuckey M: Short-term group treatment of bulimia: A preliminary report. *Int J Eat Dis* 2:199–208, 1983.
7. Lacey JH: Bulimia nervosa, binge eating, and psychogenic vomiting: A controlled treatment study and long-term outcome. *Br Med J* 286:1609–1613, 1983.
8. Pyle RL: Psychotherapy for bulimia: the role of groups. Presented at the Annual Meeting, American Psychiatric Association, Los Angeles, 10 May 1984.
9. Connors M, Johnson CL, Stuckey M: Treatment of bulimia with brief psychoeducational group therapy. *Am J Psychiatry* 141:1512–1516, 1984.
10. Walsh BT, Roose SP, Glassman AM, et al: Eating disorders and depression, Presented at the Annual Meeting, American Psychiatric Association, New York, 4 May 1983.
11. Hatsukami D, Eckert ED, Mitchell JE, et al: Affective disorder and substance abuse in women with bulimia. *Psychol Med* 14:701–714, 1984.
12. Hudson JI, Pope HG, Jr, Jonas JM, et al: Phenomenologic relationship of eating disorders to major affective disorder. *Psychiatry Res* 9:345–354, 1983.
13. Herzog DB: Are anorexic and bulimic patients depressed? *Am J Psychiatry* 141:1594–1597, 1984.
14. Hudson JI, Pope HG, Jr, Jonas JM, et al: Affective symptoms in bulimia: a controlled study. Presented at the Annual Meeting, American Psychiatric Association, Los Angeles, 9 May 1984.

15. Hudson JI, Pope HG, Jr, Jonas JM, et al: Family history study of anorexia nervosa and bulimia. *Br J Psychiatry* 142:133–138, 1983.

16. Gwirtsman HE, Roy-Byrne P, Yager J et al: Neuroendocrine abnormalities in bulimia. *Am J Psychiatry* 140:559–563, 1983.

17. Stern SL, Dixon KN, Nezmer E, et al: Affective disorder in the families of women with normal-weight bulimia. *Am J Psychiatry* 141:1224–1227, 1984.

18. Thompson WD, Orvaschel H, Prusoff B, et al: An evaluation of the family history method for ascertaining psychiatric disorder. *Arch Gen Psychiatry* 39:53–58, 1982.

19. Winokur G, Clayton PJ, Reich T: Manic Depressive Illness. St. Louis: CV Mosby Co, 1969.

20. Hudson JI, Pope HG, Jr, Jonas JM, et al: Hypothalamic-pituitary-adrenal axis hyperactivity in bulimia. *Psychiatry Res* 8:111–117, 1983.

21. Mitchell JE, Pyle RL, Hatsukami D, et al: The dexamethasone suppression test in patients with the bulimia syndrome. *J Clin Psychiatry* 45:508–511, 1984.

22. Carroll BF, Feinberg M, Greden JF, et al: A specific laboratory test for the diagnosis of melancholia: standardization, validation, and clinical utility. *Arch Gen Psychiatry* 37:747–757, 1981.

23. Hirschfeld MA, Koslow SH, Kupfer DJ: The clinical utility of the dexamethasone suppression test in psychiatry, *JAMA* 250:2171–2172, 1983.

24. Edelstein CK, Roy-Byrne P, Fawzy FI, et al: Effects of weight loss on the dexamethasone suppression test. *Am J Psychiatry* 140:338–341, 1983.

25. Kay WH, Gwirtsman HE, Ebert MH, et al: Neurobiology of binging and vomiting behavior. Presented at the Annual Meeting, American Psychiatric Association, 10 May 1984.

26. Loosen PT, Prange AJ: Serum thyrotropin response to thyrotropin-releasing hormone in psychiatric patients: a review. *Am J Psychiatry* 139:405–416, 1982.

27. Kupfer DJ, Foster FG, Cable P, et al: The application of EEG sleep for the differential diagnosis of affective disorders. *Am J Psychiatry* 135:69–74, 1978.

28. Hudson JI, Jonas JM, Pope HG, Jr, et al: REM latency in bulimia. Presented at the Annual Meeting, American Psychiatric Association, Dallas TX, May 1985.

29. Moore DC: Amitriptyline therapy in anorexia nervosa. *Am J Psychiatry* 134:1303–1304, 1977.

30. Rich CL: Self-induced vomiting: psychiatric considerations. *JAMA* 239:2688–2689, 1978.

31. Shader RI, Greenblatt DJ: The psychiatrist as mind sweeper. *J Clin Psychopharm* 2:233–234, 1982.

32. Pope HG, Jr, Hudson JI: Treatment of bulimia with antidepressants. *Psychopharmacology* 78:167–179, 1982.

33. Walsh BT, Stewart JW, Wright L, et al: Treatment of bulimia with monoamine oxidase inhibitors. *Am J Psychiatry* 139:1629–1630, 1982.

34. Sabine EJ, Yonace A, Farrington AJ, et al: Bulimia nervosa: a placebo-controlled double-blind therapeutic trial of mianserin. *Br J Clin Pharmacol* 15:195s–202s, 1983.

35. Hamilton M: A rating scale for anxiety. *Br J Med Psychol* 32:50–55, 1959.

36. Hamilton M: A rating scale for depression. *J Neurol Neurosurg Psychiatry* 23:56–65, 1960.

37. McGrath PJ, Quitkin FM, Stewart JW, et al: An open clinical trial of mianserin. *Am J Psychiatry* 138:530–532, 1981.

38. Pope HG, Jr, Hudson JI, Jonas JM, et al: Bulima treated with imipramine: a placebo-controlled double-blind study. *Am J Psychiatry* 140:554–558, 1983.

39. Pope HG, Jr, Hudson JI, Jonas JM, et al:

40. Walsh BT, Stewart JW, Roose SP, et al: Treatment of bulimia with phenelzine: a double-blind, placebo-controlled study. *Arch Gen Psychiatry* 41:1105–1109, 1984.

41. Garner DM, Garfinkel PE: The eating attitudes test: an index of the symptoms of anorexia nervosa. *Psychol Med* 9:273–279, 1979.

42. Hughes PL, Wells LA, Cunningham CJ, et al: Treating bulimia with desipramine: a placebo-controlled double-blind study. *Arch Gen Psychiat*, in press.

43. Mitchell JE, Groat R: A placebo-controlled, double-blind trial of amitriptyline in bulima. *J. Clin Psychopharm* 4:186–193, 1984.

44. Braithwaite RA, Goulding R, Theano G, et al: Plasma concentration of amitriptyline and clinical response. *Lancet* 1:1297–1300, 1972.

45. Zeigler VE, Clayton PJ, Biggs JT: A comparison study of amitriptyline and nortriptyline with plasma levels. *Arch Gen Psychiatry* 34:607–612, 1977.

46. Kupfer DJ, Hanin I, Spiker DG, et al: Amitriptyline plasma levels and clinical response in primary depression. *Clin Pharmacol Ther* 22:904–911, 1977.

47. Ong YL, Checkley SA, Russell GFM: Suppression of bulimia symptoms with methylamphetamine. *Br J Psychiatry* 143:228–293, 1983.

48. Kaplan AS, Garfinkel PE, Darby PL, et al: Carbamazepine in the treatment of bulimia. *Am J Psychiatry* 140:1225–1226.

49. Ballenger JC, Post RM: Carbamazepine in manic-depressive illness: a new treatment. *Am J Psychiatry* 137:782–790, 1980.

50. Damlouji NF, Ferguson JM: Trazodone in the treatment of bulimic patients. Presented at the First International Conference on Eating Disorders, New York, 8 April 1984.

51. Damlouji NF, Ferguson JM: Trazodone-induced delirium in bulimic patients. *Am J Psychiatry* 141:434–435, 1984.

52. Wold P: Trazodone in the treatment of bulimia (letter). *J Clin Psychiatry* 44:275–276, 1983.

53. Hsu LKG: Treatment of bulimia with lithium. *Am J Psychiatry* 141:1260–1262, 1984.

54. Chevlen EM: The adjunctive use of lithium carbonate in the management of bulimia resistant to antidepressant therapy. Presented at the First International Conference on Eating Disorders, New York, 8 April 1984.

55. NIH shaken by death of research volunteer. *Science* 209:475–479, 1980.

56. Various authors: Nomifensine. *J Clin Psychiatry* 45 (section 2): 4–105, 1984.

57. Pope HG, Jr, Herridge PL, Hudson JI: Treatment of bulimia with nomifensine. Presented at the Annual Meeting, American Psychiatric Association, May 1985.

58. Horne RL: Bupropion in the treatment of bulimia. Presented at the First International Conference on Eating Disorders, New York, 8 April 1984.

59. Emrich HM, Von Zerssen D, Kissling W: The effect of sodium valproate on mania: the GABA hypothesis of affective disorder. *Arch Psychiatr Nervenkr* 229: 1–16, 1980.

60. Puzynski S, Klosiewicz L: Valproic acid amide (VAA) in the therapy of affective disorder. Presented at the Seventh World Congress of Psychiatry, Vienna, July 1983.

61. Herridge PL, Pope HG, Jr: Treatment of bulimia and rapid-cycling bipolar disorder with sodium valproate: a case report. *J Clin Psychopharm,*

62. Pope HG, Jr, Hudson JI, Jonas JM: Antidepressant treatment of bulimia: preliminary experience and practical recommendations. *J Clin Psychopharm* 3:274–281, 1983.

63. Brotman AW, Herzog DB, Woods SW: Antidepressant treatment of bulimia: the relationship between bingeing and depressive symptomatology. *J Clin Psychiatry* 45:7–9, 1984.

64. Stewart JW: Antidepressant treatment of bulimia (letter). *J Clin Psychiatry* 45:443, 1984.

65. Green RS, Rau JH: Treatment of compulsive eating disturbances with anticonvulsant medication. *Am J Psychiatry* 131:428–432, 1974.

66. Weiss T, Levitz L: Diphenylhydantoin treatment of bulimia (letter). *Am J Psychiatry* 133:1093, 1976.

67. Greenway FL, Dahms WT, Brag DA: Phenytoin as a treatment of obesity associated with compulsive eating. *Current Therap Res* 21:338–342, 1977.

68. Green RS, Rau JH: The use of diphenylhydantoin in compulsive eating disorders: further studies. In Vigersky RA (ed): Anorexia Nervosa. New York, Raven Press, 1977, pp 377–382.

69. Rau JH, Green RS: Soft neurological correlates of compulsive eating. *J Nerv Ment Dis* 166:435–437, 1978.

70. Rau JH, Struve FA, Green RS: Electroencephalographic correlates of compulsive eating. *Clin Electroencephalography* 10:180–188, 1979.

71. Wermuth BM, Davis KL, Hollister LE, et al: Phenytoin treatment of the binge-eating syndrome. *Am J Psychiatry* 134:1249–1253, 1977.

72. Bogoch S, Dreyfus J: The Broad Range of Use of Diphenylhydantoin: Bibliography and Review. Vol. I. New York, Dreyfus Medical Foundation, 1970.

73. Bogoch S, Dreyfus J: DPH, 1975, A Supplement to the Broad Range of Use of Diphenylhydantoin: Bibliography and Review. Vol. II. New York, Dreyfus Medical Foundation, 1975.

74. Stephen JH, Shaffer JW: A controlled replication of the effectiveness of diphenylhydantoin in reducing irritability and anxiety in selected neurotic outpatients. *J Clin Pharmacol* 13:351–356, 1973.

# CHAPTER 12

# Anorexia Nervosa and Bulimia: The Role of the Nurse

## Constance A. Walsh, R.N.

Although I began my work as a psychiatric nurse approximately six years ago, I did not see a case of anorexia nervosa until 3 years ago and did not encounter bulimia until later. The first case of anorexia to appear at my hospital was a 17-year-old girl admitted to the psychiatric unit weighing 69 lbs. I immediately became interested in this girl. (I hesitate to use the term "anorectic" since it feeds into the special identity which these people seem to place on themselves through their illness. I will, therefore, refer to them as "victims.") My concern for this 69-pound victim lead to my interest in her illness. But, unfortunately, I found nothing to fall back on. It was obvious that she needed to eat. But this was the thing she could not and would not do. I went back to my nursing textbooks with no success and could not even recall the disorder being reviewed during my training. I made a trip to the library but, at that time, there was limited material on this disorder, especially material geared toward nursing. I should note here that today volumes of material are available.

As a nurse, I wanted to do something to help this patient and decided that my only recourse was to go to her—the victim herself—and try to find out what had happened and possibly to gain some understanding of how it had happened. During our talks, she would sometimes brag about how good she felt, how healthy she was, and how other girls envied her. But then there were times when she would talk about how she had to lose more weight and how frightened she was of the prison she felt enclosed in, the prison she could not get out of. She would feel her skinny arms, legs, and abdomen and say, "I can still feel softness—that's fat. I have to feel hardness, I have to feel my bones."

Her thinking seemed confused. She avoided food, yet she was thinking about it constantly. She talked about her cookbook collection and how she had plans to become a chef or nutritionist. She told me of the elaborate meals she prepared at home for her family and how everyone enjoyed her specialties. She, meanwhile, would eat lettuce leaves.

One day she came to me with a picture cut from a magazine and said, "I want to try and show you how I feel when food is placed before me." The picture was an advertisment which showed a tiny kitten with its limbs drawn close to its body in a crouching position, ready to spring, or cowering in fear as it looked up at a huge bowl of milk looming overhead. It was at this moment that I began to get some kind of handle on what she had been trying to tell me. I began to understand the confused logic behind statements such as "I am hungry, but to eat means losing control," and "I may not be able to stop eating and I will surely get fat." After showing me that cowering kitten, she began to talk about her prison, about the fear of staying inside it and the opposing fear of leaving its confinement. She wanted help, but help instilled fear. She felt she was in control, and that medical and psychiatric help would take away that control. Of course, she was out of control, but the point here is that for her the idea of losing the one control she thought she had—the ability not to eat—was overwhelming.

My interest in eating disorders continued and as more victims came in for treatment it became clear that in order to adequately treat these individuals we needed a unit designed especially for their treatment—a controlled environment in which the negative behavior could be stopped. We needed professionals who had training in working with eating disorders patients and who were committed in working with the victims of these disorders.

We had to have a unit specifically geared to treating anorexia nervosa and bulimia patients. Treating them on a general psychiatric unit led to certain problems. Some psychiatric patients who feel they are doing the right thing will eat or help dispose of the anorexia nervosa patient's unwanted food and liquid supplements. Trying to control a bulimic or help one stay in control is all but impossible. It is easy for the bulimic to have foods brought in from the outside. Also, there is generally a lot of food on a psychiatric unit—patients sometimes return from a day pass with their favorite cakes or cookies. Some patients of anorexia can manipulate psychiatric patients to stand guard at their room door so they can exercise.

174

In group therapy, eating disorder patients feel isolated. Other psychiatric patients cannot understand someone who simply refuses to eat or someone who vomits after eating. Consequently, they receive little or no understanding from other patients and retreat further into their isolation. In some cases, the psychiatric patients begin to feel that the eating disorder patients think they're special. The staff spends a good deal of time just trying to settle misunderstandings.

Eating disorder patients need a group therapy setting in which they can receive feedback from others who can relate to what they are expressing rather than negative feedback from those who can't. I could go on and on about the problems of treating eating disorder patients within a larger general psychiatric population, but I think the ones I've mentioned will help you understand why Dr. Larocca saw the need for an eating disorder unit. I am extremely pleased to have been a part of its beginning.

Eating disorders patients can recover, but it takes time. The hospital nurse's role in that treatment is extremely important. Utilizing a team approach of physician, therapist, dietician, with the nursing staff as coordinators, is an effective approach. It helps maintain a structured environment and helps the eating disorder patient to regain control in a healthy way.

As soon as a patient is admitted, it is important to obtain a thorough nursing history. The first assessment to make is measuring the patient's motivation: did the patient come at the insistence of the parents or other significant persons? "What brought you here today?" is a good leading question. Some answers one might hear are: "I'm scared, I vomited blood this morning," or "I tried to stop this but I can't do it by myself, I need help," or "I passed out this morning and my parents got upset." On the other side of the coin, one may hear, "My parents just brought me here, I don't know what they're upset about," or "My parents think I need to gain weight, but I'm just fine."

Assessment of motivation is important since motivation is an important tool in the treatment process. At times it can be difficult helping to perpetuate motivation. The nurse will always, of course, need to assess for suicidal ideations and depression. The care plan is individualized for each patient since few eating disorders patients fit a stereotyped description.

The goal is the same for all hospitalized patients: to interrupt the destructive behavior that caused hospitalization. Psychotherapy is not begun initially. Rather, food is the treatment of choice. After getting a thorough history, the nurse then explains to the patient the treatment program and the policies of the unit. In a sense the nurse should imply that the treatment team is in charge until the patient is able to regain control. It is important that the nurse relay this message in a supportive attitude. A punitive attitude has no place in treatment for eating disorders patients. Many times the patient immediately feels some relief from the pressure she has been under prior to hospitalization.

While in the hospital patients participate in a daily routine. They are expected to eat three meals a day. Food and eating are handled matter-of-factly. When a patient says, "I don't feel like coming to the dining room to eat because I'm really not hungry," the nurse can investigate the symptoms if she feels it necessary. If the symptoms and complaints are vague and seem to be just manipulative behavior to avoid being around food, instruct the patient in a firm manner that she is expected to come to the dining room at meal time.

Eating is her own responsibility, however. Do not coax patients into eating. If the nurse sees someone who seems to be having difficulty, he or she should approach her later and acknowledge the situation. Also, never praise a patient for eating her food.

I remember a patient who on her first day on the unit resisted coming to the dining room for her first meal. This patient had had anorexia nervosa for several years and had been to other centers not geared specifically to the treatment of eating disorders. She was put on hyperalimentation feedings when she refused to eat and then discharged, only to lose the temporarily gained weight and return for more treatment—her weight was severly subnormal.

On her first day, she retreated to her room when the food cart arrived for mealtime. After I approached her she did come to the dining room, but displayed underlying anger. She sat with her arms folded stiffly in front of her, staring at her food without touching it. When the allotted time for the meal was over, she got up and walked briskly out of the room. When I indicated to her my concern and asked if we could talk, she turned on me and said with anger that while we could make her come to the dining room we could not make her eat. Maintaining a calm and supportive tone, I told her that eating was her responsibility and that no one was going to make her do it. I acknowledged how difficult it would be for her, I also emphasized that everyone else in that dining room was having a difficult time but was trying hard. At that, she whirled around and stomped away.

Later that day she came back and in a much calmer tone told me that she had been angry with me, but that it had nevertheless been a turning point for her. She went on to say that she had never stopped to think that everyone else was experiencing the same fear and anxiety at mealtime, and was trying to do something about it. By pointing this out, I had helped her to realize that getting well was something she was going to have to do for herself. "I'm not saying that I'll eat everything on my plate at the next meal, but I've become aware of what I have to do to help myself."

Nurses provide support, not sympathy. Our message to the patient is "I'm here to help you with your problem, but you have to want that help for yourself. I will support you, but I will not support your illness."

Patients who are observed exercising but who don't need the exercise are confronted with their behavior. Such activity may take the form of constant walking up and down the halls or some other area on or off the unit. This is a compulsive behavior they cannot stop. If suggestions of substitute activities fail to control the walking, such patients may have to be placed on bedrest. Because they quickly figure out the times routine night rounds are made and can burn a lot of calories between bed checks, certain patients might require extra monitoring during the night. One benefit which results from having eating disorder patients together on one unit is that those who are progressing well in the program tend to police the others and may alert nursing staff about peers who are in need of more monitoring.

Most of our patients are weighed every morning, although some are weighed once a week. Their weight is never told to or discussed with them. The nurse must be careful of her facial expressions and manner when a patient is making positive gains, particularily the patient with anorexia. A remark such as "you're getting some meat back on those bones, your face is starting to fill out," or "you're really starting to look better," or "you are making good gains, you gained a whole pound today," only instills fear in the patient with anorexia. Her interpretation is "I'm fat, I'm out of control." It may be necessary at some point during their weight gain to remove their jeans and have the family substitute more realistically sized clothing for them.

Nurses need to be aware of the various techniques patients use to make the scale go up in their favor. We have found tube socks tied around waists with size D batteries tucked inside, underpants and bras stuffed with numerous objects, weights concealed in hands, jewelry hidden in socks. The patient, when discovered, is confronted in a supportive way away from other patients. It is also a common behavior for a patient with anorexia to drink large amounts of water during the night. We have found the best way to counteract this behavior is to have them weighed in a hospital gown only, and to have them empty their bladders prior to weigh-in. Still, some patients will manage to get water. In some severe cases we have had to remove their bed from a water supply at night.

Understand that although the patient is aware of what she is doing it doesn't mean she can stop. One patient told a nurse that she was relieved that she was finally caught drinking large amounts of water during the night because it was getting painful trying to hold it in. Yet, even with the discomfort she was unable to stop until we took measures to help her.

The personal belongings of all patients are also checked thoroughly on admission by the nursing staff for food, laxatives, diuretics, diet pills, etc. If it is suspected that such items are in someone's possession, a room search may be necessary, although some patients will voluntarily turn over to the staff "illegal" purchases made in a weak moment while out on a day pass.

Patients with bulimia can require constant monitoring for binging. Upon admission to the hospital many will decide to eat as little as possible—you need to be observant for this behavior because they are simply setting themselves up for a binge without realizing it. Do not allow food brought in from the outside or food not eaten at mealtime to be taken to the room. Any overdependence on the staff must be dealt with also. The nurse has to help the patient to take control and to be able to recognize that she can do it.

One interesting case involved a 22-year-old girl who did quite well on her first admission, only to have a severe relapse some time after discharge. She lived a distance away and was unable to utilize the support systems provided. On the second admission, she did well initially and seemed in control when suddenly she began to be demanding on the staff. She had reached a point at which she knew what she had to do for herself, but she still wanted her dependence on the staff. She was afraid to let go, afraid of another failure.

We discovered that she was going to other floors of the hospital with her off-unit privileges and eating food from the food carts. She was restricted to the unit. She then began measures to try to sneak additional food from other units onto her floor. The nursing staff used exhaustive means to monitor her, but she accused them of not caring because they didn't stop her from binging. She demanded more restrictions and held the staff responsible for her behavior—behavior which in fact was her way of saying, "I'm scared to give up my illness and exercise my own control, because I know I'll fail. I'm hopeless." We had to help her realize that she could indeed take control and that being scared was okay.

One evening she managed to sneak approximately 10 small containers of ice cream from the food cart in the nursing core area and purposely marched by the nurses station with the containers cradled in her arms for all the staff to see. We decided to take a risk and see what she would decide on her own to do. She knew we cared since we all had been so much involved in her treatment. We knew she felt our concern, yet we also knew that it was time for her to recognize her own strengths and take responsibility.

The risk paid off. In a few minutes she came back up the hall still carrying the ice cream. She approached her nurse and handed over the containers inquiring why she wasn't stopped. The nurse replied, "because I knew you could stop yourself." It was important for this particular patient to recognize and use the strengths which she had acquired during her hospitalization.

I think this case helps to illustrate how closely the nursing staff must work with these patients and how important it is to have dedicated and trained professionals make up that staff. I would not advocate trying the above approach with every bulimic patient, however. As I mentioned earlier, each case is different and treatment should be individualized.

It is best to have patients who vomit or exercise stay in the dining room after their meal for a certain length of time. Even if they need to go to the bathroom after eating they are asked to stay in the dining room for approximately 45 minutes. If they insist it is an emergency, a staff member will accompany them to the bathroom where they need to be monitored—many can vomit in silence. We encourage a patient to come to us when she feels the urge to binge or vomit and while we spend time helping her to verbalize her feelings, the urge will most likely pass. The difficulty is for the patient to be able to come to the staff before giving into the urge. Many will call the unit while on a pass when the urge to binge becomes overwhelming and, if talking for awhile doesn't seem to help, we tell them to come back to the unit.

Patients with anorexia who are refractory will many times require NG tube feeding. The patient is always informed this will have to be considered if she cannot change her behavior. We favor NG tube feeding over hyperalimentation because it is less traumatic, has fewer complications, and for the patient who gains privileges, is easier for mobility.

When NG tube feeding is ordered by the physician, the nurse explains the procedure to the patient and the tube is passed in the usual procedure. Usually, if you have a good rapport with the patient, there is no difficulty in getting the tube down. Many patients will request a particular nurse to pass the tube. For patients who have not yet formed any type of trusting relationship it really won't matter who passes the tube, and the presence of two nurses may offer some support to the patient.

Do not offer sympathy—offer reassurance and support. It is best to explain the procedure and then go on calmly and professionally. If you hesitate, they hesitate. Most patients will say later, "I knew it would come to this and in some way I'm relieved."

Tube feeding is continuous and accompanies the three daily meals and liquid supplements. We have found it advantageous to provide a bedside commode for patients on tube feedings, since this will eliminate 50 trips a shift to the bathroom—trips which can mask attempts to exercise or to vomit. For those on tube feedings who have to stay in bed a puff pad is ordered, in order to prevent skin breakdown—especially around the coccyx. Sensitive skin areas also need to be checked frequently.

The nurse will also want to check patients often for exercising while in bed and, since they eat their meals in their rooms, check too for food rolled up in napkins and stuffed under mattresses, inside luggage and articles of clothing. If the urine in the bedside commode appears to be a strange color, check what fluids the patient was given on her tray and find out if she poured them into the commode before getting alarmed. Most times patients are honest—again, it depends on the nurse's manner in confronting this behavior.

It is important to keep bed linens and the bedside commode clean. Offer patients a washcloth before meals and bring their oral care to the bedside before breakfast. While on tube feedings they may be able to gain privileges such as the right to wash their hair, to take a shower instead of a bed bath, or to eat meals in the dining room. All tube feeding patients do attend group therapies, taking their tube feeding apparatus with them. Many patients will decorate their machine with balloons and bows and even give it a name. The nurse will need to check the machine often, however, many patients soon learn how to regulate the rate and turn it off. Some will even disconnect the tubing and allow the fluid to run into a trash can, tissues, bed linens, or onto the floor if nothing else is handy.

Be aware also of the importance of checking for residuals after tube feeding is instated. Many patients have some difficulty with absorption in the beginning, so follow your hospital's procedure for this complication. Watch for diarrhea, vomiting and constipation. It may be necessary to change to a more hypertonic feeding solution. Patients may request throat lozengers to suppress hunger. Be suspicious of any prolonged use and arrange an ENT consult to determine if continued complaints of sore throat are valid. Remember, these patients are hungry.

Working with eating disorder patients requires a nurse who has a definite interest in this type of patient and illness. Burn-out can occur quickly. The nurse also needs to have some understanding of eating disorders, but I believe that if the interest is there the understanding comes easily. They reach out to their nurse in their struggle. When they get anxious and scared they come to their nurse for reassurance and support. The nurse spends time talking with them and listening to them verbalize their feelings. The nurse become the sounding board for the patient's pent-up rage.

Throughout treatment, it is also essential that the nurse recognize his or her own feelings. While working with these patients nurses will feel anger, pity, helplessness, many frustrations, and, many times want to give up. It is imperative that the staff meets on a regular basis with the physician. Feelings can be ventilated and shared with colleagues.

With education, confrontation and support nurses help these patients to explore their feelings, build their self-esteem and realize their self-worth.

I would now like to give some signs and symptoms of anorexia nervosa and bulimia which may be seen:

*Anorexia Nervosa*

1. Emaciated appearance

2. Hyperactivity
3. Denial of hunger
4. Failure to see themselves as emaciated
5. Over-sensitivity to cold temperatures
6. Amenorrhea
7. Numerous rituals at mealtime. Cutting food into tiny pieces—
   re-arranging food on plate to make it appear they have eaten.

*Bulimia*

1. Darkened or discolored teeth
2. Swollen parotid glands
3. Scars on the knuckle of forefinger
4. Going to bathroom immediately after eating
5. Irregularity of menstruation
6. Arrythmias

## REFERENCES

Larocca, Felix E.F., An inpatient model for the treatment of eating disorders, The Psychiatric Clinics of North America, June 1984.

Lehman, Allie, Emancipation by Emaciation, The Canadian Nurse, November 1982.

McNamara, Rhonda, The Role of the Nurse at the Bedside, The Canadian Nurse, November 1982.

CHAPTER 13

# Anorexia, Bulimia, and Obesity in Adolescence: The Sociocultural Perspective

**Gwen Weber Burch and**
**Paul H. Pearson**
Today's adolescents are exposed to psychologically sophisticated media—e.g. television and magazine commercials. These sociocultural messages may be primary factors in the increasing prevalence of eating disorders. They may confuse adolescents who are trying to establish an ego ideal self. They add stress and conflict in a society where themes of success, independence, and egocentrism dominate personal feelings of inadequacy, isolation, and future uncertainties. This chapter discusses some of the social culture factors that influence adolescents today and identifies those specific factors thought to have an influence upon the potential development of eating disorders.

A multidimensional model that includes the context of social cultural influences best illustrates the complex nature of eating disorders. The individual's psychobiology, system influences of the family, and the individual's perceptual interpretations of peer and social relations, all contribute to the development of an eating disorder. Although the epidemiology of eating disorders does reveal associated social cultural risk factors—e.g., age, sex and socioeconomic status—it does not define the other specific etiological mechanisms within the individual's life that makes them more vulnerable toward developing an eating disorder than other individuals.

## INCREASE OF EATING DISORDERS

The impact of serious eating disturbances is now high enough to be considered a significant health problem. Current data demonstrates the continued increase in the incidence of anorexia nervosa and bulimia. For example, recent surveys give the prevalence of anorexia to be 1–4% of teenage females[16, 29] and for bulimia to be present among 12–20% of surveyed high school and college females.[26] Obesity occurs among 11–21% of adolescents.[12, 18, 27, 36]

To date there are no large epidemiological studies to show the incidence of bulimia in the general population.[24] Recent reports have shown an increase of binge-eating and self-induced vomiting among young college women of normal weight.[7, 26, 43] Hawkins and Clement[28] found that 3.5% of a sample of 255 college women engaged in self-induced vomiting. Button and Whitehouse[7] found among their female sample (N-466) from a technical college that 39% of this group engaged in self-induced vomiting.

Other large population studies have demonstrated an increase of anorexia nervosa.[31, 42] High risk populations of young girls were surveyed by Crisp et al.[16] They found a prevalence of one severe case of anorexia in approximately every 200 girls under the age of 16 in private schools, one in 100 among girls age 16–18 in private schools, and one in 250 of all adolescent girls in both private and public schools. One in every 150 Scandinavian adolescent women[35] were found to suffer from anorexia.

Schwartz et al.[39] recently discussed the current dilemma of efforts to provide reliable data on the prevalence of bulimia. They did agree with findings which demonstrated its increased prevalence. They believed, however, that improved record keeping, the absolute numerical increase in the adolescent population, and the increased awareness by the public and professionals influenced the estimated number of eating disorders now reported. They recently found 5,000 patients reported in studies[40] as compared to perhaps 250 cases described in literature up until 1950.

## SEX DISTRIBUTION

Females continue to far exceed males in being identified as having an eating disorder. In fact, women account for 90–95% of all eating disorder cases.[2, 30] The frequency of male cases has been shown to have decreased or remained the same,[6,20] except in Russia where the distribution of those hospitalized increased to one male to every five females.[22] One could hypothesize that male eating disturbances are less likely to gather attention or are related to physical training programs associated with athletics. They are perhaps more socially acceptable, therefore, and not as apt to be clinically identified as a disorder.

## SOCIAL CLASS DISTRIBUTION

Anorexia nervosa among women has repeatedly been found in the past to be of greater incidence in upper social classes.[5, 16, 30] In recent years, however, it appears to be more equally distributed in all social classes. There is no good data on the incidence of bulimia, however, the increased prevalence found among college women surveyed possibly reflects the middle, upper socioeconomic attitudes towards achievement, success, etc. Studies on the effect of the social environment on obesity are conflicting. Of the two largest North American studies, one found obesity increased in a higher socioeconomic class compared to a lower socioeconomic class—except for late adolescent females[9]—while Stunkard et al.'s studies (covering only white populations) found increased obesity in lower socioeconomic classes. They reported 29% of lower-class girls were rated obese as compared with only 3% of the upper-class girls.[41] Males identified with eating disorders do not show such social class distributions.[15, 32]

## SOCIOCULTURAL DEVELOPMENTAL TASKS OF ADOLESCENCE

Adolescence marks the period of development that moves the child through a series of physical, emotional and intellectual stages as he or she matures. Rapid physical changes and pubescence cause a greater awareness of one's sexuality, physical capacity, and social presentation. Sociocultural mores establish standards for these processes and prescribe "ideal" role models which the adolescent strives to achieve.

Adolescence may be inherently more difficult for females than males. Bardwick[1] found girls are not often significantly stressed until puberty while boys are more likely to experience many preadolescent social-development crises. The social norms for female psychosocial sexual development have changed so substantially over the past thirty years that the current social norms are unclear and potentially threatening to the adolescent female. Crisp[11, 14] has suggested that anorexia reflects a "phobic avoidance" of the conflicting issues given to young females' psychosexual maturity. McKenzie's research has suggested that starvation for the woman with anorexia represents her effort to stay a child. McKenzie sees this as an effort to remain closer to the father rather than an effort to avoid adult sexual relationships.[34] Other young women seek to hide sexual physical changes through obesity. While avoiding such sexual issues is not the only motivation present, the physical self can become the focal point of the struggle to cope with conflicting demands.[1]

During adolescence, the developmental tasks of emancipation and establishing a self-identity dominate the social codes for a successful adolescent experience. The youth becomes a more active participant in his or her achievements and moves from familial dependence towards social independence. Social standards for sexual expression, sex role behavior and identity are integrated into one's own perceptions and attitudes. A confident sex role identity is often sought by a trial and error process. An idealized adult model is formulated.

Young women soon discover the current contradictory roles and expectations that affect all women in modern society. If they lack sufficient psychological resources to face such ambiguous or contradictory female role definitions, the turmoil over traditional and modern values for women causes anxiety. There is the potential desire to become a "wonder woman" who seeks to achieve both domesticity and vocational achievement. A sense of failure occurs if this is not accomplished. The delicate processes of self-expression in heterosexual relationships causes fear and uncertainty. Such male-female relationships become the complex entities where issues of self-actualization occur heterosexual relationships intensify the fears of either "losing oneself" in a relationship, or to suffer the potential loss of the relationship in order to maintain personal autonomy. Success, independence, self-confidence, and self-sufficiency as reflected in a male oriented society are experienced by many women as isolation and loneliness.[25]

Such social, interpersonal, and personal dilemmas create confusion and a sense of inadequacy if these developmental issues are not resolved. Ensuing fears create regression, rigidity, pseudoconfidence or other compensations. The struggle to become independent as socially prescribed while actually feeling fearful increases vulnerability in relationships.

When feeling "out of control" the young woman uses available coping mechanisms in an effort to manage the perceived, and often real, threat to her emerging identity. If it is impossible to control or master that which is painful or threatening, then an effort is made to gain control over those facets of life that are possible to control. Establishing a greater sense of security through compulsive, disciplined behavior or rituals in a specific, often restricted environment helps to alleviate the anxiety. Others cope by submitting to such pressures and instead let go—perhaps to over indulge, regress or to escape these growing-up responsibilities.

Any other added stress may contribute to the potential development of an eating disorder. A loss or separation from a significant other, a problem in handling some extreme emotion, or trying to deal with some prolonged conflict increases the likelihood of a disorder. As Wooley and Wooley[46] observed, for many women weight management becomes a symbol of control for other areas of personal functioning. Obsessive self-discipline in restrictive eating habits reflects the symbolic regaining of mastery over one's self. Loss of control—e.g. binging, or binging and purging behaviors—often leads to self-destructive behaviors. All too often the search for quick pleasures or rigorous discipline fail. This results in increased feelings of depression, self-depreciation, and a repeated "loss of control" even more profound than before. This added fear of helplessness leads to an addictive obsession that can become all consuming and further thwart both self-fulfillment and maturity.

Food often becomes a friend as well as an enemy to these young women. Ritualistic eating habits may become a preoccupation for good self-performance and an effort to achieve perfection.[17] Social ascriptions—especially those enhanced by family themes about food and dieting—exacerbate the likelihood that a woman will resort to behaviors so prospectively safe and pleasurable yet so obstensibly threatening to one's physical shape. The binge for immediate pleasure and the purge to escape potential weight gain initially may be experienced as a panacea for those deprivations in one's personal development. Self-restricting dieting behaviors are reinforced personally and are socially perceived as assets of self-discipline and control. For example, Branch and Eurman[4] found at least 50% of the relatives and friends of patients with anorexia "admired" the appearance of the patient and "envied" their self-control and discipline around food. The thinness gained from restrictive eating is socially reinforced with the current trends in women's fashion. It all appears positive at the onset of such behavior.

Some young women indulge in overeating behavior and become overweight or obese. The prevailing negative stereotypes associated with obesity in culture affect females much more than males.[45] Their obesity may provide protection for them from social relationships, sexual intimacy, and competition with the cultural female idea promoted in the media. The ambivalence of obesity causes frustration and often leads to extreme dieting efforts: abuse of laxatives, diet pills, diuretics, and many other forms. Once there is weight loss the individual often will give in to an impulse binge—an "I deserve it" indulgent consumption. The prospective regaining of body weight reinstates the depressed feelings and sense of loss of control.

# FAMILY DETERMINANTS

The family is the medium through which social codes are interpreted by the child. Family themes, or rules about diet and food may be a significant influence in the development of an eating disorder. Many families are found to have abnormal attitudes about eating and food and have concerns about weight issues.[5] The adolescent eating disturbance may be a metaphor of these family messages or symptomatically serve as a source of helplessness, power, control, manipulation, or provide the opportunity for the individual to withdraw or isolate themselves from family stresses or enmeshed relationships.[35]

Often the individual with the eating disorder is struggling with rigid parental expectations over conformity, perfections, achievement and compliance to the family's quest for upward mobility. The difficulty in expressing oneself, emancipating or disengaging from the overprotective environment, and personal tendencies to suppress or internalize anxiety in an effort to comply with social codes leaves the adolescent feeling isolated, uncared for, and helpless.[35] Food serves as a means to express individual assertion, gain attention, and indirectly gain control of the family in an effective manner that enables her or him to remain dependent, yet to have a personal sense of independence.

Other environmental influences have been described in those families with individuals who have an eating disorder. Family environments are often egocentric and chaotic and yet function with a conventional facade of normality.[5] Members are expected to comply, deflect tensions and deny their self-expression to maintain family harmony. Often family codes emphasize achievement, success, perfectionistic performance, and self-discipline. The mind over body is a sign of self-discipline and control. Physical appearance is viewed as important for one's successful image. Fathers are often appearance conscious and aspire for their daughter to be physically fit and beautiful.[5] Mothers often feel competitive towards their daughters or sense a personal lack of worth. Their general sense of inadequacy is compensated for with authoritarian styles of parenting which can smother the child.[5] The potential for the daughter to become triangulated in the possible "loveless" marriage increases the risk of added family problems. The eating disorder can become a stabilizing force in the family's interactions and relations and the victimized adolescent prevented from emancipating herself.

Dietz[18] studied the social and family environment of obese infants, children and adolescents. The risk for obesity in childhood increased when there were obese parents and the child was either an only child or younger child in a large family. Parents were found to often be possessive, overprotective and discouraged the child from developing a separate identity. Excessive feedng and overprotective measures may be compenstory acts from insecure parents. Food may symbolize love, security, and satisfaction.[5] Increased parental age, a single parent household, and separation also increase the likelihood of obesity.[18] The family interactions that focused on the child's obesity were often stabilizing factors.[5]

In general, family interactions and attitudes towards food, diet, and physical appearance may influence the development of an eating disorder in adolescent children. There does not appear to be any one specific family constellation or parent-child relationship that causes eating problems. A variety of variables—culturally and individually determined—predisposes an adolescent towards an eating disorder. The dynamic interactions of all family members and their respective roles in relation to each other account for the developmental processes that either enhance the youth development or deter it. These symptoms are used to maintain the existing equilibrium among family member relations.

## OTHER CULTURAL DETERMINANTS
### Fear of Becoming Fat

In an era where threats of inflation, nuclear war, increased violent crime, and poverty persist, 38% of the American public (N-500) told pollsters that what they feared most in the world was "getting fat."[10] These feelings are established early in life. Studies utilizing reference tests show normal children consistantly rank obese children below children with other obvious physical deformities.[18] This discrimination is further demonstrated by college acceptance rates that are significantly lower for obese adolescent girls than for girls of normal weight.[18]

The public now spends more than ten billion dollars a year at weight control businesses. Women—whose bodies naturally have more fat content than men—are especially preoccupied with body image and the desire to be thin. (50th percentile girls go from 7% total body fat at age 10, to 17% by age 17, while 10-year-old males go from 3% to 8% by age 18.[8]) A study in the February, 1984 issue of *Glamour* magazine, found that 75% of the respondents felt "too fat." Sixty six percent believed that they should diet even though only 25% were over weight—45% were actually underweight. Only 6% of those 33,-000 women surveyed were "very happy" with their bodies.

Such a national mania for thinness distorts women's perceptions of their own bodies. As Chernin[10] denotes, "We have entered an era of cultural life when everyone is preoccupied with a woman's body but few women, whether fat or thin, feel comfortable living inside the body they possess. (p. 35) Women live out their lives in these bodies as if they were enemies, struggling against them, and inflicting penances upon them . . ." (p. 149) Crisp[13] has described anorexia as a "fat phobia" in which there is the intense drive to resist those impulses of gluttony and culinary consumption that the culture has branded as evil, taboo, or repulsive.

Some vocational selections increase the likelihood of eating disorders among youth. Career pressures to maintain a thin shape and a higher incidence of anorexia have been correlated among models and dance students.[21] Weight control has been suggested to be one of the few areas of women's lives where actual competition among women has been encouraged or fostered.[46]

## THE MORAL IMPERATIVE - SELF CONTROL AND WEIGHT

Anthropologist Margaret McKinzie has pointed out that the fear of fatness (central to both anorexia nervosa and bulimia), may arise at least in part from a culture that sees obesity "As one symbol of failure to achieve elemental moral virtues, e.g., self-control."[34] Being slender is essential for self-confidence and success. She points out that in earlier times glutony was simply considered a sin. Today it has been medicalized into a preventable disease: "The price paid for the medicalization of moral problems, however, is high. In exchange for removing the stigma of sin the cost is accepting the diagnosis of inadequate will power . . . There are few wounds to rival that of being seen as incompetent in achieving moral restraint."[34]

McKinzie contrasts this with those cultures where people of high social status are fat—i.e., Pacific islanders. There it would be difficult to convince any one that being fat was a sign of moral failure. In most Western societies today, however, it would be hard to convince most people otherwise. Our culture defines an adult as "Self-controlled, competent, morally responsible, rational, productive, and independent. The obese contradict every one of these central American values."[34]

McKinzie also feels contemporary society has, in this area, become "More puritan than the puritans. In striving for self-control and in feeling guilty when it eludes us, we have a fear of pleasure . . . There is ambivalence about enjoying food, guilt follows in an instant after the slightest indulgence . . . People (e.g. the anorectic) demand unrelenting control of themselves."[33]

## DRIVE FOR THINNESS

The image of the ideal female shape has changed over the past 50 years. Current fashion now emphasizes a lean, tubular body shape. As the Dutchess of Windsor popularly noted, "You can never be too rich or too thin." A thin body shape is considered by women to be the most salient aspect of physical attractiveness.[3] Socially sensitive young women become desperate for a positive idealized self, image and social approval. They resort to extreme measures in efforts to control their body size and achieve thinness. Such cultural standards have a greater impact upon women than men.[44] Youth, success, positive personality attributes, athleticism, nonreproductive sexuality, and a kind of androgenous social independence are all symbolized in thinness (comparisons of the centerfolds of Playboy magazine and candidates for Miss America's over the previous twenty years show the consistent trend of thinner women as the "idealized" standard).[23]

## DIETING

Dieting has become a socially accepted approach to achieve ideal thinness. There has been an increase of public information on dieting. Garner,[21] for example, found an increase of dieting articles in women's magazines. Dwyer et al.[19] found that 61% of high school women had dieted and 37% were dieting on the actual day of the survey, some through extreme measures such as fasting, excessive use of diet pills, laxatives, etc. Ninety five percent of the memberships in diet organizations are women.[10] Little social regard has been given to the factual data that quick weight reduction strategies have been unsuccessful for most women. Approximately eighty-five percent of those who reduce quickly regain the lost weight and actually tend to gain back more.

## CHANGE IN EATING HABITS

Social eating habits have altered among society-at-large. Many social experiences and group activities center around food. The recent changes now offer more opportunity for disturbed eating patterns to develop. Family meals shared together are no longer a ritual in many households. More food is being purchased in restaurants or fast food places, and more prepared foods are available for a "quick to fix" meal.

Eating has become a primary recreational, social activity especially among young people. Eating alone is often described by many single individuals to be one of the most stressful activities of living alone. There is more opportunity not to eat regularly. The potential to develop unhealthful eating patterns—overeating, having a "binge," and identifying social significance to one's eating—is much easier to do in the present environment.

## EXERCISE AND PHYSICAL FITNESS

Ninety five percent of health spa memberships are women.[10] They promise a "lean slender look" through exercise and diet, and reinforce the current values of exercise and fitness. Women have learned that increased exercise reduces "ugly" body fat, and helps "lose" those unwanted pounds. "The more the better" becomes the motto for many figure conscious young women. Anorectics are known for their often extensive, rigorous exercise regimen.

Recent legislation has also provided adolescent women with more equal opportunities to develop their physical skills in athletic areas. Individual and group competitive sports activities have increased. The training of these young women becomes a rigorous, disciplined activity that encourages strict weight control and physical training. Dieting or bulimic behaviors are often used to control weight and are even taught by coaches. For example, Cathy Rigby described in a recent article in

*People* magazine[38] her binging and purging up to six times a day as a means to maintain her weight throughout her career as a gymnast. The increased emphasis and opportunity for young adolescent women to become involved in athletic and sports activities has increased the potential for eating disorders.

## CONCLUSION

A combination of factors contribute to the development of anorexia nervosa, bulimia, and obesity. Biogenic and psychological vulnerability, family relationships and their generated stresses, and current sociocultural pressures together make a profound impact upon the individual adolescent's adaptative responses. The increased pressures to achieve complex developmental tasks when the social codes—especially for young women—are more diverse creates uncertainty.

While it is difficult to prove scientifically, most authorities seem to agree that there has been a real and significant increase in the prevalence of anorexia nervosa and bulimia in the past decade. Since there is no reason to postulate an increase in biogenetic vulnerability, we must look to other factors in an effort to account for this increase. This chapter has explored some of the sociocultural factors forced upon families and the adolescent female during her struggle with the developmental tasks necessary to achieve maturity.

## REFERENCES

1. Bardwick, J. (1971). *Psychology of women: a study of bio-cultural conflicts.* New York: Harper and Row.

2. Bemis, K. M. (1978). Current approaches to the etiology and treatment of anorexia nervosa. *Psychol. Bull.,* 85:593–617.

3. Berscheid, E., Walster, E., & Bohrnstedt, G. (1973). The happy american body: a survey report. *Psychology Today,* 1:119–131.

4. Branch, C. H. H., & Eurman, L.J. (1980). Social attitudes toward patients with anorexia nervosa. *Am. J. Psychiatry,* 137:631–632.

5. Bruch, H. (1973). *Eating disorders.* New York: Basic Books.

6. Bruch, H. (1978). *The golden cage.* Cambridge: Harvard University Press.

7. Button, E. J., & Whitehouse, A. (1981). Subclinical anorexia nervosa. *Psychol. Med.,* 11:509–516.

8. Carruth, Betty R. and Iszler, Jacelyn. (1981). Assessment and conservative management of the overfat adolescent. *J. Adolesc. Health Care,* 1:289–299.

9. Center for Disease Control. (1972). *Ten-State Nutrition Survey 1968–1970.* Center for Disease Control (DHEW Publication No. HSM 72–8131. Atlanta.

10. Chernin, K. (1981). *The obsession, reflections on the tyranny of slenderness.* New York: Harper Colophon Books.

11. Crisp, A. H. (1965). Some aspects of the evolution, presentation and follow-up of anorexia nervosa. *Proc. R. Soc. Med.,* 58:814–820.

12. Crisp, A. H., Douglas, J. W. B., Ross, J. M., et al. (1970). Some developmental aspects of disorders of weight. *J. Psychosom. Res., 14,* 313–320.

13. Crisp, A. H., (1970). Premorbid factors in

adult disorders and weight with particular reference to primary anorexia nervosa (weight phobia): a literature review. *J. Psychosom. Res., 14,* 1–22.

14. Crisp, A. H. (1980). Sleep, activity and mood. *Br. J. Psychiatry,* 137:1–7.

15. Crisp, A. H. & Toms, D. A. (1972). Primary anorexia nervosa or weight phobia in the male: Report on 13 cases. *Br. Med. J.,* 1:334–338.

16. Crisp, A. H., Palmer, R. L., & Kalucy, R.S. (1976). How common is anorexia nervosa? A prevalence study. *Br. J. Psychiatry,* 218:549–554.

17. Dally, P. J. (1969). *Anorexia nervosa.* New York: Grune and Stratton.

18. Dietz, Wm. (1981). Obesity in infants, children, and adolescents in the United States. Part II. *Causality Nutrition Research,* Vol. 1, pp. 117–137, 193–208, 289–301.

19. Dwyer, J. T., Feldman, J. J., & Mayer, J. (1970). The social psychology of dieting. *J. Health Soc. Behav.,* 11:269–287.

20. Garfinkel, P. E., & Garner, D. M. (1982). *Anorexia nervosa: a multidimensional perspective.* New York: Brunner/Mazel.

21. Garner, D. M., & Garfinkel, P. E. (1980). Socio-cultural factors in the development of anorexia nervosa. *Psychol. Med.,* 10:647–656.

22. Garner, D. M., Garfinkel, P. E., & Bemis, K. M. (1982). A multidimensional psychotherapy for anorexia nervosa. *Int. J. Eating Disorders,* 1:3–64.

23. Garner, D. M., Garfinkel, P. E., Schwartz, D., & Thompson, M. (1980). Cultural expectations of thinness in women. *Psychol. Reports,* 47:483–491.

24. Garner, D., Garfinkel, P., and Olmsted, M. (1983). An overview of sociocultural factors in the development of anorexia nervosa in Darby, P., Garfinkel, P., Garners, D. and Coscima, D. *Anorexia Nervosa, Recent Developments in Research.* New York: Alan R. Liss, Inc. pp. 65–82.

25. Gilligan, C. (1982). *In a different voice.* Cambridge: Harvard University Press.

26. Halmi, K. A., Falk, J. R., & Schwartz, E. (1981). Binge-eating and vomiting: a survey of college population. *Psychol. Med.,* 11:697–706.

27. Hamptom, M. C., Huenemann, R. L., Shapiro, L. R., et al. (1966). A longitudinal study of gross body composition and body conformation and their association with food and activity in a teen-age population. *Am. J. Clin. Nutr.,* 19:422–435.

28. Hawkins, R. C. & Clement, P. F. (1980). Development and construct validation of a self-report measure of binge eating tendencies. *Addict. Behav.,* 5:219–226.

29. Hill, O. W. (1977). Epidemiologic aspects of anorexia nervosa. Advan. *Psychosom. Med.,* 9:48–62.

30. Jones, D. J., Fox, M. M., Babigan, H. M., & Hutton, H. E. (1980). Epidemiology of anorexia nervosa in Munroe County, New York: 1960–1976. *Psychosom. Med.,* 42:551–558.

31. Kendall, R. E., Hall, D. J., Hailey, A., & Babigan, H. M. (1973). The epidemiology of anorexia nervosa. *Psychol. Med.,* 3:200–203.

32. Marshall, M. H. (1978). Anorexia nervosa: dietary treatment and re-establishment of body weight in 20 cases studies on a metabolic unit. *J. Nutr.,* 32:349–357.

33. McKenzie, M. (1979). Fear of Fatness, the pursuit of self-control and the distrust of pleasure. Unpublished, personal communication.

34. McKenzie, M. (1983). Self control and moral responsibility, competence and rationality: obesity as failure in American culture. Unpublished, personal communication.

35. Minuchin, S., Rosman, B., & Baker, L. (1978). *Psychosomatic Families.* Cambridge: Harvard University Press.

36. National Center for Health Statistics. Height and weight of youth 12–17 years. *U.S. Dept. of Health, Education and Welfare Pub.,* No. HSM 73:1606.

37. Nylander, I. (1971). The feeling of being fat and dieting in a school population: epidemiologic, interview investigation. *Acta. Sociomed. Scan.,* 3:17–26.

38. People Magazine, October 22, 1984.

39. Schwartz, D. et al. (1984). Eating disorders and the culture. In P. Darby et al., ed., *Anorexia nervosa, recent developments in research.* New York: Alan R. Liss, Inc. pp. 83–94.

40. Schwartz, D. M., & Thompson, M. G.

(1981). Do anorectics get well? Current research and future needs. *Am. J. Psychiatr.,* 138:319–324.

41. Stunkard, A., D'Aquili, E., Fox, S., & Fillion, R. D.L. (1972). Influence of social class on obesity and thinness in children. *J. Am. Med. Assoc.,* 221:579–584.

42. Theander, S. (1970). Anorexia nervosa, a psychiatric investigation of 94 female patients. *ACTA Psychiatric Scand.* (Suppl) 214:1–194.

43. Wardle, J., & Beinart, H. (1981). Binge eating: a theoretical review. *Br. J. Clin. Psychol.,* 20:97–109.

44. Wooley, O. W., Wooley, S. C., & Dyrenforth, S. R. (1979). Obesity and women. II. A neglected feminist topic. *Women's Studies Int. Q.,* 2:81–92.

45. Wooley, S. C. & Wooley, O.W. (1979). Obesity and women. I. A closer look at the facts. *Women's Studies Int. Q.,* 2:67–79.

46. Wooley, S. C., & Wooley, O. W. (1980). Eating disorders: obesity and anorexia. In Brodsky A, Hare-Mustin R. (eds): *Women and psychotherapy: an assessment of research and practice.* New York: Guilford Press.

## CHAPTER 14

# Current Treatment of Obesity

by
Pauline S. Powers, M.D.
and
Alexander Rosemurgy, M.D.

## INTRODUCTION

The physiological hazards of significant obesity are well known and include predisposition to hypertension, diabetes mellitus, gout, gallstones, joint disease, and possibly coronary artery disease. Two large epidemiological studies—the Framingham Study[1] and a seven nation cross-cultural study reported by Keys and colleagues[2]—have documented an association between increasing obesity and increases in systolic and diastolic blood pressures. Insulin regulation is also involved in fat metabolism: clinically relevant alterations begin to occur in patients who are more than 25–35% above ideal body weight (IBW). Four percent of patients 25–35% above IBW have the diagnosis of diabetes mellitus and 10% of patients 35–45% above IBW have diabetes mellitus.[3] Although it is widely believed that mild obesity predisposes a patient to atherosclerosis this has not been proven. Those mildly obese individuals with high blood pressure, diabetes mellitus or elevated cholesterol levels are more likely to develop coronary artery disease. But those without these risk factors may be no more prone to coronary artery disease than age-matched normal weight individuals.[3,4]

Patients more than 100% above ideal body weight (so called "morbid" obesity) are prone to an impressive number of physiological complications including coronary artery disease, cerebrovascular disease, and diabetes mellitus. There is also an increased incidence of osteoarthritis, lower extremity venous disease, the Pickwickian Syndrome and cholelithiasis. The mortality for such patients is reported to be twelvefold higher for patients between the ages of 25 and 34, sixfold higher between the ages of 35 and 44, and threefold higher between the ages of 45 and 54.[5] This increased mortality rate helps explain why morbidly obese patients older than 65 are seldom encountered.

The psychological hazards of obesity in a culture obsessed with slenderness are important. More than two decades ago, Canning and Mayer[6] demonstrated discrimination against obese girls applying to college. The attitudes of normal weight children toward obese children has been shown to be more censorious than toward any other group of handicapped children.[7,8] The attitudes of physicians and other health personnel is similarly highly critical. It has been postulated that the downward social mobility of many obese individuals may be partly due to the discrimination they experience.[9,10]

Another important psychological facet of obesity is body image. Body image is the perception that one has of one's self and the sum of emotional attitudes toward that perception. Many, but certainly not all, obese individuals perceive themselves as larger than they are in reality and have very negative attitudes toward their bodies.[11] Patients who have been obese as children or adolescents and who subsequently lose weight, often retain a distorted perception of themselves as very obese.[12] Leon and colleagues[13] have recently shown that the attitudinal aspect of body image tends to improve in obese individuals who have lost weight even though the perceptual aspect may remain unchanged—that is, they may continue to view themselves as large and ungainly even though they may have a more positive attitude toward themselves.

In the last few years there has been an increased awareness that weight loss and its maintenance are issues that must be addressed separately.[14] Most programs focus on weight loss although there have been attempts—especially in certain behavioral programs—to address the issue of maintenance. Some self-help groups—notably TOPS (Take Off Pounds Sensibly)—have separate groups (KOPS, Keep Off Pounds Sensibly) for members who have achieved their target weight and are striving to maintain these losses. The Protein Sparing Modified Fast (PSMF) developed by Bistrian[15], and Linder and Blackburn[16] includes a significant emphasis on weight maintenance.

The hazards of certain treatments for obesity have been recognized for decades—nutritionists have an extensive body of knowledge about the characteristics of fad diets and the likelihood that weight lost on these diets will be regained. More subtle dangers have been identified, however. Although most of the documented physiological hazards of obesity do not occur until a person is 25–30% or more above IBW, the intense preoccupation with slenderness and the widespread dieting among normal weight and near normal weight individuals may be partly responsible for the near epidemic prevalance of bulimia (perhaps as high as 10–15% of college co-eds[17]) and the twofold increase in anorexia nervosa[18]. The belief that slenderness confers additional health benefits is a difficult idea to dispel. The outcry which greeted the 1983 Metropolitan Height and Weight Tables[19]—in which desirable weights were higher than those in the 1959 tables—is only partly accounted for by methodological criticisms of the collection and description of the data. After all, the insurance company earns its money by insuring people most likely to be long-lived. Keys[4] has reported on a ten year follow-up of 12,763 men is seven countries around the world and found that the lowest mortality rate during that period was among that group which was slightly above average weight. These and other data argue for a revision of our cultural beliefs about "ideal" body weight.

## CLASSIFICATION SYSTEMS

There are multiple classifications systems for obesity detailed elsewhere[20] but division into mild, moderate and severe (or "morbid") is a practical system that has implications for treatment. Although there are well-documented circumstances in which fat content is more or less than expected from various height-weight tables, these are useful as preliminary guides. Mild obesity is defined as 30% or less above the norms of the 1983 Metropolitan Height and Weight Tables[19]; moderate obesity is 30–100% above these norms; morbid obesity is greater than 100% above the norms. The special circumstances which require more accurate determination of fat content include patients under 20 or over 50 years of age, those in unusual occupations or with unusual amounts of exercise. For example, several decades ago, football players were shown to be overweight but underfat.[21] Similarly, sedentary individuals at normal weights may have an excessive fat content.[22] Patients with repeated weight fluctuations or binge-eating and purging behavior may also have fat contents different than expected from the height-weight tables.

An improvement in determining actual fat content can be attained with the body mass index (BMI) which is defined as weight divided by height squared ($W/H^2$) for men and weight divided by height raised to 1.5 power ($W/H^{1.5}$) for women. Of the relative weight indices, it appears to be the most valid and reliable index of obesity and shows the least correlation with height and the highest correlation with independent measures of body fat.[23,24]

# EVALUATION

The initial evaluation is crucial in selecting an effective treatment plan and the procedure followed in the Eating Disorders Clinic at the University of South Florida will be briefly described. The evaluation includes a psychiatric and medical history, mental status examination, physical examination, estimation of fat content, tests for the presence or absence of body image disturbances and selected laboratory tests.

## Questionnaire

Patients are asked to complete a questionnaire which elicits socioeconomic data and information on the history of their obesity and attempts to lose weight. The questionnaire serves several purposes. Patients who complete a lengthy questionnaire are more likely to keep their appointments and certain information can be collected efficiently and quickly.

## Psychiatric History

A psychiatric history including a mental status examination should be an integral part of the evaluation process for several reasons. First, the patient may be in a precarious psychological balance which depends upon remaining obese—weight loss may precipitate a crisis unless factors which determine this balance are detected and considered. Second, there may be conjoint psychiatric disorders, such as schizophrenia or affective disorder, which may influence the effectiveness of treatment unless recognized and managed. Third, psychological responses to previous weight loss efforts need to be known. Stunkard and Rush[25] have described a "dieting depression" during the first few weeks of weight loss. These patients have a euphoric mood and extravagant ideas about the effects of weight loss followed by weeks or months of depression. Psychotic reactions have been reported following weight loss[26]. The nature of the weight loss regimen may be important—one morbidly obese patient in our clinic hallucinated whenever his calorie intake fell below 1,000 calories per day.

Fourth, patients who have disturbances in body image may have psychiatric disorders. Stunkard and Mendelson[11] postulated that emotional disturbances seemed to be a necessary prerequisite for body image disturbances. This may account for the fact that weight loss The results of the psychoanalytic study of obesity reported by Rand and Stunkard[27] lend support to this idea—obese patients in psychoanalysis not only lost weight but had an improvement in body image. There are data, however, which go against the thesis that emotional disturbances are a pre-condition for a body image disturbance. Large percentages of women from the normal population have been found to have disturbances in body image[28]. This may represent sampling error but may also indicate that body image disturbances are related to cultural beliefs as well as to psychopathology.

A fifth reason for a psychiatric evaluation is that there are two syndromes associated with obesity which may be primarily psychiatric disorders. The first, "the binge-eating syndrome"[29], is characterized by impulsive episodic overeating of huge quantities of food within a short period of time. Episodes are usually triggered by stress and patients feel guilty and dysphoric afterward. This condition may be identical to, or a variant of, the syndrome bulimia as defined in the DSM-III[30]. "Thin fat people" described by Bruch[31] may have a similar condition. The second condition that may have significant psychiatric ramifications is the night eating syndrome[32]. This condition is characterized by evening hyperphagia, insomnia, and morning anorexia—this pattern has been associated with a poor prognosis in weight loss programs and has been associated with significant psychopathology.

## Medical History and Physical Examination

In eliciting the history of obese patients it is important to determine weights at various ages as well as significant life events which preceded or followed weight gain or weight loss. Since there is evidence that juvenile-onset obesity (i.e., obesity which began in or continued through adolescence) may be more refractory to treatment than adult-onset obesity, it is important to determine when obesity began. Weight loss efforts as well as successes or failures at maintenance efforts need to be determined. Activity levels need to be determined since it has been known for decades that a sedentary life style fosters the development of obesity.

The signs and symptoms of various rare diseases that can result in obesity (for example, Cushing's syndrome, hypothyroidism, pituitary or hypothalamic tumors, and various ovarian conditions) should be evaluated, although fewer than 5% of patients have an identifiable organic cause for their obesity[33]. Patients with headaches or visual symptoms should be evaluated for hypothalamic or hypopituitary syndromes with a visual field examination. Pituitary tumors occasionally present with obesity and bitemporal hemianopsia. Obese patients with hypertension and plethora should have a dexamethasone suppression test to rule out Cushing's syndrome. A normotensive mildy obese patient with lethargy, cold intolerance, coarse dry skin, slow speech or hypoactive reflexes should be evaluated for hypothyroidism. Hirsute or amenorrheic females should be evaluated for the virilization syndromes. Finally, obese youngsters may have one of the rare genetic syndromes associated with obesity such as the Prader Willi syndrome.

Perhaps even more important is the accurate detection of the much more common consequences of obesity (for example, diabetes mellitus, hypertension and coronary artery disease). Diabetes can be suspected in the obese patient who heals poorly, has skin infections or vaginal monilia or who complains of polyuria or polydipsia. On physical examination, fungal skin infections may also be present or there may be evidence of peripheral neuropathy (for example, a decrease in vibratory sense). Hypertension can be identified accurately using a sphygmomanometer wide enough to compress approximately one-third of the length of the arm and which contains a rubber bag long enough to cover the entire circumference of the arm.[34] Other conditions in which obesity is a contributing factor are gout, menstrual irregularities and reproductive problems and abnormalities of heart size and function.

## Estimation of Fat Content

Measurement of the thickness of certain skinfolds provides a simple, relatively accurate, office estimate of fat content. A skinfold caliper is used to determine the biceps, triceps, suprailiac and subscapular skinfolds. The age, sex, weight and the sum of these four measures can be used to determine fat content using tables designed by Durnin and Womersley.[35] Normal fat content is difficult to define, but figures often given are approximately 25% for women and 18% for men at age 25[36].

### Psychological Testing

Although there are a number of psychological tests which can provide valuable information about a patient's functioning and personality style, we have found the Beck Depression Inventory[37] to be useful. Similarly, tests which detect perceptual or attitudinal disturbances in body image can be helpful in deciding if patients will require conjoint psychiatric treatment during any weight loss program. The Open Door Test devised by Simonson[38] is a simple office procedure: the patient is asked to open the door as wide as necessary to just squeeze by sideways and then the patient's actual width is determined. Patients who make significant overestimation or underestimation errors have a perceptual disturbance in body image. Attitudinal disturbances can be detected by asking the patient how he feels about how he looks or there are a variety of self report measures such as the Body Parts Satisfaction Questionnaire[39] or the Fisher Body Distortion Questionnaire[40] which can be administered.

### Laboratory Testing

Screening for diabetes mellitus should be done in any patient more than 30% above ideal body weight. Fasting blood sugars greater than 140 mg/dl on more than one occasion is diagnostic of Type II Diabetes[41]. Although it is unusual for hypothyroidism to cause significant obesity, thyroid screening should probably be done routinely since many patients suspect that "glandular" problems are contributing to their obesity. Triglyceride and cholesterol levels should be obtained on all patients. Any other laboratory testing should be obtained on an individual basis when signs or symptoms dictate.

## TREATMENT OF MILD OBESITY
### Patient Selection

Some patients who are less than 30% above IBW probably require no treatment. The physiological hazards of obesity generally do not occur until this level and few weight loss regimens for this group have proven to produce and maintain weight loss. Repeated dieting followed by weight gain may result in an increase in total body fat content even if the starting and final weights are the same.[42,43] This is especially true on fad diets followed for short periods (two or three weeks) in which the weight loss is primarily lean body tissue—weight regained quickly may not return to the lean body stores but may be stored as fat. Thus, at the next weight loss effort the patient may have a greater fat content and the same diet may result in less weight loss (although it is still likely to be primarily lean body tissue that is lost). The weight regained may then result in a further increase in fat stores. A vicious cycle may be set up in which ever more stringent diets result in less weight loss each time. Thus, a mildly obese patient who is in no physiological danger and who has maintained a stable weight for several years may be best advised to avoid dieting. Some of these patients may benefit from a moderate exercise program which may result in improved vitality and perhaps some weight loss with fewer risks. The patient who follows this advice may need assistance in coping with the rigid cultural expectations for thinness.

Some midly obese patients may need a weight loss regimen if they are progressively gaining weight or if they have serious physiological complications such as hypertension or diabetes. Careful analysis of weight loss efforts in the past may suggest which strategy to recommend. Patients who develop a dieting depression on stringent calorie restricted diets may benefit from a graduated exercise program. Brisk walking for one or two miles 4–5 times per week combined with a modest reduction in calories may be useful.

## Self Help Groups

Self help groups such as Weight Watchers, Take Off Pounds Sensibly (TOPS) or Overeaters Anonymous (OA) may be helpful for some mildly obese patients. Weight Watchers is a commercial group which prescribes a specific calorie intake and recently this group has introduced the Quick Start Program, which has fewer calories. Both Weight Watchers and TOPS have attempted to incorporate some of the principles of behavior therapy into their programs. Generally, TOPS has been more willing to allow scientific scrutiny of their programs[44]. TOPS is a non-profit organization, unlike Weight Watchers. Overeaters Anonymous[45] follows many of the principles of Alcoholics Anonymous—the major premise of this group is that its members are compulsive overeaters who feel powerless over food. Like Alcoholics Anonymous this group has twelve steps which are suggested as a program of recovery. These include admission that the person is powerless over food and a belief in the power of God to restore sanity.

Local chapters of all three of these parent self-help groups vary tremendously and these differences need to be taken into account when a patient is referred. A group with a willingness to accept medical input into a dietary or exercise regimen is most likely to be effective. Some groups have a distinctly anti-medical stance and patients who require specific treatment in addition to a self-help group may be caught between the recommendations of the physician and the behests of the group.

The effectiveness of self-help groups in promoting weight loss or maintenance of weight loss remains to be established. The report by Levitz and Stunkard[44] in which the usual TOPS program was combined with behavior therapy resulted in a loss of less than 2 kgs. This finding is discouraging but may underestimate the potential effectiveness of these groups. The TOPS members in this study were more than 30% above IBW, may have already failed at several other programs and therefore may have been more resistant to treatment. Also members may have already lost some weight by the time the study began. It may be that such self-help groups are best suited for those who are mildly obese and who have not failed at other treatments.

### Behavior Modification

Behavior modification methods have been widely used in treating mildly and moderately obese individuals in brief treatment programs.[46-48] Studies utilizing behavior modification techniques have shown a consistent modest benefit in producing weight loss although generally the programs have been short (twelve weeks or less). Often patients do not lose to IBW and weight losses are not necessarily maintained. Nonetheless, there have been important benefits from the behavior modification studies of obesity. First, the more rigorous design and report methodologies generally characteristic of behavior therapists have increased scientific interest in the topic of obesity. Second, from behavior studies it has become clear that weight loss and weight maintenance are different problems.[14,49]

There have been attempts to produce "treatment packages" in which behavior therapy is combined with cognitive therapy or other alternative ways of coping with emotions (such as relaxation therapy or assertive therapy). These have not generally improved effectiveness of weight loss, perhaps because each patient needs an individualized prescription.

Another defect in the behavior therapy studies is that generally the programs have been so short that on a conservative weight loss regimen patients would not be expected to lose dramatic amounts of weight. Most programs have not attempted to continue for a year or more which may be necessary for clinically significant weight losses. Brightwell[50] has described a study of obese veterans in which patients participated in a study for a year and has found some indications that those who lost weight to IBW were more likely to maintain their losses than those who did not achieve IBW. This result suggests the possibility that obesity may be similar to anorexia nervosa in that achieving IBW and maintaining it for relatively long periods of time (perhaps six months or a year) may be necessary for long-term positive outcomes in terms of weight maintenance.

There are four major aspects of behavior programs for obesity.[51] *First,* the behavior to be controlled is described and documented, often via a daily food intake or exercise diary. The patient records the time he ate, what he ate, the amount and the stimuli associated with eating. The stimuli include the environment, people present, emotional feelings and whether or not he or she was hungry. *Second,* the stimuli that precede eating or exercising are identified by analyzing the diaries. Several sequences may be identified. Anxiety may be a stimulus which results in eating and leads to a calmer mood—a consequence that reinforces the likelihood that the overeating may reoccur. *Third,* a plan is designed to control the act of eating. This includes altering what has been described, probably inaccurately,[52] as "the obese eating style" (rapid ingestion of large bites of food and hypersensitivity to environmental food cues) by eating slower, taking smaller bites and confining eating to certain situations. Patients are advised to eat in one place and to isolate eating from all other activities. These techniques are designed to decrease the power of certain environmental cues which have come to be associated with eating. New discriminative stimuli are developed to assist in the development and maintenance of new eating patterns. The patient may be asked to purchase a distinctive place setting or eat only in certain places. *Fourth,* the consequences of the altered behavior are modified. Small changes in eating behavior are reinforced with individualized immediate rewards. Likewise, small increments in exercise are reinforced. The patient may award himself a certain number of points for eating slowly, eating at certain times or in certain places or for walking up a flight of stairs or parking the car farther from his work place. These points can be converted into concrete rewards such as clothes or books. Although praise for changing eating habits has been found to be effective, it is often not as spontaneous as criticism for poor eating habits.

## MODERATE OBESITY

Patients with moderate obesity (i.e. 30–100% above IBW) are more likely to develop hypertension, diabetes mellitus or other complications and thus treatment should be considered for this group. The Protein Sparing Modified Fast (PSMF) is a regimen which may prove to be effective in assisting this group exchange moderate obesity for mild obesity and thus decrease the likelihood of developing significant physiological complications.

### History

Bloom, in 1959,[53] studied patients on a short-term total fast who lost clinically significant amounts of weight with no apparent complications. Subsequent studies demonstrated that total fasts produced dramatic quick weight reduction associated with the loss of hunger. But later studies found that the weight was quickly regained.[54] Also, several deaths were reported during fasting or refeeding but these generally occurred during or following total fasts lasting longer than two months.[55]

In addition, with the total fast there is a significant loss of lean body mass.[43] In an attempt to design a regimen that would be both safer and produce primarily loss of fat tissue rather than lean body tissue, protein and electrolytes were added to the fasting regimen. Bistrian[15] and Blackburn and Lindner[16] have carefully investigated the Protein Sparing Modified Fast in medically well-supervised research settings. Bistrian[15] and Vertes and colleagues[56] have reported that in this situation, death attributable to the PSMF did not occur in over 2,000 patients.

Unfortunately, in 1976, the Last Chance Diet Book[57] became a best seller and led to the widespread use of liquid protein products that were used without medical supervision. Furthermore, these products provided 300–400 kilocalories per day as collagen hydrolysate, a protein low in biologic value. One hundred thousand patients had used these products by the end of 1977 and 60 deaths among this group had been reported to the Centers for Disease Control.[58,59] Seventeen of these deaths were attributed to the diet.[58,60] In the next year the Federal Drug Administration issued warnings about the diet and the well-supervised, scientifically-credible Protein Sparing Modified Fast fell into disrepute along with the Last Chance liquid protein diet.

Against this historical backdrop, it is emphasized that the PSMF must be undertaken under closely monitored, informed medical supervision and should include all the elements of the regimen outlined below. Furthermore, we still consider it a research technique—much remains to be understood about the physiological and psychological consequences of the fast. And, perhaps most importantly, if such a regimen is to remain potentially useful, further efforts must be directed towards maintenance of weight loss achieved.

## Patient Selection[15,16,61]

Patients should be more than 30% above IBW (since there is a risk to the treatment that probably outweighs the risk from mild obesity) and less than 100% above IBW (since morbidly obese patients are probably more safely and effectively treated with gastric partition procedures). More conservative measures (for example, supervised weight loss programs and/or exercise regimens) should have been tried and have failed. Children and adolescents should be excluded since, despite attempts to minimize loss of lean body mass, there is some. These losses may interfere with growth. (Lebow[48] has described novel behavioral approaches to the treatment of obesity which are probably more suitable for children.)

Pregnant and lactating women should neither fast nor diet. Patients with a history of psychosis or depression associated with dieting should be excluded or carefully monitored by a psychiatrist during the fast. Patients with any of the psychiatric conditions or complications noted earlier should be seen conjointly by a psychiatrist. Patients with gout, hyperuricemia, or a family history of gout should either be excluded or, if on a fast, should be monitored closely. Patients with a recent myocardial infarction or cerebral vascular accident should be excluded since hypotension occurs in almost all patients and may decrease perfusion to the heart or brain. Patients with chronic renal disease should not be on the PSMF. Hepatic disease is a relative contraindication and depends on the type of disease. Fatty liver disease that occurs in obesity may improve with weight loss. Cancer, Type I diabetes, lithium therapy and overt psychosis are absolute contraindications.

## Nutritional Content of Protein Sparing Modified Fast

Different groups have proposed either formula feedings containing high quality protein with vitamin and mineral supplements[16] or animal protein (meat, fish or fowl) served in food form.[62] The former regimen has been more commonly used and its proponents have argued that it is easier and promotes compliance. Proponents of animal protein contend that patients are more likely to learn to cope with conventional foods. Although both approaches have been equally effective, there has not been a comparison of possible relative merits[61]

It has been assumed that maintenance of lean body mass is equivalent to the preservation of body protein and that changes in lean body mass can be estimated by determining nitrogen balance. Although this assumption may be valid, measuring nitrogen balance is difficult and influenced by a number of factors including the amount and quality of dietary protein, age and sex of the individual, hormones and electrolyte content. Bistrian and colleagues[63] have recommended that relatively large amounts of protein be used—1.5 grams of protein per kilogram of IBW. They believe that nitrogen balance is likely to be achieved more rapidly with this amount of protein.

For the moderately obese man with an IBW of 70 kilograms, a typical prescription utilizing conventional animal protein would be as follows:

(1) The patient is advised to consume 105 grams of protein per day; the ounces of animal meat required are calculated by using the following formula: 1 ounce = 7 grams of protein. Thus 15 ounces of animal meat is divided into three to five servings.

(2) Fluid intake of at leat 1500 to 2000 cc (eight or more 8 ounce glasses) per day is required.

(3) The patient is advised to use table salt at each meal in order to consume three to five grams of sodium chloride.

(4) three grams of potassium (prescribed as 25 meq. potassium twice a day)

(5) multivitamin capsule daily containing both iron and zinc.

(6) calcium supplementation of 400–800 miligrams.

## Monitoring During the PSMF

Prior to starting the PSMF a complete blood count, urinalysis, SMA6, fasting SMA18, chest x-ray (PA and lateral) and EKG are obtained. Each three months on the fast the SMA6 and 18 are repeated. Serum uric acid is repeated each week for the first two months and then monthly. If uric acid levels rise above 10 mg. percent (normal 4–8 mg percent) for two successive weeks, drug therapy is instituted until serum uric acid levels return to normal for two successive weeks. Electrolytes (SMA6) are determined monthly unless there are some signs or symptoms of electrolyte depletion in which case they are monitored weekly. If serum potassium falls 10% below the lower limits of normal, potassium supplementation is increased. If sodium falls 20% below the lower limits of normal sodium chloride supplements are increased. If hypokalemia is suspected (even if serum potassium is normal) a strip EKG is obtained in which the most prominent T waves occur (usually standard lead 2) to determine if there has been a decrease in the amplitude of the T waves. If potassium or sodium chloride supplementation is required, the supplementations may be decreased to the usual levels after two successive weeks of normal serum levels.

Fasting blood sugar, serum albumin/globulin (A/G) ratio, BUN, serum creatinine and a complete urinalysis should be obtained monthly. If serum A/G ratios fall, patients should be questioned to determine if they are taking the prescribed amount of protein since some patients may attempt to speed up weight loss by consuming less protein. If they are consuming less than prescribed, they should be encouraged to follow the diet and A/G ratios determined weekly until they return to normal—levels are then checked monthly.

If mean corpuscular hemoglobin concentration drops 10% below lower limits of normal, 5 grains of ferrous gluconate three times a day is prescribed and when this measure returns to normal the additional supplementation is discontinued. If serum creatinine or BUN rise above 10% of the upper limits of normal, patients should be reminded to drink 8 to 10 eight-ounce glasses of fluid per day. Values usually return to normal.

At weekly visits patients are weighed, lying and standing blood pressures are obtained and urine is checked for ketones. During the weight loss phase, the patient is seen weekly and is required to participate in individual or group nutritional counseling. Through such education the patient begins to learn and practice the principles of behavior modification. Patients are also encouraged to engage in an exercise program. The initial behavior modification in this phase can be directed toward substitution of activities for eating and can be utilized to reinforce increases in exercise.

### Complications

In a well supervised program, side effects are usually mild.[61] Orthostatic hypotension is common but easily corrected with salt supplementation and adequate fluid intake. Constipation is common and can be controlled either with mild laxatives or by the addition of vegetables with low carbohydrate content. Cold intolerance is common but dry skin, brittle nails, hair loss and dizziness have been observed to occur in fewer than 10%[64] of patients. Women may have menstrual irregularities. Patients may have bad breath from the ketonemia.

### Integration into Comprehensive Treatment Program

Bistrian[15] and Blackburn and Lindner[16] have advocated a three phase program. In the first phase, patients are not only evaluated, but must pass a series of screening tests that these investigators think may select patients more likely to succeed. During this phase, patients are asked to keep a diary and also are started on a 1200–1400 calorie diet. Patients are not allowed to proceed to the second phase unless they keep their diary and until weight changes correspond with their dietary records. Patients meet in group sessions several times weekly in this phase for education in nutrition, exercise and behavior modification. When patients have begun an exercise regimen and passed tests in nutrition and behavior modification they are permitted to enter the second phase of the program.

During this second phase the patient follows the PSMF and dramatic weight loss occurs. The careful monitoring described earlier occurs in this phase and patients continue in their behavior modification and nutrition education groups. This phase in their program lasts an average of seventeen weeks but in other programs has lasted up to twenty-four weeks.[64]

211

Phase three is the refeeding and weight maintenance phase. Refeeding occurs over 4–6 weeks using milk, milk products, vegetables, fruit, lean meat, fish and fowl. Simple sugars are introduced gradually to prevent an abrupt increase in fluid.[65] During the refeeding and maintenance phase, there is an emphasis on behavior modification methods and nutritional counseling as well as increased physical activity.

## Efficacy of Weight Loss

Wadden and colleagues[61] have reviewed eight major studies using very low calorie diets, some of which have included small amounts of carbohydrates. These studies included at least 25 patients each. Treatments lasting at least twelve weeks produced average weight losses of 18.7 kg. Shorter treatment (4 weeks) resulted in losses of 7–10 kg[66] and longer treatments resulted in greater losses of 31–41 kg.[64,67] These reviewers note that these losses are much greater than with other conventional non-surgical treatments such as supervised diets or behavior modification which generally produce losses of less than 7 kg[68]. There are a number of factors which may result in selection of highly motivated patients including large fees for the programs and required participation in teaching or research programs. Nonetheless, the weight losses achieved with these programs are impressive.

## Maintenance of Weight Losses

Unfortunately, the maintenance of weight losses is not nearly as impressive as the initial weight loss. Fifty-six percent of the patients of Genuth and colleagues[69] had regained more than 50% of weight lost by follow-up at 22 months. The study by Lindner and Blackburn[16] reported the most positive findings with mean weight losses of 67 subjects 20.8 kg; 14.5 kg of the weight lost was maintained at follow-up between 18–24 months later, although 22% of patients were lost to follow-up. Their findings may have important implications for maintenance. Not only did these investigators stress behavior modification techniques in the beginning of their program but they also required certain evidence of capacity to comply with instructions before allowing patients to even begin the PSMF. Since there are hazards associated with this program, it may be that such stringent entrance criteria are justified if weight loss is to be maintained.

### Psychological Responses

Although there are few reports of untoward psychological responses, there have also been few formal studies. Wise and colleagues[70] have suspected a change on the performance scale of the Shipley Hartford in the early weeks of the fast. The changes in cognition in semi-starved volunteers studied by Keys and colleagues[71] may have implications for the PSMF. Cook and colleagues[72] have given the Beck Depression Inventory[37] on a serial basis and found that there were modest improvements. This finding may reflect the euphoria secondary to fasting, perhaps due to a rise in endorphins.

# MORBID OBESITY: DESCRIPTION

Common definitions of morbid obesity are patients 100% or 100 pounds over IBW, or 100% or 100 pounds over "desirable weight for height." Approximately 600,000 Americans are at least 100% heavier than their IBW.[73]

There is an excessive incidence of morbidity and mortality in patients that are morbidly obese. The adjective "morbid" is used to emphasize the serious health hazards associated with extreme obesity. The increased mortality is due to the increased incidence of coronary heart disease, cerebrovascular disease, and diabetes mellitus and its complications.[74] There is also an increased incidence of hypertension, gout, cholelithiasis, osteoarthritis, lower extremity venous disease, Pickwickian syndrome, and endometrial cancer.[74,75] Apart from the medical aspects of morbidity associated with morbid obesity, there is an associated social morbidity. The social morbidity of morbid obesity is ofttimes severe: immobilization, discrimination, social isolation and decreased self-respect are all prominent in patients with morbid obesity.

# MORBID OBESITY; INDICATIONS FOR SURGERY

### Ideal Surgical Procedure

The ideal bariatric operation should be safe with little associated morbidity and no mortality. There should be few longterm sequelae. There should be satisfactory and permanent weight loss. There should be easy reversibility of the operation should late problems develop. Bariatric surgery has been done for more than 15 years, however, and as of yet, no operation completely fits these criteria. There are three general categories of bariatric operations currently being done: gastric partitioning operations, gastric bypass operations, and small intestine bypass operations.

## Risk/Benefit Ratio of Surgery

There is evidence that weight loss in patients with morbid obesity ameliorates or eliminates some risk factors for premature cardiovascular disease, such as diabetes mellitus, hypertension, and hyperlipemia.

Unfortunately, patients with morbid obesity, in general, do not lose much weight in medically supervised dietary programs, or tend to lose weight only temporarily. Additionally the medical consequences of morbid obesity—venous insufficiency, coronary heart disease, cerebrovascular disease, or osteoarthritis—are serious and difficult to treat. Therefore, many think that morbid obesity in and of itself is an indication for surgical therapy.

Patients with morbid obesity are operated upon to decrease their risk of illness and death brought on by their obesity and to improve their quality of life. The premise of surgical intervention is that morbid obesity is a disabling and life-threatening disease and that surgery can bring about significant weight reduction.

## Patient Selection

To qualify for bariatric surgery, a patient must meet several strict criteria. Each patient must weigh 100% or 100 pounds over IBW for at least the last two years and must have failed in a supervised dietary program. Additionally, metabolic causes of obesity must be ruled out. Each patient must have a psychiatric evaluation and demonstrate adequate support to sustain them in the postoperative period. Each patient must resolve to lose weight and to participate in a protocol, which should involve long-term follow-up.

There are extenuating circumstances that enable a person not morbidly obese by strict weight criteria to qualify for bariatric surgery. If a patient is having complications of obesity which could be corrected by weight reduction, then the patient may be considered for bariatric surgery, even though not 100% or 100 pounds over IBW.

Patients are excluded from bariatric surgery if they are alcoholics, psychiatrically unstable, less than 18 or older than 60 years of age, weigh more than 225 kg, have other significant disease (renal failure, inflammatory bowel disease, cirrhosis, active hepatitis, and others), or are prohibitive surgical risks. Patients who are between the ages of 50 and 60 or who are sedentary need to be considered on an individual basis. Patients should also be excluded from bariatric surgery if they fail to grasp the intent of the surgery, if they have food addictions or if they have unreasonable expectations of the surgery. They must comprehend that bariatric surgery is intended to exchange morbid obesity for moderate obesity, not for IBW.

The preoperative work-up should focus on the medical and psychiatric health of the patient. An in-depth medical evaluation is in order, particularly one that identifies surgical risk. Abnormalities that can be corrected preoperatively should be corrected. This may involve treating diabetes, hypertension, or cardiorespiratory disease preoperatively. Weight reduction is ofttimes necessary preoperatively to decrease the operative risks. A patient weighing more than 225 kilograms preoperatively should undergo a medically-supervised weight reduction program until weighing less than 225 kilograms to reduce perioperative morbidity and mortality. Such a program may involve wiring the patient's jaws together to obtain preoperative weight reduction.

The social, motivational, and support makeup of the patient with morbid obesity should be investigated. Also, psychological problems should be addressed preoperatively. If uncorrectable, the patient should be omitted from bariatric surgical protocols. Support mechanisms should be developed for patients undergoing bariatric surgery —they can significantly affect results. Postoperative office visits, for example, correlate well with the amount of weight loss.[76]

Preoperatively it is of paramount importance to appreciate the necessary anesthetic care pre-, intra-, and postoperatively. Airway management and vascular access can be difficult in morbidly obese people. Anesthetic drug metabolism is altered by the patient's size. The frequency and severity of aspiration is increased in morbidly obese patients because they have a high incidence of gastric reflux and are hypersecreters of gastric acid with a low fasting gastric pH and a high fasting gastric volume.[77] Last, patients with morbid obesity are higher anesthetic risks because they tend to have oxygenation problems due to a decreased functional residual capacity and increased closing volumes.

Bariatric surgery cannot be discussed without some attention to the process of consent for operation. Medicolegal problems must be addressed. There must be a clear understanding by the patient that morbid obesity will be exchanged for moderate obesity. There must be a discussion of the risks and benefits of the operation. This discussion is made difficult because the long-term benefits of bariatric surgery are not well understood. The perioperative risks, however, are known and must be made clear to the patient. The intent of the operative procedure, malabsorption or restricted intake, must be understood by the patient.

# MORBID OBESITY: JEJUNOILEAL BYPASS

Small intestine bypass operations have long been utilized in the treatment of patients with morbid obesity. Jejunoileal bypass is the most frequently performed small intestine bypass operation. Jejunoileal bypass operations have been done in more than 100,000 patients to date. Over 12,000 such bypasses have been reported in the literature.

There are two basic types of jejunoileal bypass. They are based upon the type of jejunoileal anastomosis. In one, 35 cm of proximal jejunum is anastomosed in an end to side fashion to the distal ileum, 10 cm proximal to the ileocecal valve.[78] In the other basic type, 30 cm of proximal jejunum is anastomosed end to end to 15, 20, or 30 cm of distal ileum.[79] Here the distal end of the bypassed small bowel segment is anastomosed in an end to side fashion to either the sigmoid colon, transverse colon, or cecum. The jejunoileal bypass that involves the end to end jejunoileal anastomosis is generally preferred because the associated weight loss is generally larger.[80] When the excluded small bowel is drained end to side into the cecum, the end to end jejunoileal bypass is considered the "gold standard" of small intestine bypass operations.

The operative mortality is 0–3%.[79,81] Mortality is usually secondary to myocardial infarction, pulmonary embolus, liver failure, or sepsis. Perioperative morbidity is generally due to wound complications.[78,79]

## Weight Loss after Bypass

After jejunoileal bypass, patients with morbid obesity lose approximately 1/3 of their weight within the first year.[78,81] The weight loss brought about by jejunoileal bypass is thought to be principally due to malabsorption. The foremost cause of malabsorption is diarrhea.

Diarrhea occurs in all patients following jejunoileal bypass and is an expected result. Immediately postoperatively, there are usually 8 to 12 watery bowel movements per day. With intestinal adaptation and medication this may decrease to 3 to 4 semisolid bowel movements per day by the end of the first postoperative year.

There are many causes of diarrhea. There is a decrease in the absorptive surface, a decreased transit time, and an increase in the bile acid content, in the dissaccharide content, and the fatty acid concentration of intestinal chyme.[81]

Malabsorption, however, does not account for all the weight loss after jejunoileal bypass. The stool does not contain enough calories to explain the weight loss. Also involved in weight loss is a decrease in consumption[74], which may be due to an unpleasant association of eating and diarrhea, or may be due to a loss of taste for certain foods.

After 18 months weight loss generally reaches 40 to 50% of the preoperative weight.[81] At this time there may be a small weight gain. This gain is often due to adaptation of the small bowel. This results in a decrease of the malabsorption. Adaptation involves lengthening of the bowel in circuit, villus hypertrophy, increased mucosal blood flow and increased mucosal enzyme activity.[81] At two years, if the operation has not failed, it probably won't—the adaptation is not progressive beyond that point.[81] Eventually, the weight loss is near two-thirds of the excess preoperative weight[74,81], but may be as high as 80%,[82-84] Unfortunately, while no one disputes that a correctly performed jejunoileal bypass will result in weight loss, because adaptation of the small bowel in circuit occurs to a varying degree, weight loss for a given patient cannot be predicted.

### Complications of Jejunoileal Bypass

Most patients have complications after the jejunoileal bypass, many of which are severe.[78,79,81] There is a 30–40% rehospitalization rate within the first year after surgery for treatment of any of the numerous complications associated with this procedure.[78,79] In addition, 58% of the patients undergoing jejunoileal bypass in one series[85] either died, required reversal, had life-threatening complications, or required a major reoperation.

Hepatic dysfunction is the foremost complication associated with this procedure.[78,79] It accounts for 1/3 of all operations in patients following jejunoileal bypass and is the most common cause of reoperation. Hepatic dysfunction may be a nutritionally induced problem, although the exact deficiency is not known. It appears with contracting body cell mass, most commonly at 6-12 months postoperatively, near the time of maximum weight loss. It may be due to protein malnutrition, vitamin malabsorption, fat malabsorption, altered methionine metabolism[86], or carbohydrate/protein imbalance due to the preferential absorption of carbohydrate.[74] It may also be due to a production of a hepatotoxin in the excluded segment of small bowel.[74,81]

Hepatic dysfunction presents itself clinically as lassitude, hepatomegaly and right upper quadrant tenderness on physical examination. The liver injury is not picked up by laboratory examination[74,78,81] although elevated serum bilirubin and depressed serum albumin levels are findings that call for take-down of the jejunoileal bypass.[78] A liver biopsy is needed to diagnose hepatic dysfunction.[74] Fatty degeneration, cholestasis, periportal inflammation, centrilobular fibrosis or frank cirrhosis is seen histologically. Hepatic dysfunction is often successfully treated with IV protein supplements.[87] Weight stabilization[88] or restoration of intestinal continuity usually improves the histologic and biochemical status of the liver.[89] It is fatal in 1 to 3% of the patients.[74]

Fluid and electrolyte imbalances are brought about by intestinal fluid and electrolyte losses associated with diarrhea.[78] Specific losses in volume, potassium, calcium, magnesium, and bicarbonate are often serious and are frequent causes of rehospitalization. The intestinal adaptation that occurs following jejunoileal bypass helps alleviate the seriousness of these losses. Nonetheless, these imbalances are a frequent cause of dismantling the jejunoileal bypass.

Nephrolithiasis is a significant problem following jejunoileal bypass.[78,81] This may occur in 10 to 15% of patients[78,90,91] after jejunoileal bypass. Free fatty acids—which are not absorbed because of the intestinal bypass—combine with calcium causing hyperoxaluria. This leads to nephrolithiasis. Ingestion of calcium salts is often helpful in the treatment of nephrolithiasis.

Specific absorption defects are also a common complication. Specifically, amino acid malabsorption, vitamin malabsorption, and fatty acid malabsorption occurs. While it is the intent of the operation to cause malabsorption, the degree of malabsorption determines the type of malabsorptive complications that develop.

Polyarthralgias are seen in 20% of the patients 3 years after jejunoileal bypass.[81] In 7% of the patients, these are very severe.[78] The specific cause of the polyarthralgias are unknown, although there are some suggestions that this is due to altered 25-OH vitamin D absorption and metabolism. The malabsorption may be due to a decreased intestinal absorption surface, steatorrhea, diarrhea, liver disease, and/ or the blind loop syndrome.[81]

Bowel disorders are a frequent complication of this procedure.[78,87,92] Flatulence and "gas bloat" are also frequent complications. Bowel obstructions can develop, as after any operation, because of postoperative adhesions. Additionally, intussusception of the excluded small bowel can occur, resulting in obstruction. A bypass enteropathy has been described[93] which is probably due to increased bacterial levels in the excluded bowel. This usually begins with the onset of fever and abdominal tenderness. Bypass enteropathy is best treated with antibiotics and can be considered a complication of the blind loop syndrome.[94]

There are other complications associated with jejunoileal bypass which are nonspecific in nature and are presumably due to the deterioration in general nutritional health.[74,87] These include hair loss, dermatitis, muscle wasting, immune complex related kidney disease, and increased lithogenicity of the bile secondary to alterations in bile salt and cholesterol metabolism. Anorectal problems are also common, presumably because of the diarrhea that all patients experience.

Complications of the jejunoileal bypass often require that the bypass be revised or dismantled.[87] Revisions are usually done to correct either inadequate or excessive weight loss. Revisions are now infrequent before dismantling the bypass.

The most frequent complications that precipitate dismantling jejunoileal bypass procedures are hepatic insufficiency, electrolyte or fluid depletion, and severe lassitude or fatigue. While re-anastomosis after jejunoileal bypass is a major undertaking, the mortality and morbidity rate is low, unless the event precipitating re-anastomosis has resulted in a significant deterioration of the patient's health. If the bypass is dismantled—for whatever reason—the weight gain that occurs often results in a final weight that exceeds the pre-bypass weight.[95] If plans are made to dismantle a jejunoileal bypass, consideration should be given to performing a concommitant operation that limits intake.

In conclusion, there are a plethora of serious complications associated with jejunoileal bypass. Because of these complications, jejunoileal bypass procedures have been removed from the routine armamentarium of bariatric surgery. If used, preoperative selection criteria must be strict and patients with preoperative renal disease, hepatic disease, or gastrointestinal disease must be excluded.

### Alternative Intestinal Bypass Procedures

Complications of the jejunoileal bypass may be more common when the jejunoilostomy is constructed in an end to end manner.[94,95,96] This is due to chronic colonic contamination of the bypassed small bowel. Since the bypassed small bowel, or the blind loop, is often implicated in the development of complications after jejunoileal bypass, two proposals to eliminate the functionally excluded small bowel have gained attention.

The first of these is a biliointestinal shunt[97] in conjunction with an end to side jejunoileal bypass. Here the gallbladder is anastomosed to the proximal end of the excluded small bowel.

The other proposal is a biliopancreatic bypass in conjunction with an end to end jejunoileal bypass.[98] This proposal involves a partial gastrectomy with closure of the duodenal stump and reconstruction that uses both a roux-en-Y gastrojejunostomy and distal jejunum. The excluded segment includes proximal jejunum which is anastomosed in an end to side fashion to the distal ileum. With this type of bypass the excluded segment drains the biliary system and the pancreas in a normal anatomic fashion. This latter type of bypass causes malabsorption of carbohydrates and fat while leaving the enterohepatic circulation intact. The ability of these two modifications to eliminate the complications of jejunoileal bypass is under investigation.

# MORBID OBESITY: GASTRIC RESTRICTION PROCEDURES

### Historical Perspective

Gastric restriction operations are used to reduce the volume of food ingested. They have replaced operations aimed at creating malabsorption in the treatment of patients with morbid obesity. Because of their intent, gastric restriction operations require patients to accept the premise of eating less. This type of operation should not be done on patients who are food or cola addicts or alcoholics. A history of ulcer disease or of gastroesophageal reflux may also exclude patients from this type of operation, but this has not yet been proven.

Edward Mason, a pioneer in the field of gastric restriction operations, published a clinical series in the 1960's describing gastric bypass operations for the treatment of morbid obesity.[99] This operation entailed division of the stomach and construction of a loop gastrojejunostomy, 20 mm in diameter, to the proximal gastric pouch, 100 cc's in volume. This operation—developed as an outgrowth of laboratory and clinical experience in the surgical treatment of peptic ulcer disease—resulted in a loss of 42% of the mean excess weight by two years.

This design was altered by Alden[78]—another pioneer in this field—in the late 1970's. He partitioned the stomach rather than dividing it, leaving a 100 cc proximal gastric pouch which was anastomosed in a side to side fashion to a jejunal loop. This modification decreased the morbidity and mortality associated with the initial gastric bypass operation of Mason. Patients undergoing Alden's gastric bypass operation lost weight at about the same rate as patients undergoing jejunoileal bypass operations.[78] Additionally, they returned to energetic health more rapidly and consistently than patients undergoing jejunoileal bypass.

The gastric bypass operation was further modified by Ward Griffin in the late 1970's.[79] He performed a roux-en-Y gastrojejunostomy to a proximal gastric pouch to decrease the incidence of bile reflux gastritis. As with Alden's operation, the gastric pouch was created by high transverse gastric partitioning rather than by gastric division. In a randomized prospective trial, he compared patients undergoing this gastric bypass to patients undergoing a jejunoileal bypass. The weight loss (30% of preoperative weight) by two years after gastric bypass compared favorably with that achieved after end to end jejunoileal bypass. In this series gastric bypass operations were associated with fewer complications.

### Gastric Bypass Procedures: Operative Procedure

Clinical experience with gastric bypass operations reveal they can be done with low operative morbidity and mortality.[100,101] Gastric bypass operations can result in a significant postoperative weight loss when certain principles are followed. A secure partition, a small gastric pouch, and a narrow gastrojejunostomy are essential in producing satisfactory results.[101,102]

A secure gastric partition is best obtained by two applications of a double row stapling device. The gastric pouch should be less than 50 cc's, and possibly as small as 10 to 30 cc's.[82,103] The gastrojejunostomy should be mechanically calibrated to less than twelve millimeters in diameter to promote weight loss.[101] Some[82] have suggested a more narrow gastrojejunostomy (less than 10 mm) to promote additional weight loss. Ideally, it is best when the gastrojejunostomy is reinforced to prevent dilatation.[104] Most commonly this is done by reinforcing the gastrojejunostomy with running prolene suture or with silastic tubing. Silastic tubing reinforcement seems to be associated with the best results.[93,103] Reinforcement of the gastrojejunostomy, however, may be associated with a higher incidence of gastric pouch outflow obstruction.[102,104,105]

Gastric bypass operations have produced rewarding results. Mason[106] and Knecht[107] showed that 60% to 74% of the excess body weight can be lost by two years following gastric bypass operations. Unfortunately, in trying to predict who would and who would not lose weight, only age and weight were found to be accurate predictors of weight loss.[101] Weight loss was greatest in young patients[101,104] and heavy patients.[101] Morbidly obese patients older than 50 years experience less weight loss than younger patients[108], presumably because of decreased caloric requirements brought on by their sedentary nature.

## Gastric Bypass Procedures: Complications

The gastric bypass operations have been associated with few complications, as long as decreased intake is considered an expected result. Patients undergoing this operation do not experience the problems associated with jejunoileal bypass such as diarrhea, fatigue, nephrolithiasis and polyarthritis (Table I)[78,79,87]. The complications associated with gastric bypass operations occur generally in the immediately postoperative period[79], unlike those associated with jejunoileal bypass. Complications associated with gastric bypass operations are many in variety, but few in incidence. The incidence of complications varies with the skill and experience of the surgeon.

Splenectomy—one complication of gastric bypass operations in morbidly obese patients—occurs with an incidence of from less than 1% to approximately 4 to 5%.[78,108]

Wound complications occur with a range of from 2%[78,105], to 25%[79] in morbidly obese patients following gastric bypass operations.

Wound infections are more difficult to diagnose in morbidly obese patients than in patients of normal size. Many of the symptoms and signs of wound infection—pain, erythema, and induration—are not seen in morbidly obese patients. Wound hernias occur with an incidence of from 1 to 5%.[78,79] Associated with wound infection and herniation is an incidence of wound dehiscence that is high for elective surgery, near 1%.[78,105]

Deep venuous thrombosis and pulmonary embolization is also a complication of gastric bypass operations due to the sedentary nature and venous abnormalities of morbidly obese patients. Suprisingly, fatal pulmonary embolization seldom occurs.[109] Most, but not all, surgeons use subcutaneous heparin therapy in the hospital. Many also use compression stockings to prevent venous stasis in the lower extremities. Intraoperative maneuvers such as leg wrappings, leg elevation, and pneumatic compressing stockings are also used by many surgeons to minimize venous stasis and deep venous thrombosis.

In the immediate post operative period, pneumonia and atelectasis are a significant problem. Atelectasis occurs to some degree in all patients, while pneumonia is a clinical problem in approximately 2% of patients undergoing gastric bypass operations for morbid obesity.[110] In general this condition is prevented by, and responsive to, vigorous pulmonary toilet.

Peritonitis in the postoperative period, although uncommon, occurs more frequently following gastric bypass operations than following jejunoileal bypass operations.[87] Since the stomach is no longer divided in the course of gastric bypass operations, this is usually secondary to gastrojejunostomy leaks, which occur in from 1% to 6% of the gastric bypass operations[79,104,105,107]. When peritonitis occurs without evidence of a gastrojejunostomy leak, it is presumed that the antecedent contamination occurred from a transient leak in the gastric partitioning. In general, these leaks and the subsequent peritonitis are difficult to diagnose in morbidly obese patients. Early symptoms and signs include malaise, epigastric or upper abdominal pain, tacycardia, and tachypnea. Physical findings on abdominal examination are quite limited. A chest x-ray and a gastrograffin swallow should be obtained if a postoperative anastomotic leak or partition leak is suspected.

Intra-abdominal and subphrenic abscesses can develop after gastrojejunostomy or gastric partitioning leaks. Their incidence ranges from 2%[107] to 6%.[105] Subphrenic abscesses are more common in patients that have undergone incidental splenectomy, presumably due to the creation of dead space.

Late complications associated with the gastric bypass operation are few as long as it is understood that decreased intake and vomiting with excessive intake is expected.

Bile gastritis is a potential problem following gastric bypass with a loop gastrojejunostomy. Chances of this are minimized, however, if a small gastrojejunostomy is made. The chance of bile gastritis is further minimized when the gastric bypass design includes a roux-en-Y gastrojejeunostomy.

Obstruction of the gastrojejunostomy is an infrequent but serious complication following gastric bypass operations. In general, less than 5% of patients undergoing this operation have this complication.[100] Though nasogastric suction, intravenous fluids, and endoscopic dilatation generally allow this to resolve, reoperation is occasionally required.[100]

Dumping, to some degree, occurs in many patients[104,106] but is clinically significant in few (3%) patients[78] after gastric bypass operations. Dumping symptoms are often felt to be partially responsible for reduced intake in patients after gastric bypass operations and thereby aid in producing long term weight loss.

Reflux esophagitis is also seen after gastric bypass operations, as are marginal ulcers. Both are infrequent complaints, however. Marginal ulcers occur in approximately 3% of patients undergoing gastric bypass.[110] Ulcers in the bypassed stomach are similarly uncommon.[110] The smaller the proximal gastric pouch the less the incidence of stomal ulcers.[101,110,111] Serum gastrin[101] and the gastric secretory response to a meal[112] are reduced following gastric bypass operations for morbid obesity. Gastric bypass operations are not ulcerogenic.

The most common problem that occurs after gastric bypass operations is that of "insufficient weight loss." If "insufficient weight loss" is defined as weight loss of less than 25% of the preoperative weight, then this complication occurs in approximately 6% of the patients.[107] An excessively large gastric pouch, staple line dehiscence and gastrojejunostomy dilatation can result in insufficient weight loss.[105,106] Meticulous attention to detail is the best guard against operative failure.

Metabolic complications other than those associated with weight loss are infrequent with this operation. There have been reports of polyneuropathy, which, in general, have been responsive to thiamine therapy and vitamin B complex repletion.[100] Liver failure, renal failure, electrolyte disturbances, polyarthralgias, arthritis, diarrhea, and anorectal problems are virtually nonexistent. This is not so with jejunoileal bypass.

## Gastric Partition Procedures

Another group of operations designed to decrease the amount of ingested food are gastric partitioning operations. They were devised in an attempt to simplify gastric bypass operations and to eliminate some of the problems associated with gastric bypass operations—anastomatic leaks and dumping—while maintaining intestinal continuity. In general, gastric restriction operations should be designed with the same principles that have proven to be of success in gastric bypass operations. Namely, gastric restriction operations should have a secure partition, a proximal gastric pouch less than 50 cc's, and a reinforced outflow conduit with a diameter of 9–12 millimeters.

Gastric partitioning operations can generally be divided into two groups: first, those with a transverse gastric partition and second, those with a fundus excluding partition. This latter group involves staple lines that parallel the lessor curvature of the stomach, thereby excluding the fundus of the stomach.

Early attempts at gastric partitioning, such as by Mason and Printen[110] in 1971, failed because the proximal gastric pouch was too large and its outflow canal was too wide.

The first partitioning operation of any popularity involved a transverse gastric partition operation. It was developed by Pace and his colleagues[113] at Ohio State. Initially this involved one application of a double row stapling device after 3 staples from the mid portion of the stapler had been removed, thus creating a mechanically calibrated stoma in the mid portion of the transverse staple line. This was associated with a high failure rate until a second double row of staples was added, again with a mechanically calibrated stoma in the mid portion of the transverse gastric partition[114]. Even still, the rate of failure was high unless a liquid diet was consumed for 8 weeks postoperatively.[114] Currently some surgeons use this transverse gastric partitioning operation, with a liquid diet until the goal weight has been reached.[114]

One modification of the transverse gastric partitioning operation

225

involves two transverse applications of a double row stapling device followed by a mechanically calibrated gastrogastrostomy. A further modification described by Laws[115] involves the use of a silastic collar to reinforce the gastrogastrostomy. Results with these modifications— mean initial weight loss near 25%—have not been appreciably better than those with the double row transverse gastric partitioning operation.

Gastric partitioning operations that exclude the gastric fundus seem to have a more desirable success rate. There are currently many gastric partitioning operations that fit the definition of a lesser curvature gastroplasty. The most popular of these is a vertical banded gastroplasty popularized by Mason at the University of Iowa.[106] This operation involves the use of an EEA Stapler to create a hole in the anterior and posterior walls of the stomach. Two double row staple lines are then created between this hole and the greater curvature near the angle of His. Again using this hole a 6.5 cm band of marlex mesh, 1.5 cm wide, is wrapped around a 1.5 cm long conduit along the lesser curve, connecting the small proximal gastric pouch (30–40 cc) to the remaining stomach. This mesh wrapping is overlapped to construct a reinforced conduit with a 5 cm circumference.

Results with the vertical banded gastroplasty have been good in Mason's series[106]. At six months, there has been a 42% loss of excess body weight following vertical banded gastroplasty. This is to be compared to a 38% loss after a similar time period following gastric bypass with a roux-en-Y gastrojejunostomy, reconstruction, and 44% loss after gastric bypass with loop gastrojejunostomy.[106]

## Results of Gastric Partition Procedures

Gastric partitioning operations should lead to results comparable to those associated with gastric bypass operations as long as the same principles that have proven to be of success in gastric bypass operations are utilized in designing gastric partitioning operations. A small gastric pouch, a secure gastric partitioning, and a small (.9 to 1.2 centimeter diameter) outflow conduit from the pouch must be constructed. In general, gastric partitioning operations have not quite matched weight loss results associated with gastric bypass operations. Bypassing the distal stomach, duodenum and proximal jejunum may contribute to weight loss after gastric bypass by adding a component of malabsorption.

Obstacles to successful gastric partitioning are in may ways the same as those with gastric bypass operations. Migration of staple lines are an on-going problem and contribute to morbidity and mortality, although it is low. Another obstacle to successful gastric partitioning operations is gastric pouch dilatation. Enlargement of the gastric out-flow is another obstacle, and seems best treated by wrapping the outflow conduit with polyproplene mesh or marlex mesh. Mechanically reinforcing the outflow conduit with nonabsorbable suture has not proven successful in obtaining conduit diameter.[93]

Significantly, reoperation is required after 10–20% of gastric partitioning operations because of wound complications (2–3%), insufficient weight loss, stomach obstruction, or gastric pouch leaks.[113,116] Complications of gastric partitioning operations seem to be less frequent than complications of gastric bypass operations because an anastomosis is avoided and because intestinal continuity is preserved. If patients overeat, emesis should not be considered a complication but an expected result. Operative mortality approaches 1%.[106,107]

**TABLE I:** Comparison Of Complications Of Jejunoileal (JI) Bypass With Gastric Restriction Procedures

|  | Jejunoileal bypass | Gastric restriction |
|---|---|---|
| Mortality rate (%) | 0-5 | 0-5 |
| Rehospitalization (%) | 33 | 10 |
| Revision rate | 1-25% | 0-10% |
| Conversion | To gastric restriction is common | To JI bypass is rare |
| Excess Weight loss (%) | 70-80 | 60-80 |
| Hepatic failure (%) | 5% | 0 |
| Liver dysfunction | common | rare |
| Liver histology | deteriorates | no change or improved |
| Urolithiasis (%) | 5-20 | rare |
| Cholelithiasis (%) | 36-50 | ? |
| Osteomalacia (%) | Common | rare |
| Diarrhea | common | rare |
| Dumping | minimal | Uncommon after bypass, never after partitioning |
| Electrolyte or Mineral Depletion | common | rare |
| Hypovitaminosis | common | rare |
| Transient emesis | minimal | minimal |
| Marginal ulceration | minimal | 1-2% |

227

## REFERENCES

1. Kannel, W.B., LeBauer, E.J., Dawber, T.R., McNamara, P.M.: Relation of body weight to development of coronary heart disease: The Framingham study. Circulation 35:734–744, 1967.
2. Keys, A., Aravanis, C., Blackburn, H., et al., Coronary heart disease: overweight and obesity as risk factors. Ann. Intern. Med. 77:15–27, 1972.
3. Westlunk, K.: Ten year mortality and morbidity related to serum cholesterol. Scana. J. Clin. Lab. Invest. 30, Supp. 127:1–24, 1972.
4. Keys, A.: Seven countries. A Multivariate Analysis of Death and Coronary Heart Disease. Cambridge, Harvard University, 1980.
5. Drenick, E.J., Bale, G.S., Seltzer, F., Johnson, D.G.: Excessive mortality and causes of death in morbidly obese men. J.A.M.A. 243:443–445, 1980.
6. Canning, H., Mayer, J.: Obesity - its possible effect on college acceptance. N.Eng. J. Med. 275:1172–1174, 1966.
7. Goodman, N., Richardson, S.A., Dornbusch, S.M., Hastorf, A.H.: Variant reactions to physical disabilities. Am. Sociolog. Rev. 28:429–435, 1963.
8. Richardson, S.A., Goodman, N., Hastorf A.H., Dornbusch, S.M.: Cultural uniformity in reaction to physical disabilities. Am. Sociolog. Rev. 26:241–247, 1961.
9. Monello, L.F., Mayer, J.: Obese adolescent girls: An unrecognized "minority" group? Am. J. Clin. Nutr. 132:35–39, 1963.
10. Stunkard, A.J.: From explanation to action in psychosomatic medicine: The case of obesity. Psychosom. Med. 37:195–236, 1975.
11. Stunkard, A., Mendelson, M.: Obesity and the body image. I. Characteristics of disturbances in the body image of some obese persons. Am. J. Psychiatry 123:1296–1300, 1967.
12. Glucksman, M.L., Hirsch, J.: The response of obese patients to weight reduction. The perception of body size. Psychosom. Med. 31:1–7, 1969.
13. Leon, G.R., Eckert, E.D., Teed, D., Buchwald, H.: Changes in body image and other psychological factors after intestinal bypass surgery for massive obesity. J. Behav. Med. 2:39–59, 1979.
14. Stunkard, A.J., Penick, S.B.: Behavior modification in the treatment of obesity: the problem of maintaining weight loss. Arch. Gen Psychiatry 36:801–806, 1979.
15. Bistrian, B.R.: Recent developments in the treatment of obesity with particular reference to semistarvation ketogenic regimens. Diabetes Care 1:379–384, 1978.
16. Lindner, P.G., Blackburn, G.L.: Multidisciplinary approach to obesity utilizing fasting modified by protein-sparing therapy. Obesity/Bariatric Med. 5:198–216, 1976.
17. Halmi, K., Falk, J., Schwartz, E.: Binge-eating and vomiting: a survey of a college population. Psychol. Med. 11:697–706, 1981.
18. Willi, J., Grossman, S.: Epidemiology of anorexia nervosa in a defined region of Switzerland. Am. J. Psychiat. 140:564–567, 1983.
19. Metropolitan Life Insurance Company Health and Safety Division: 1983. Metropolitan height and weight tables, New York, 1983.
20. Powers, P.S.: Obesity. The Regulation of Weight. Williams and Wilkins, Baltimore, 1980, pp 14–26.
21. Welham, W.C., Behnke, A.R., Jr.: The specific gravity of healthy men: body weight divided by volume and other physical characteristics of exceptional athletes and of naval personnel. JAMA 118:498–501, 1942.
22. Keys, A.J., Brozek, J.: Body fat in adult men. Physiolog. Rev. 33:245–325, 1953.
23. Womersley, J., Durnin, G.A.: A comparison of the skinfold method with extent of overweight and various weight-height relationships in the assessment of obesity. Br. J. Nutr. 38:271–284, 1977.
24. Keys, A.J., Fidanza, F., Karvonen, M.J. et al.: Indices of relative obesity, J. Chron. Dis. 25:329–343, 1972.
25. Stunkard, A.J., Rush, J.: Dieting and depression re-examined; a critical review of reports of untoward responses during weight reduction for obesity. Ann. Intern. Med. 81:526–533, 1974.

26. Robinson, S., Winniks, H.: Severe psychotic disturbances following crash diet weight loss. Arch. Gen. Psychiatry 29:559–562, 1973.

27. Rand, C.S., Stunkard, A.J.: Obesity and psychoanalyis. Am. J. Psychiatry, 135:547–551, 1978.

28. Garfinkel, P., Garner, D.: Anorexia Nervosa: A Multidimensional Perspective. Brunner/Mazel, New York, 1982.

29. Stunkard, A.J.: Eating patterns and obesity. Psychiat. Q. 33:284–294, 1959.

30. Diagnostic and Statistical Manual of Mental Disorders (DSM III): 3rd ed. Am. Psych. Assoc., Washington, 1980.

31. Bruch, H.: Thin fat people. J. Am. Wom. Assoc. 28:187–208, 1973.

32. Stunkard, A.J., Grace, W.M., Wolff, H.G.: The night-eating syndrome: A pattern of food intake among certain obese patients. Am. J. Med. 19:78–86, 1955.

33. Douglass, T.S.: Endrocrinological and other uncommon causes. In Powers P.S.: Obesity. The Regulation of Weight, Williams and Wilkins, Baltimore, 1980, pp 81–96.

34. Orma, E., Karvonen, M.J., Keys, A.: "Cuff" hypertension. Lancet 2:51, 1960.

35. Durnin, J., Womersley, G.: Body fat assessed from total body density and its estimation from skinfold thickness: measurements on 481 men and women aged 16 to 72 years. Br. J. Nutr. 32:77–97, 1974.

36. Powers, P.S.: Obesity. The Regulation of Weight. Williams and Wilkins, Baltimore, 1980, pp 1–18.

37. Beck, A.T., Ward, C.H., Mendelson, M., et al.: An inventory for measuring depression. Arch. Gen. Psychiat. 4:561–569, 1961.

38. Simonson, M.: Lecture at conference: The management of obesity. Johns Hopkins Medical Institutions, Feb. 13–16, 1978.

39. Berscheid, E., Walster, E., Bohrnstedt, G.: The happy American body: a survey report. Psychology Today 11: 119–131, 1973.

40. Fisher, S.: Body Experience in Fantasy and Behavior, New York, Appleton-Century-Crofts, 1970.

41. Classification and Diagnosis of Diabetes Mellitus and Other Categories of Glucose Intolerance, National Diabetes Data Group. Diabetes 28:1039–1057, 1979.

42. Ball, M., Canary, J., Kyle, L.H.: Comparative effects of caloric restriction and total starvation on body composition in obesity. Ann. Int. Med. 67:60–67, 1967.

43. Runcie, J., Hilditch, T.E.: Energy provision, tissue utilization and weight loss in prolonged starvation. Brit. Med. J. 2:352–356, 1974.

44. Levitz, L.S., Stunkard, A.J.: A therapeutic coalition for obesity: behavior modification and patient self-help. Am. J. Psychiat. 131:423–427, 1974.

45. Overeaters Anonymous: A program for compulsive eaters. World Service Office, 2190 190th St., Torrance, CA 90504.

46. Leon, G.R.: Current directions in the treatment of obesity. Psycholog. Bull. 83:557–558, 1976.

47. Leon, G.R.: Treating Eating Disorders: Obesity, Anorexia Nervosa and Bulimia. Lewis Publ. Co., Lexington, 1983.

48. LeBow, M.: Child Obesity: A New Frontier of Behavior Therapy. Vol. 12, Springer Series on Behavior Therapy and Behavior Medicine. Springer Publ. Co., New York 1984.

49. Kingsley, R.G., Wilson, G.T.: Behavior therapy for obesity: A comparative investigation of long-term efficacy. J. Consult. Clin. Psychol. 45:288–298, 1977.

50. Brightwell, D.: Grand Rounds, University of South Florida, Tampa, 1984.

51. Brightwell, D.R.: New Eating Behavior: Practical Management of Obesity. I. Physician's Guide to Behavior Therapy in Treating Obesity. New York, Penwalt Corp., 1975.

52. Mahoney, M.J.: Fat fiction. Behav. Ther. 6:416–418, 1975.

53. Bloom, W.L.: Fasting as an introduction to the treatment of obesity. Metabolism 8:213–220, 1959.

54. Drenick, E.: Weight reduction by prolonged fasting. In Obesity in Perspective. Fogarty International Center Series on Preventive Medicine. G. Bray, editor, U.S. Govt. Printing Office, Washington, DC, 1977, pp 341–360.

55. Garnett, E.S., Barnard, D.L., Ford, J., et al.: Gross fragmentation of cardiac myofibrils after therapeutic starvation for obesity. Lancet 1:914–916, 1969.
56. Vertes, V., Genuth, SM., Hazelton, I.M.: Precautions with supplemental fasting. J.A.M.A. 238:2142 1977.
57. Linn, R., Stuart, S.L.: The Last Chance Diet Book. New York, Lyle Stuart, 1976.
58. Isner, J.M., Sours, H.E., Paris, A.L., et al.: Sudden, unexpected death in avid dieters using the liquid-protein-modified-fast diet: observations in 17 patients and the role of the prolonged QT interval. Circulation 60:1401–1412, 1979.
59. Schuyker, R.E., Gunn., W.J.: A national survey of the protein products used in conjunction with weight reduction diets among American women. Altanta: Centers for Disease Control, 1978.
60. Sours, H.E., Frattali, V.P., Brant, C.D., et al.: Sudden death associated with very low calorie weight reduction regimens. Am. J. Clin. Nutr. 34:453–461, 1981.
61. Wadden, T.A., Stunkard, A.J., Brownell, K.O.: Very low calorie diets: Their efficacy, safety, and future. Ann. Int. Med. 99:675–684, 1983.84, 1983.
62. DeHaven, J., Sherwin, R., Hendler, R., Felig, P.: Nitrogen and sodium balance and sympathetic-nervous-system activity in obese subjects treated with a low-calorie protein or mixed diet. NEJM 302:477–482, 1980.
63. Bistrian, B.R., Blackburn, G.L., Flatt, J.D., et al.: Nitrogen metabolism and insulin requirements in obese diabetic adults on a protein sparing modified diet. Diabetes 25:494–504, 1976.
64. Vertes, V., Genuth, S.M., Hazelton, I.M.: Supplemented fasting as a large scale outpatient program. J.A.M.A. 238: 2151–2153, 1977.
65. Bistrian, B.R., Hoffer, L.J.: Obesity. In Conn. H., ed. Current Therapy. Philadelphia, W. B. Saunders Co., 1982, pp 444–447.
66. Howard, A.N., Grant, A., Edwards, O., et al.: The treatment of obesity with a very-low-calorie liquid-formula diet: an inpatient/outpatient comparison using skimmed milk as the chief protein source. Int. J. Obes. 2:321–332, 1978.
67. Genuth, S.M., Castro, J.H., Vertes, V.: Weight reduction in obesity: a comparision of methodology and clinical results. Int. J. Obes. 3:261–272, 1979.
68. Wing, R.R., Jeffrey, R.W.: Outpatient treatments of obesity: a comparison of methodology and clinical results. Int. J. Obes. 3:261:272, 1979.
69. Genuth, S.M., Vertes, V., Hazelton, J.: Supplemented fasting in the treatment of obesity. In Bray G., ed. Recent Advances in Obesity Research, London, Newman, 1978, pp 370–378.
70. Wise, T., personal communication.
71. Keys, A., Brozek, J., Henschel, A., et al.: The Biology of Human Starvation. Univ. Minn. Press, Minneapolis, 1950.
72. Cook, R.F., Howard, A.N., Mills, I.H.: Low dose mianserin as adjuvant therapy in obese patients treated by a very-low-calorie diet. Int. J. Obes. 5:267–272, 1981.
73. New weight standards for men and women. Stat. Bull. Metropol. Life Ins. Co., 40:1–4, 1959.
74. Van Itallie, T.B., Kral, J.G.: The dilemma of morbid obesity. J.A.M.A. 246:999–1003, 1981.
75. Van Itallie, T.B.: Obesity: Adverse effects on health and longevity. Am. J. Clin. Nutr. 32:2723–33, 1979.
76. Halverson, J.D., Koehler, R.E.: Gastric bypass: analysis of weight loss and factors determining success. Surg., 90:446–55, 1981.
77. Benedict, C.: Anesthesia and intensive care management of the obese patient. Can. J. Surg., 27:133–134, 1984.
78. Alden, J.F.: Gastric and jejunoileal bypass: A comparison in the treatment of morbid obesity., Arch. Surg. 112:799–806, 1977.
79. Griffin, W.O., Young, V.L., and Stevenson, C.C.: A prospective comparison of gastric and jejunoileal bypass procedures for morbid obesity., Ann. Surg., 186:500–507, 1977.
80. Sherman, C.D. Faloon, W.W., Flood, M.S.: Revision operations after bowel bypass for obesity. Am. J. Clin. Nutr., 30:98–102, 1977.
81. Thorlakson, T.K.: Overview of jejunoileal bypass. Can. J. Surg 27: 127–28 1984.
82. Salmon, P.A.: Weight loss following hori-

zontal gastroplasty with rigid stoma and variable pouch size: Comparison with intestinal bypass. Can. J. Surg., 27: 234–35, 1984.

83. Scott, H.W., Land, D.H.: Clinical appraisal of jejunoileal shunt in patients with morbid obesity., Am. J. Surg., 117: 246–253, 1969.

84. Stone, A.M. Friedman., M. Rothenberg, H.: Intestinal bypass for morbid obesity., J. Abdom., Surg., 17:225, 1975.

85. Halverson, J., In discussion of: Griffin, W.O., Young, V.L., Stevenson, C.C.: A prospective comparison of gastric and jejunoileal bypass procedures for morbid obesity., Ann. Surg., 186: 500–507, 1977.

86. Rhoads, J.E.: In discussion of Pace, W.G, Martin, E.W., Tetrick, T., Fabri, P.J. Carey, L.C.: Gastric partitioning for morbid obesity., Ann. Surg., 190: 392–397, 1979.

87. Halverson, J.D.: Obesity surgery in perspective. Surgery, 87: 119–127, 1980.

88. Payne, J.H., Dewind, L., Schwab: Surgical treatment of morbid obesity: 16 years of experience. Arch. Surg., 106: 432–437, 1973.

89. Soyer, N.T., Ceballos, R., Aldrete, J.S.: Reversability of severe hepatic damage caused by jejunoileal bypass after re-establishment of normal intestinal continuity. Surg. 79: 601–604, 1976.

90. Fikri, E., Cassella, R.R.: Jejunoileal bypass for massive obesity: results and complications in 52 patients., Ann. Surg., 460–464, 1974.

91. Halverson, J.D. Wise, L., Wayna, M.F.: Jejunoileal bypass for morbid obesity: a critical appraisal. Am. J. Med., 64: 461–475, 1978.

92. Ackerman, N.B. Abou-Mourad, N.N.: Obstructive, pseudoobstructive, and enteropathic syndromes after jejunoileal bypass. Surg. Gynecol. Obstet., 148: 168–174, 1979.

93. MacLeon, L.D., Rhode, B.M.: The history of surgery for morbid obesity., Can. J. Surg., 27: 126–27, 1984.

94. Passaro, E., Drenick, E., Wilson, S.E.: Bypass enteritis: a new complication of jejunoileal bypass for morbid obesity. Am. J. Surg. 131: 169–171, 1976.

95. Halverson, J.D., Gentry, K., Wise, L.: Reanastomosis after jejunoileal bypass. Surgery 84: 241–249, 1978.

96. Gaspar, M.R., Movius, H.J., Rosenthal, J.J., A comparison of Payne and Scott operation for morbid obesity., Ann. Surg., 184: 507–515, 1976.

97. Hallberg, D., Holmgren, U.: Biliointestinal shunt. Acta Chir Scand., 145: 405–408, 1979.

98. Holian, D.K.: Biliopancreatic bypass for morbid obesity. Contemp. Surg., 21: 54–65, 1982.

99. Mason, E.E., Ito C.C.: Gastric bypass., Ann. Surg., 170: 329–339, 1969.

100. Peltier, G., Hermreck, A.S., Moffat, R.E., Hardin, C.A., Jewell, W.R.: Complications following gastric bypass procedures for morbid obesity. Surgery 86: 648–654, 1979.

101. Mason, E.E., Printen, K.J., Hartford, C.E., Boyd, W.C.: Optimizing results of gastric bypass. Ann. Surg., 182: 405–413, 1975.

102. Halverson, J.D., Koehler, R.E.: Assessment of patients with failed gastric operations for morbid obesity. Am. J. Surg., 145: 357–363, 1983.

103. Linner, J.H., Drew, R.L.: Technique of anterior wall roux-en-Y gastric bypass for the treatment of morbid obesity. Contemp. Surg., 26: 46–59, 1985.

104. Deitel, M.: Horizontal gastric partitioning for morbid obesity. Can. J. Surg., 27: 237–38, 1984.

105. Buckwalter, J.A., Hervst, C.A.: Complications of gastric bypass for morbid obesity. Am. J. Surg., 139: 55–59, 1980.

106. Mason, E.E.: Vertical banded gastroplasty for obesity. Arch. Surg., 117: 701–706, 1982.

107. Knecht. B.H.: Mason gastric bypass: long-term follow-up and comparison with other gastric procedures. Am. J. Surg., 145: 604–608, 1983.

108. Printen, K.J., Mason, E.E.: Gastric bypass for morbid obesity in patients more than fifty years of age. Surg. Gyncol. Obstet. 144: 192–194, 1977.

109. Printen, K.J., In discussion of Alden, J.F.: Gastric and jejunoileal bypass: a comparison in the treatment of morbid obesity. Arch. Surg. 112: 799–804, 1977.

110. Mason, E.E.: Surgical treatment of obesity. Philadelphia, W.B. Saunders, 1981.

111. Printen, K.J., Scott, D., Mason, E.E.: Stomal ulcers after gastric bypass. Arch. Surg. 115: 525–527, 1980.

112. Mason, E.E., Ito, C.: Gastric bypass in obesity., Surg. Clin. N. Amer., 47:1345–1351, 1967.

113. Pace, W.G., Martin, E.W., Tetirick, T., Fabri, P.J. Carey, L.C.: Gastric partitioning for morbid obesity. Ann. Surg. 190: 392–397, 1979.

114. Carey, L.C., Martin, E.W., Mojyisik, C.: The surgical treatment of morbid obesity. Current Prob. Surg., 21: 7–8, 1984.

115. Laws, H.L.: Standardized gastroplasty orifice. Am. J. Surg., 141: 393–94, 1981.

116. Palmer, J.A., Roncari, D.A., Rotstein, L.E. Piecszonka, R.: Treatment of morbid obesity by gastric partitioning. Can. J. Surg., 27: 233, 1984.

# CHAPTER 15

# Burn-Out and Eating Disorders Therapists

J. Bradley Rubel, Th. D.

## BURN-OUT AND EATING DISORDERS THERAPISTS

In recent years burn-out—a cyclical disillusionment with work that can lead to chronic debilitation—has been recognized as a near universal occupational hazard in the helping professions.[6] Burn-out reduces therapist effectiveness, wastes time and money, and deprives clients of optimal care.

Also in recent years, the number of individuals who develop anorexia nervosa (voluntary starvation) and bulimia (the binge/purge syndrome) has increased dramatically.[8] Many therapists, either in hospital eating disorders programs or in private practice, are working primarily with anorectic and bulimic clients. Given the inherent dynamics of these two disorders, therapists who are restricted to this client population may be particularly vulnerable to burn-out. If clinicians can recognize their personal burn-out symptoms before their resources are exhausted, they can make constructive changes and avoid many of the long-term complications described below.[10]

### What Is Burn-Out?

Burn-out is a progressive depletion of idealism, energy, and motivation coupled with increasing feelings of futility, anger, frustration, and cynicism.[6,11] Most individuals who burn out report feeling physically and emotionally exhausted. One social worker commented, "I'm sucked dry . . . an empty shell, a desiccated husk." Burned out therapists are vulnerable to doubt and disillusionment as well as various psychosomatic complaints such as headaches, sleeplessness, ulcers, sexual problems, back pain, and frequent colds and flu. Many develop a sense of sardonic omnipotence; almost all detach from and become angry at their clients for not improving more rapidly. The clients in turn respond to their burned out therapists with deterioration, disorganization, and crisis. The personal resources of burned out clinicians may be so depleted that they have trouble managing their private lives. Some abuse alcohol, other drugs, or food—especially if they have had previous problems in those areas. Burn-out erodes therapist effectiveness and self-esteem, and it robs clients of optimally functioning, caring professional helpers.

According to Herbert Freudenberger, M.D., a psychoanalyst who specializes in burn-out, the syndrome includes more than just stress, depression, and simple job dissatisfaction, although all of those factors can contribute to the problem. Burn-out is a process that occurs in recognizable stages. If allowed to continue unchecked, it can result in chronic loss of therapist self-esteem.[7]

## Stages of Burn-Out

Naive or beginning therapists are often surprised to learn that the first stage of burn-out consists of zealous enthusiasm for work fueled by high optimism and unrealistic expectations. These become a set-up for future disillusionment. Usually therapists in this stage do not fully understand the realities of their jobs. They focus most of their energy on their work, putting in long hours, and perhaps making themselves available to clients during nonbusiness hours. These therapists expect their work to provide much benefit to those they serve, and therefore much satisfaction to themselves. As they invest most of their time and energy in their work, they ignore their needs to develop other areas of their lives: family relationships, friendships, creative activities, recreation, and other interests. Their work is their life.

The second stage of burn-out begins when therapists discover some of the harsher realities of their jobs, and when they realize their work never will be a substitute for satisfying outside activities. As their initial enthusiasm wanes, they become dissatisfied, still performing adequately on the job, but, unlike before, also wanting tangible rewards for their efforts: money, fewer hours, and better working conditions. Their jobs are no longer their sole source of satisfaction.

If burn-out is not interrupted, therapists may find themselves in the third stage of burn-out—they move from a relatively vague sense of dissatisfaction to more disturbing feeling of futility. They begin to feel powerless to make any significant differences in the lives of their clients. They also feel powerless to improve their working conditions through the regular channels. Hospital bureaucracies, are seen as serious impediments to career advancement, funding for programs, and assistance for clients. Third-stage burned-out therapists can swing from grandiose feelings of compassion and omnipotence ("Those poor, suffering people! I *know* I can cure them. If only I try hard enough, I *will* make them better!") to anger and aggression against clients who do not improve ("Those lazy defectives! They don't want to get well; they're just wasting my time. I hope no one shows up for the next group meeting!") These therapists question not only the effectiveness of their work but its value as well.

In this frustrated state clinicians become vulnerable to severe physical, emotional, and behavioral problems. In view of the secondary gain derived from anorexia nervosa and bulimia,[2,3,5] there seems to be a real danger at this point that therapists who themselves have experienced an eating disorder will regress back to their old patterns of dieting or binge/purging in order to establish some semblance of order and control in their lives.

The fourth stage of burn-out is a defense against chronic frustration. Therapists who cannot change their circumstances because they need their jobs or practices for economic survival usually become apathetic, adopting a strategy of "getting by" so they can continue to collect their salaries. They develop pessimism about the chances of any of their clients making significant improvement. They resent demands made on them by clients. Realizing how little power they have to change client behavior, or the existing system of medical and mental health care, fourth stage burned-out therapists put in minimum hours, avoid clients whenever possible, and resent extra hours required for in-service trainings and continuing education. To protect themselves against further disillusionment, they avoid new job responsibilities and withdraw into an apathetic shell.

## Causes of Burn-Out

Burn-out seems to be caused by problems in three areas: (1) chronically stressful working conditions, (2) frustrating psychopathologies and client expectations, and (3) personal qualities and unrealistic expectations of therapists.

*Stressful Working Conditions:* The initial enthusiasm therapists bring with them when they begin clinical work is dissipated by the realities of the helping professions. Since these factors have been well documented elsewhere,[6,7,10,11,13] they will be listed here only briefly with minimal discussion.

1. The job requires too many hours and too many responsibilities.
2. The financial rewards to not compensate for efforts expended.
3. Bureaucratic regulations demand too much paperwork.
4. Therapists have no specific methods of measuring their effectiveness. Quantifying client progress and cure in many cases is impossible, leaving clinicians questioning their worth as helpers.
5. Possibilities of career advancement are limited unless therapists are willing to assume administrative duties (and headaches) which reduce time spent working directly with clients.
6. Budgets and funding are inadequate. Sources of financial assistance for clients are likewise inadequate.
7. Therapists are not sufficiently trained to handle all the problems they encounter on the job—problems with "the system" as well as problems with clients.
8. Therapists are regarded with distrust by the general public. Clients do not appreciate efforts made on their behalf by therapists.
9. Supervisors and administrators do not appreciate efforts made by staff therapists.
10. Administration will not support important decisions or policy changes.
11. Sexist attitudes influence job descriptions, job assignments, and performance standards.
12. Medical and mental health care systems too often spend their resources processing red tape and are not optimally responsive to the needs of their clients.
13. Agency policy or economic necessity may dictate that therapists accept every client that comes through the door, even those people who do not respond to intervention regardless of the skill of the clinician.
14. Office politics and personality conflicts interfere with client care.

As a result of a combination of a few or many of the above factors, therapists begin to respond to demands made on them by supervisors, administrators, and clients with feelings of frustration.

*Frustrating Psychopathologies and Client Expectations:* People with eating disorders are difficult to treat.[3,8,14] Anorectics often insist their emaciated bodies are normal and more attractive than they were before they began to diet. Bulimics usually feel embarrassed and guilty about their binge/purge behavior, believing that to ask for help would be confirmation of their personal inferiority. Both anorectics and bulimics tend to mistrust authority figures. They resent what they interpret as interference in their lives by people whom they believe do not really understand them but who only want to manipulate them. Many eating disordered individuals state they do not want to change their behaviors. Others do want to change, but often they want to cure themselves without outside help. A great majority of those who want to stop starving or binge/purging also want to remain thin—a condition which seems to biologically precipitate continued problems with anorexia nervosa and bulimia.[1,9]

Once eating disordered individuals have entered therapy—whether voluntarily or because family members have insisted—they are usually ambivalent at best about changing their behaviors. Because of the significant amount of secondary gain they derive from their symptoms (feelings of power and control;[3] a unique identity;[3] a way of avoiding adult responsibilities;[5] an outlet for tension, anxiety, and suppressed hostility and rage[2]), they overtly or covertly sabotage attempts to help them. They resent on the one hand, what they interpret as interference, but fear, on the other, rejection if they fail to please the therapist.

Anorexia nervosa and bulimia are spectrum disorders.[8] Some eating disordered clients have relatively minor psychopathologies and are less difficult to treat than others who, in addition to their eating disorders, present with borderline personality or severe psychosis. These individuals will require long-term treatment and after many months may make only a few improvements—or none at all. Therapists who have several of these clients in their case loads will almost certainly begin to question their effectiveness when no measurable successes are observed.

Eating disordered individuals frequently come from dysfunctional family systems—they participate in symbiotic relationships that retard their growth towards adult autonomy.[12] They will (unconsciously) try to recreate similar relationships in therapy. They become exceedingly dependent on their therapists, making ever increasing demands for attention. At the same time, because of a fear of true intimacy, they usually keep therapists at emotional arm's length, thus preventing development of a committed therapeutic relationship.

Although all eating disordered individuals seem to have problems trusting other people, two subgroups have acute difficulty in this area: those who have been victims of sexual abuse and those who are children of alcoholic parents. (Therapists are wise to specifically ask about these possibilities since many clients will not report this kind of information spontaneously.) These people find it hard to fully enter into therapeutic—or any other—relationships. They fear violation of their boundaries, disregard of their needs, and betrayal if they invest themselves in a committed relationship. Client distrust often emerges as a belief that therapists are extensions of non-nurturing parents whose only goal is "to make me fat" (which can be translated as, "I fear you are going to take away what little power I do have and my identity as well.") Although therapists can understand their clients' reluctance to trust them, many find themselves disillusioned about their ability to help when these frightened people either drop out of therapy prematurely or remain but make minimal or no progress.

The expectations of their clients can exacerbate burn-out for many therapists. Anorectic and bulimic individuals tend to polarize their experiences of the world and other people into black and white dichotomies.[8] For example, after initial resistance has been decreased, eating disordered clients expect their therapists to be all-wise and all-compassionate, but at the same time clients still fear exploitation. They expect, or demand, their therapists to be constantly available, and always understanding. At the first sign of confrontation, clients usually withdraw to a victim position where they become hostile. They may travel a cycle between dependent adoration of their therapists and defensive criticism. Therapists in turn become confused about where they stand with these clients. The lack of consistent trust prevents progress and growth.

There is no question but that anorectics and bulimics are difficult to treat. These individuals have been labeled resistant by therapists whose best interventions have been frustrated by their insecure, ego-deficient clients. Therapists whose case loads are heavily weighted with anorectic and bulimic clients may experience enormous amounts of frustration when those clients do not improve or make only minimal changes in personalities and behaviors.

*Personal Qualities and Unrealistic Expectations of Therapists:* People who become psychotherapists usually begin their careers with genuine enthusiasm and a deep desire to help others. In too many cases, however, formerly dedicated professionals come to the point where they dread work each morning, avoid clients whenever possible, and describe those previously valued clients as "stubborn, spoiled princess-wimps who are so locked into their defenses, pay-offs, and manipulation that they will never change or appreciate what I'm trying to do for them." In addition to stressful working conditions and frustrating psychopathologies, one other factor contributes to burn-out: certain personal characteristics and unrealistic expectations brought to the job by therapists themselves.

Certain personalities seem to be more vulnerable to burn-out than others. Individuals who need to always maintain an image of poised control are at risk—so are people who do not delegate responsibilities. The latter seem to prefer exhaustion to trusting others with control of job duties. Others susceptible to burn-out are those who do not know how to pace themselves. They focus intense energy on every client and every project, quickly depleting their own resources. Exhausted therapists achieve fewer and fewer successes, becoming doubtful of their effectiveness as helpers. It is important to note that many individuals who are presently working with anorectic and bulimic clients have themselves had an eating disorder and may still have problems with the very issues that predispose helpers to burn-out.

Therapists who have an idealized image of what helping professionals are supposed to be and do, and who at the same time realize how far they and their work are from that ideal, are vulnerable to burn-out. Novels and television present images of therapists who always intervene at exactly the right moment to save a life and solve major problems. Clinicians in real life, who cannot quickly "cure" complex psychopathologies in spite of their best efforts, can become frustrated and self-critical when they fail to achieve the dramatic successes of their media counterparts.

Some therapists need to have concrete evidence they are making progress with clients. Unfortunately, quantifying the progress of any client in therapy is almost impossible. Trying to judge whether an anorectic or bulimic client is improving, deteriorating, or standing still is even more difficult given the resistance these clients bring into the therapeutic setting. Some eating disordered clients *do* respond to intense, brief therapies and improve rapidly;[2] many others require years of intense treatment.[3,14] A few experiences with the former can set therapists up for frustration when they encounter the latter. If therapists need to have frequent concrete evidence of their effectiveness, they would do well to look for it in areas other than their work with anorectic and bulimic clients.

In addition, there is much controversy in the field of eating disorders about what are, or are not, effective treatments. Researchers debate whether anorectics and bulimics can ever recover totally from their disorders. Behavioral therapists contend with insight-oriented clinicians, and psychopharmacologists discount psychotherapy altogether.[15] One group insists on a multidimensional, psycho-bio-socio-familial treatment plan[8] (which seems to have considerable merit, but which is not available to clients and clinicians outside metropolitan areas). Therapists who believe there ought to be reliable strategies to predictably achieve success become frustrated and burned-out when they realize there are no such proven interventions thus far (and there may never be) in the treatment of anorexia nervosa and bulimia.

A certain number of therapists have a need to treat everyone who approaches them for help. They would be far wiser to apportion their resources, saving their energy for those individuals who will truly benefit from their efforts.

Some therapists have a strong desire to be needed. When they work with eating disordered clients they may unconsciously collude with patients to maintain mutually dependent relationships. Thus, while the therapists' needs for relatedness are satisfied, their needs for success with clients are frustrated, which can contribute directly to burn-out.

Also vulnerable to burn-out are therapists who have a need for power—not necessarily power that will hurt or abuse others, although that does happen, but rather power that will make a significant impact on the world. As Edelwich[6] notes,

> Burn-out, in its most general and universal sense, occurs when this wish is frustrated, whether because of mundane bureaucratic obstacles to effective treatment or the inherent difficulty of changing what another person does and is. It occurs when one sets out to move the world, only to find oneself with the world pressing down on one's shoulders. (p. 35)

Professionals who work with anorectic and bulimic clients need to keep in mind how easily eating disordered individuals can precipitate a power struggle, how frightened they are of change, and how rigidly they cling to old patterns in an attempt to maintain some sense of power in their lives. Therapists need to evaluate how much power they really do have to produce behavior changes. Those who avoid burn-out will not expect themselves to quickly produce dramatic, positive changes in their clients.

Therapists at risk for burn-out may consciously or unconsciously have entered the helping professions to learn more about themselves. They may be trying to receive therapeutic help vicariously by helping others. This situation is analogous to one in which an anorectic seeks pleasure from food by cooking for others while she herself does not eat. In both cases the goal is worthy, but the strategies for achieving it are ineffective.

Some naive, eating disorder therapists believe there are simple explanations and solutions for these conditions. Techniques such as prayer, special diets, art and movement therapy, week-end sensitivity trainings, meditation, and journal writing can be powerful tools for change when they are appropriately integrated into a comprehensive treatment plan. When they are applied indiscriminately as global panaceas, however, they are usually not only ineffective, but may also be harmful to clients, leaving them with doubts about whether or not recovery is possible. Many anorectics and bulimics come into treatment after years of severe psychopathology. Therapists who expect simplistic techniques to make major changes in their clients' behaviors are setting themselves up for burn-out.

Idealistic therapists who believe all their eating disordered clients are highly motivated to "get well" are also susceptible to burn-out. Therapists must remember that both anorexia and bulimia provide significant secondary gain to those who develop these disorders. By starving, anorectics achieve attention, status among peers, and a sense of control.[3,8,14] They can avoid the responsibilities of adulthood by remaining childlike in a prepubertal body.[5] Binge/purgers quite literally can "have their cake and eat it too" in a society that demands a slim, fit appearance.[4,8]

Binge/purging can also serve as a method of releasing tension and anger.[2] Many bulimics turn to food to fill unstructured time. Others find their food activities allow them to avoid the responsibilities of relationships. Therapists who expect their clients to give up their symptoms (and pay-offs) quickly and easily are vulnerable to burn-out.

Consciously or unconsciously, some therapists want to control other people. When their clients do not react and recover according to some arbitrary schedule, therapists vulnerable to burn-out can become angry and sometimes retaliatory.

Many therapists begin their careers expecting to spend most of their time working directly with clients. They become burn-out candidates when they find they must also schedule agency paperwork, insurance forms, various reports, monthly billings, staff meetings, continuing education, committee responsibilities, and other administrative duties.

# MANAGING BURN-OUT

Eating disorder therapists who want to protect themselves from burn-out must first of all understand the syndrome and then learn to recognize their own personal symptoms. Then they can design strategies to help them (1) make realistic improvements in working conditions, (2) accept the difficulties inherent in working with anorectics and bulimics, and (3) bring their unrealistic expectations more in line with the givens of the helping professions.

*Stressful Working Conditions:* Obviously an important first step in reducing burn-out is to improve working conditions whenever possible. However, as Edelwich[6] has stated,

> No matter how much the work environment is modified, some of the deepest causes of burn-out cannot be altered. It is beyond the power of the most well-intentioned administrators to do away with clients' resistance to change, the scarcity of funds for human services, the tendency of people living in our society to engage in bureaucratic and political manipulation, and (probably the most important) the profound frustration of being unable to exert as much influence on the world as one would wish. No intervention can do away with the pain and suffering that make the helping professions necessary while sometimes defeating their best efforts. (p. 193)

After analyzing working conditions, therapists can decide what they can expect to change and what they will have to accept. To make specific improvements in work conditions, therapists can

1. Arrange for flexible hours that permit a balance between work and satisfying outside relationships and activities.
2. Organize or attend workshops that generate specific, concrete

changes in policy and procedure. If workshops are to lead to long-term relief, those who attend must make and then implement specific plans for change. If sessions are nothing more than opportunities to ventilate frustrations, the group will develop a "workshop high" which will quickly dissipate, leaving therapists in the old burned-out routine.

3. Organize an in-house counseling program focused specifically on burn-out and problems resulting from work conditions.
4. Organize or join a peer supervision or peer review group that provides positive feedback as well as constructive criticism.
5. Participate in a research project. The enthusiasm and gratification derived from formulating a hypothesis, gathering data, consulting with colleagues, writing reports, and finally publishing results can serve to counteract discouragement and burn-out.
6. Leave the agency or institution and enter private practice which provides more autonomy and flexibility.
7. Leave private practice to affiliate with an agency or institution that will provide not only new challenges but also peer support.
8. Leave the helping professions and develop a new career if not willing to accept the realities of the profession.

*Frustrating Psychopathologies:* The second step in reducing burn-out includes acceptance of the fact that anorexia and bulimia are difficult problems to treat. In view of this reality, eating disorders therapists can

1. Learn more about anorexia, bulimia, and various treatment options. Books, professional journal articles, and short-term conferences are good places to start. Resident training programs may be expensive and difficult to arrange but necessary to the mental health and effectiveness of clinicians.
2. Limit the number of anorectic and bulimic clients in the case load. Two or three are enough for many therapists.
3. Screen clients and accept only those who give reasonable indications they can be helped. Refer the rest.
4. Do group therapy with a co-therapist in addition to individual sessions. The co-therapist can provide support and another perspective during planning and evaluation sessions.
5. Become a member of a treatment team (psychiatrist, psycholo-

gist, dietitian, social worker, rehabilitation counselor, exercise physiologist, etc.) so that case responsibilities are shared and multiple resources are available.

6. Focus on client growth and success, not failure. In spite of the frustrating nature of anorexia and bulimia, many clients *do* persist in treatment, eventually entering into trusting relationships with their therapists where they make significant progress towards recovery. In general, after the difficult initial resistance has decreased, therapists find their eating disordered clients to be people who possess a large capacity for growth and development. Working with them can become rewarding and satisfying.

*Personal Qualities and Unrealistic Expectations of Therapists:* In many cases therapists must accept as givens stressful working conditions and difficult clients. In areas of their own attitudes and expectations, however, they can make major changes—if they are willing to exert the required effort. Therapists who incorporate one or more of the following items into their belief structure will be protecting themselves against burn-out. To bring their erroneous expectations more in line with reality, therapists can

1. Expect periods of burn-out and plan strategies for relieving frustration before it becomes chronically debilitating.
2. Expect difficult work with insufficient financial rewards and little appreciation from clients, peers, and the community.
3. Expect problems because training was inadequate.
4. Expect difficult clients, disagreeable supervisors, and stifling bureaucratic requirements.
5. Expect work with clients to be inconsistent and uneven.
6. Expect some clients to improve, others to remain the same, and still others to deteriorate.
7. Find measures of success other than recidivism rates. Not waiting for major, dramatic recoveries, therapists with healthy self-esteem congratulate themselves, and their clients, for small, positive steps that indicate client growth and progress.
8. Set realistic goals for themselves and encourage clients to do the same. Grandiose, absolute goals ("I'll cure this person of anorexia in two months," and "I'll never binge or purge again") are guaranteed set-ups for failure.
9. Schedule breaks in the daily routine by becoming available for

presentations to school personnel, students, and civic organizations. Therapists can increase their knowledge of and enthusiasm for the field of eating disorders by organizing and participating in in-service trainings, symposia, and community education efforts.

10. Take career-related classes. Completing an advanced degree will open additional opportunities.

11. Find a new position or, if problems are intolerable, leave the field and enter a new area. Unless unrealistic expectations are restructured, however, burn-out may be a problem in the new setting also.

12. Learn from past experiences with burn-out. Therapists can make changes to prevent recurrences, watching for the first symptoms so the cycle can be aborted before problems become critical.

13. Separate career and personal life with firm boundaries.

14. Develop interests far removed from career pursuits.

15. Develop personal relationships that provide support.

16. Develop a wide, supportive network of friends and acquaintances. Therapists who successfully avoid burn-out usually associate with normal, healthy people outside of work and are involved in normal, healthy activities.

17. Take advantage of opportunities for personal growth and development: i.e., personal therapy, spiritual pursuits, etc. Therapists concerned about burn-out need to come to terms with personal strengths and weaknesses.

18. Set aside periods of free, unstructured time.

Therapists who best reduce the effects of burn-out remain somewhat, but not completely, detached from their clients, not taking client successes or failures personally, and realizing that failure and self-destructive behaviors are permanent facts of life. Therapists need to remember they are not responsible for the progress of their clients. In many cases anorectic and bulimic individuals are suffering the consequences of immaturity, irrational thinking, and poor decisions. The goal of therapy is to make healthier alternatives and options available to clients. The goal of therapists is to support clients while they gather the courage to experiment with new choices and behaviors. If clients choose not to change, therapists are not at fault. Clinicians who do their work the very best way they know how have every right to feel good about themselves, regardless of how their clients respond. How clients respond is the business of the clients.

Burn-out seems to be a universal occupational hazard in the helping professions. It is a complex problem aggravated by stressful work conditions, difficult psychopathologies, and unrealistic expectations on the part of therapists. The chronic, debilitating effects of burn-out, however, can be reduced by the recognition of symptoms and implementation of strategies to alleviate the underlying causes.

## REFERENCES

1. Bennett, W., and Gurin, J.: *The Dieter's Dilemma: Eating Less and Weighing More.* New York, Basic Books, Inc., 1983.
2. Boskind-White, M., and White, W.C., Jr.: *Bulimarexia: The Binge/Purge Cycle.* New York, W. W. Norton & Company, 1983.
3. Bruch, H.: *Eating Disorders: Obesity, Anorexia Nervosa, and the Person Within.* New York, Basic Books, Inc., 1973.
4. Chernin, K.: *The Obsession: Reflections on the Tyranny of Slenderness.* New York, Harper & Row, 1981.
5. Crisp, A. H.: *Anorexia Nervosa: Let Me Be.* New York, Grune & Stratton, 1980.
6. Edelwich, J.: *Burn-Out: Stages of Disillusionment in the Helping Professions.* New York, Human Sciences Press, 1980.
7. Freudenberger, H. J.: *Burn-Out.* New York, Bantam Books, 1980.
8. Garfinkel, P., and Garner, D.: *Anorexia Nervosa: A Multidimensional Perspective.* New York, Brunner/Mazel, 1982.
9. Leibowitz, S. F.: "Hypothalamic Noradrenergic System: Role in Control of Appetite and Relation to Anorexia Nervosa." *Understanding Anorexia Nervosa and Bulimia: Report of the Fourth Ross Conference on Medical Research.* Columbus, Ohio; Ross Laboratories, 4:54–60, 1983.
10. Maslach, C.: *Burnout: The Cost of Caring.* Englewood Cliffs, New Jersey, Prentice-Hall, 1982.
11. Mendel, W.: "Staff burn-out: Diagnosis, treatment, and prevention." *New Directions for Mental Health Services,* 2:75–83, 1979.
12. Minuchin, S., Rosman, B., and Baker, L.: *Psychosomatic Families: Anorexia Nervosa in Context.* Cambridge, Harvard University Press, 1978.
13. Niehoff, M.: "Burnout and alcoholic treatment counselors." *Counseling and Values,* 29(1):67–69, 1984.
14. Palazzoli, M. S.: *Self-Starvation.* New York, Jason Aronson, 1974.
15. Pope, H. G., Jr., and Hudson, J. I.: *New Hope for Binge Eaters.* New York, Harper and Row, 1984.

## CHAPTER 16

# Self-Help On an Individual Basis

By Fernando Tapia, M.D.

Self-help is a key ingredient in the successful treatment of bulimia and/or anorexia nervosa. This self-help should be directed by counselors and reinforced by group interaction, however. The confrontation by multiple individuals who "have been there" is instrumental in breaking down the defenses which the individual has set up. The group also provides a significant support structure. These groups can succeed where the one-on-one treatment approaches fail. Once the group is functioning the behavioral techniques emerge or, in some cases, a spiritual or inspirational force which propels the healing process.

Self-help on an individual basis is not an unknown. What might be considered spontaneous "cures" are part of the scene of alcoholism, anorexia nervosa, drug abuse, and other conditions of dyscontrol. Readiness for change and motivation have been ascribed as the most important ingredients in these turn-about cases. The individual becomes flushed with "willpower" and consequently triumphs over his impulses. What prompted this turn around? Where was this new strength found? What was there this day that had not existed before? Was it insight? Was it fear? Perhaps if we knew, the treatment of these conditions would be much easier.

The question now is whether a person with anorexia (A-N) or a person with bulimia (Bu) can help herself on an individual basis. Can she do this with any consistency? And, can she find any book, booklet or set of rules, etc. that might help her? For instance, books that have been evaluated for help with test taking, for improving sleep and for quitting drinking have not been shown to be effective except when therapist administered. Rosen, Glasgow, and Barrera[1] reduced snake phobias, however, by self-instruction manual as well as by a therapy. Morris and Thomas[2] in 1973 successfully treated phobias by written instructions in systematic desensitizations. They treated agoraphobia, fear of public speaking, phobias of death and insects. But the true assessment of a self-help book is difficult. For instance it should include:

1. An objective criteria for rating improvement
2. Rater should be uninformed as to the treatment received
3. Adequate statistical tests should measure the differences.

Furthermore, one would have to have: (a) a treatment and a non-treatment group, (b) randomly assign patients, and (c) both groups come from a comparable population. This becomes impossible partly because those who want self-help are self-directed and have a different motivational structure than those who don't attend voluntarily. In essence one has to measure motivation first and then put the equally motivated groups through the research design. Nevertheless, self-help books keep getting published and some become popular. The question of popularity does not seem to rest on whether they help more or less but perhaps because they are more interesting and better written.

It is an accepted fact that the treatment of anorexia and bulimia should take a holistic approach. The study done by Hsu[3] in which he reviewed the literature on anorexia from 1954 to 1978 indicated that although at two years follow-up some 75% of the patients demonstrated weight gain, there was also the problem that 25–50% of adolescents with anorexia underwent a relapse. In addressing the problem of improving the long-term prognosis one must address the treatment of the total person. In other words, how do we help the anorectic patient *after* hospitalization or *after* psychotherapy, or even *after* group therapy?

At some point in time the patient is going to have to quit being a patient and move away from therapy. It is during this transition that self-help therapy can be beneficial. Self-help also has a place in the general treatment of a patient prior to separation from the therapist. Thus the objective should be, in terms of self-therapy, to promote the growth of the patient in terms of stability, self-concept, reality testing and minimal anxiety. Certainly with a greater self-concept and/or self-esteem the individual would be less apprehensive about how they appear to others and about life's social network outside the hospital.

## SELF-HELP BOOKS

Many psychotherapy approaches have been written into self-help books. For instance, psychoanalysis has been treated in a book called "Self-Analysis".[4] Gestalt therapy has been written about by Muriel Schiffman.[5] More recently, cognitive behavior therapy has been explained in an excellent book for depression called "Feeling Good" by David D. Burns.[6] Just recently, Brian T. Yates of the American University in Washington D.C. has converted behavioral modification into an excellent comprehensive book called "Self Management".[7] Those are only four, but self-help books are legion and different approaches have been tried. Psychocybernetics, self-hypnosis, transcendental meditation, and even creative visualization are therapeutic techniques authored into self-help books.

It is not my purpose at this point to criticize self-help books but only to mention their different styles. Some of the books call for a significant amount of reader preparation: keeping a diary, listing the targeted behaviors complete with antecedent elements and consequent events. But some of the assignments are extraordinary and must test the willingness of even the most motivated to conform to a program. Two psychotherapy cliches come to mind at this point. One of them being that "you get out of therapy only what you put into it", and the other "the healthier the patient the more progress he is likely to make". Actually if these cliches are true for therapist-guided psychotherapy they might well be true for self-psychotherapy.

It may be of interest to see what some of these books call for. For instance in the book on *Gestalt Self-Therapy* the individual must on his own go through the experience and emotional catharsis that would be likely in a therapists directed Gestalt treatment.

The mode of therapy in which insight is instrumental is probably the basis for many of the popular self-help books. In the process of reading the purported psycho-dynamics of life, the individual may find himself while they are reading the book. I remember a patient of mine who had read Claire Weekes' book on Agoraphobia[10] saying "that's me, that's me, now I understand what's happening." Perhaps reading renders some insight and understanding. Reading may even provide a therapeutic impetus.

## A NEW DIRECTION AND SUSTAINING IT

The anorectic patient has been called a bulimic with will power—the bulimic has been called an anorectic without will power. These may be gratuitous and probably incorrect shibboleths. We can, however, say that both groups have concerns about how they appear to others and that their self-esteem and anxiety is reduced if they are conforming to the imputed expectations of a "normal body" size. Furthermore their fear of rejection is unrealistic and often exaggerated.

To be vulnerable to opprobrium of others is a position of jeopardy. As successful treatment progresses and the patient begins to overcome these anxieties, there is an accompanying expansion in them of greater self-esteem, better reality testing, greater stability, and less impulsivity in responding to psychic pain. It is this new direction that must be sustained to avoid later relapse.

It is at this juncture that self-psychotherapy can be employed most effectively. A common strategy utilized is to promote the patient to therapist. Going from patient to counselor heightens self-esteem and reinforces the new found sense of security. This is a continuation of the group process, however. What is needed now is a generalized growth for after hospitalization, a growth that relies on self-help. So how to do this? What are the ingredients that might particularly help the individual after she leaves a treatment program?

In my book, "The Magic Rooster, A Shortcut to Self-Psychotherapy,"[11] I have reviewed those elements which can prove effective in a patient's growth after treatment and will now discuss them further. These elements include:

    I. The conviction that growth is a personal project which must be accomplished alone and for one's own personal needs and satisfactions.

    II. Motivation that is spontaneously acquired.

    III. A method which will provide:

        A. An opportunity for change.

        B. The probability for sustaining the effort to change.

    IV. Overcoming anticipated resistances.

    V. A way of knowing when "you have arrived".

As the reader will soon note, the project is easy to get started, but sustaining interest and motivation will prove the most difficult obstacle to overcome. Hopefully the project called for gives the subject a high probability of getting well into it before the resistances arise. A significant question, however, is whether an accomplishment such as called for in any given self-help book renders emotional growth and self-esteem.

Many of us who do psychotherapy have found that therapy begins to succeed when the patient begins to assume responsibility for their own happiness and well-being. Paradoxically the anorectic individual can be said to have made this assumption—they are responsible for their own body weight and image. Furthermore, they have consistently worked away from others who they may have felt would stop them in their personalized efforts to "save themselves." This must be viewed as a "strength" which unfortunately was misapplied. The anorectic patient—once they begin to recover—discovers that they have given too much value to how they are viewed by others. When this conception is altered, the anorectic patient is on the road to recovery. Hence it is when such a reversal has begun that the anorectic patient can then use and benefit from self-psychotherapy.

Sustained motivation is probably the most difficult ingredient to put into therapy. Patients of their own have to bring it to therapy. It is the therapist's job, then, to sustain the motivation or—as it is often viewed—to remove the resistances hindering motivation. Again, motivation for change is fragile. Note the myriad of New Year's resolutions, which are usually excellent ideas and proper self-assigned tasks. So many of those New Year's resolutions are dead by March regardless of their merit. They have, as someone put it, "drowned in an ocean of old habits and established behaviors." What happened to the good resolve? Obviously the intellectual designation of something a person *should do* does not carry the impact of something a person wants to do. The "should do's" represent voices from outside the person (i.e., coming from the demanding "parent" or other guilt-inducing sources in the personality). These resolutions lack spontaneity and a true personal want. They are, for the most part, doomed. Now what strategy can be devised to find motivation of an "I want" quality which will succeed for a "should" objective?

There is an old story about a lad that was under a street light looking for something. When asked what he was doing, he stated that he had dropped a fifty-cent piece and was looking for it. When asked where he had dropped it, he pointed several yards down the street. He said that he was looking here because this was where the light was— there would be no sense looking for it where it was dark even if that was where he lost it. Such skewed thinking might be applicable in cases of bulimia and anorexia nervosa. Perhaps the therapist or patient might divert energy away from merely controlling the appetite disorder and devote time and energy elsewhere.

Examples of dealing with patients away from just the symptoms and complaints abound in the practice of medicine. One need only look at the strategy applied in the treatment of chronic pain. There, in fact, successful therapy dictates that not only the painful area (let's say the lower back) be addressed but that the total body (exercise, loss of weight, good physical status, etc.) be addressed as well. By the same token we should view the total person equally important in treating bulimia and anorexia—not just appetite and body weight but the patient's personal needs should be addressed as well. Successful therapy can be obtained by realizing the importance of a comprehensive approach and that therapeutic energy is not to be exclusively dedicated at the precise site of concern. This approach must include some means of self motivation and self-help.

The basic therapeutic premise that underlies the method of self-psychotherapy that is being offered here is to contrive a situation akin to the transactional analysis paradigm of the child growing up under the tutelage of a supportive parent. Such a child would grow to be an adult who is self-directed, secure, and has a "built in" or "endogenous" sense of belonging and of being accepted. Therefore the idea is to provide the opportunity to an inhibited and insecure person to redo their growth under more appropriate auspices. These auspices, of course, must come from within the individual (remember this is self-psychotherapy) and guidelines are offered to the individual for structuring them. In other words, if the individual is to do this for herself, she needs to trust that this is the only way to do it.

The first guideline is to set a goal and at the same time a method for achieving of it. Find out what the patient is "buggy" on. The goal is used to improve the performance. If the patient is "buggy" on dancing then she must become a better dancer and be able to assess the improvement. If it is photography, golf, tennis, whatever, she must become better at it. She must, therefore, set about in an organized way to improve herself at the selected activity. This quest for self-improvement is dictated by the premise that she was not better at dancing because she had not allowed herself to be. She had inhibited herself. The qualities that had made her vulnerable to eating disorders had participated in making her a less than satisfactory performer at dancing or golf or whatever. Now if she were to allow herself the opportunity to become a better dancer she would have to shed some of those restraining qualities along the way.

The second guideline for achieving the designated goal is the use of meditation which in this respect is called Reconstructive Meditation (R.M.). Meditation in the service of this program offers relaxation as well as opportunity for insight and planning. It also helps to sustain a concentration on the task at hand. Relaxation, furthermore, reduces the tendency for defensiveness and allows for a *change* in behavior. Meditation has the advantage that it is one of the methods of relaxation that it is most likely to be sustained—over and above biofeedback or tapes. Finally, it is most likely that new and creative thoughts will emerge to help the individual in her quest for improvement.

# RECONSTRUCTIVE MEDITATION

Meditation has gained popularity. The teaching of Transcendental Meditation (T.M.) by Maharishi Mahesh Yogi has contributed to this rise. His approach has simplified meditation to it's most basic but critical elements. The benefits to be derived from the prescribed twenty minutes, twice a day of meditation have been hailed, maybe overly so. Nevertheless, the legion of satisfied meditators certainly attests to some derived or at least perceived benefits.

In T.M., the relaxation response as described by Herbert Benson, M.D.[12], is achieved. One finds a quiet, comfortable place, lets one's mind and attitude remain passive and uses the gimmick of a mantra (the mantra is a word repeatedly conjured in silence). Such practiced repetition soon promotes the relaxed condition which translates into a passive alertness and a relaxed concentration. These contradictory states achieved simultaneously imply perhaps that both the left and right hemispheres of the brain are participating in a "more equal" way. The old problem solving concentration which generally employs the dominant hemisphere now relents and as a result a more comprehensive thinking mode emerges.

In T.M., the mantra is repeated continuously. When the individual realizes that the mind has strayed then he or she is to return to the mantra. Straying from the mantra is to be expected—the relaxed state often brings to consciousness many concerns that the individual has been recently struggling with. These concerns usually emerge in relation to the priority they have in the individual's life. In a restful moment it is not odd to suddenly be thinking that you better not forget *again* to pick up milk and bread on the way home. Many individuals who meditate twice a day find that in the morning session their thoughts often turn towards the forthcoming tasks of the day and when meditating in the latter part of the day, there seems to be a tendency to review the day's happenings. This is not universal but it is common.

In R.M., the idea is to use the meditation time in the service of the person's project (i.e., dancing, golf, etc.). This requires that the individual meditate much as is done in T.M. but that upon feeling relaxed that he or she consciously and in as relaxed a state as possible turn his or her mind to the project. Again the individual's attention will stray and it is likely items of higher priority will beseech the meditation. This is not a negative, however. As practiced in autogenics, the use of suggestion is recommended. It now follows that self-hypnosis may be part of this process. Again, this is not a negative. The essential features are mainly relaxation and concentration.

# RESISTANCES

Through Reconstructive Meditation, the anorectic has been lead to realize that whatever she is going to do is entirely up to herself and that she is to use a meditation technique to help her with the task. Now the question arises as to whether the individual will be able to continue to develop her skills in her chosen activity until such time as she has achieved a modicum of proficiency commensurate with her innate capabilities. The goal is not that the individual will play a lot of tennis and have fun but that she will become a *better tennis player.* Therefore, if the individual is to accomplish this she must a.) take lessons, b.) practice with some diligence, c.) challenge the better players, d.) overcome her weaknesses in the game, and e.) work on any personal characteristic that needs modification to enhance her tennis. It is understandable that none of the above is easy. It is a challenge, however.

It is now to be expected that the old patterns of behavior and all those rationalizations formerly used by the anorectic will emerge to hinder her progress. These qualities are the resistances against which she must now battle. Many of these resistances can be predicted. For instance, the patient's excuse of there not being enough time can be anticipated. It is then that meditation can help deal with these resistances, by helping the patient become aware of their negative quality. Meditation will also help to overcome the realistic aspects of the problem. The individual who claims to be short of time will review her priorities and examine the budgeting of time. An underlying change usually happens as the patient takes more responsibility for her own happiness and satisfaction.

Guilt and anxiety are also predominant resistances. The patient will invariably feel guilty about her new use of resources. She may even have to face individuals around her who in one way or another are bothered by her changes and therefore are unwittingly trying to get her back "in line." I consider these the people she must struggle against since they were the people who were surrounding her while she was not doing well. Yes, the struggle is an upstream one against excuses, guilt, anxiety AND a host of people that were partly responsible for creating the problem in the first place.

Anxiety, of course, is possibly the most effective enemy. The discomfort of anxiety pushes on all of us to quickly find a position that is comfortable. It is often done by a step backward, a regressive move. Thus, the anxiety that appears when one is doing something new and perhaps bolder may need to be assuaged. Meditation is prescribed as an aid in coping with anxiety. New behavior can be sustained more readily if it does not create anxiety or if the anxiety that it creates is kept at a low level. There is a need to minimize negative reinforcers and to replace them with the enjoyment of the new activity—a reward that further and positively reinforces.

Finally, many patients in therapy have the tendency to give up because "nothing is happening" and they're "not getting anywhere." Also, following a setback the overgeneralization of "I'm never going to do any better" will serve as a shove towards giving up. In individual psychotherapy it is common to have to remotivate the patient following each setback "glich." This is done by making them note that the bottom of the "glich" is still way above where the improvement graph started. The feelings of depression that surround these "gliches" only make it *seem* to the patient as if it were the end of everything.

The above bits of insight and anticipated defenses presented in advance are expected to be overcome. Hopefully they will not be allowed to make the person give up on the activity. Furthermore, the patient can reexamine her previous lifestyle and those efforts that netted her the problems. She learns to trust therapy and her project since in the end they *will deliver* the promise of helping her to become a better, more mature person.

Now there is the question of how long or how far does one go with one's project. An easy answer would be "as long as you keep improving and enjoying." However, in reality, most individuals have a limitation to their talents. These talents may be modest. There is the potential for disappointment if solid and outstanding measures of improvement are not forthcoming. It is for this reason that patients are advised to seek professional advice to help establish a reasonable level of accomplishment to go with his apparent capabilities. This professional or expert help is designed to obviate disappointment in what might seem to be lack of achievement. At the same time it will give satisfaction for the achievement that was attained. After all, the fact that she tried, stuck with it and did achieve some improvement is the medicinal part of the whole project.

## CONCLUSION

So we come to the end of a system by which a patient can in fact provide herself with self-psychotherapy. She has indeed been given permission and encouragement to be her own spontaneous self and to do something with it. She has been given a system by which she can probably make a sustained effort and which in the process allows her to make personality changes that are advantageous. The approach is tangential only in appearance. Self-psychotherapy should be a part of a treatment program. In the case of bulimia and anorexia, self-psychotherapy benefits will be enhanced by the strengths which at the height of the illness were aggravating it.

## REFERENCES

1. Rosen, G.M., Glasgow, R.E. and Barrera, M., Jr.: A controlled study to assess the clinical efficacy of self-administered systematic desensitization. *Journal of Consulting and Clinical Psychology,* 1976, vol. 44, pp. 207–217.

2. Morris, L.M. and Thomas, C.R.: Treatment of phobias by self-administered desensitization techniques. *Journal of Behavioral Therapy and Experimental Psychiatry,* 1973, vol. 4, pp. 397–399.

3. Hsu, L.K.G.: Outcome of anorexia-nervosa. Review of the Literature (1954–1978). *Archives of General Psychiatry,* vol. 37, pp. 1041–1046, 1980.

4. Horney, Karen: Self-Analysis. W.W. Horton, New York, NY., 1942.

5. Schiffman, Muriel: Gestalt Self-Therapy. Self-Therapy Press, Menlow Park, California, 1971.

6. Burns, David D.: Feeling Good. Signet, New York, NY. 1980.

7. Yates, Brian T.: Self-Management. Wadsworth Publishing Company, Belmont, California, 1985.

8. Hendrix, Gay: Learning to Love Yourself: A guide to becoming centered. Prentice-Hall, 1982.

9. Baer, Jean: How to be an assertive (not aggressive) woman in life, in love, and on the job. Signet, New York, N.Y., 1976.

10. Weekes, Claire: Simple Effective Treatment of Agoraphobia. Bantam Books, 1979.

11. Tapia, Fernando: The Magic Rooster: A Shortcut to Self-Psychotherapy. Vantage Press, New York, N.Y., 1983.

12. Benson, Herbert: The Relaxation Response. Avon Press, New York, NY., 1975.

# Index